Scoop

Scoop

Notes from a
Small Ice Cream Shop

JEFF MILLER

MINNESOTA
HISTORICAL
SOCIETY PRESS

www.mhspress.org

The Minnesota Historical Society Press is a member of the Association of American University Presses.

Manufactured in the United States of America

10 9 8 7 6 5 4 3 2 1

♾ The paper used in this publication meets the minimum requirements of the American National Standard for Information Sciences— Permanence for Printed Library Materials, ANSI Z39.48-1984.

International Standard Book Number
ISBN: 978-0-87351-943-4 (paper)
ISBN: 978-0-87351-944-1 (e-book)

Library of Congress Cataloging-in-Publication Data

Miller, Jeff, 1963–
Scoop : notes from a small ice cream shop / Jeff Miller.
pages cm
Summary: "This is the true story of a lawyer and his partner who give up their corporate lives in London to run an ice cream shop and small inn in Wisconsin's north woods. It is a tale of starting over, slowing down, and ice cream."— Provided by publisher.
ISBN 978-0-87351-943-4 (paperback) — ISBN 978-0-87351-944-1 (ebook)
1. Miller, Jeff, 1963– 2. Cooper, Dean. 3. Ice cream parlors—Wisconsin— Hayward. 4. Bed and breakfast accommodations—Wisconsin—Hayward. 5. West's Hayward Dairy (Firm) 6. McCormick House (Inn : Hayward, Wis.) 7. Career changes—Case studies. 8. Businessmen—Wisconsin—Hayward— Biography. 9. Hayward (Wis.)—Biography. 10. Hayward (Wis.)— Social life and customs. I. Title.
F589.H39M55 2014
977.5'16—dc23
2014011350

This and other Minnesota Historical Society Press books are available from popular e-book vendors.

Contents

Scoop

In a Blue Moon

I was not prone to drastic actions. I did not rush into the unknown. After fifteen years as a more or less effective lawyer, I approached decisions with a certain caution. I not only weighed the pros and cons but also examined all likely consequences and reasonably foreseeable risks. Looking back, I wondered what could have prompted me to take those initial steps down a path that would alter the course of the rest of my life armed with only an optimistic hunch and knowledge that turning back was not an option.

It was September, and the day was warm and summerlike. The town of Hayward, Wisconsin, was having its annual Fall Festival. A few of us bought ice cream and sat on a bench in front of a small ice cream shop painted like a red barn.

Dean—my partner—and I had come over from London to check on the renovations of a cabin we had bought that year on the shores of nearby Teal Lake. We met up with some friends, Matt and Dave, who also had a home in the area. I grew up with Matt in Chaska, a small town outside Minneapolis. Matt was also a lawyer, who had given up a career in Washington, DC, to return to his native Minnesota. Every Friday, though, he and Dave rushed to their lake home near Hayward in order to catch the fish fry at their favorite restaurant, and they convinced us of the merits of buying property in Wisconsin despite the impractical distance from London.

"Isn't this the life," Dave said, looking at a spoonful of maple nut ice cream. "Now that you have a place on the lake, shouldn't you move here?" he continued. "I know you bought the place because of your mom, but you might like it."

Matt laughed. "That would never happen," he said. Matt knew that from a very young age, I was determined to see the world and had no intention of moving home. I blamed it on a subscription to *National Geographic* my mother once bought me.

"Oh, we'll definitely be back here for at least two or three weeks a year—especially in the summer and fall, like this," I said. "It will be a great break from work." I looked at Dean to see if he agreed. He nodded.

"I'd like to come in the winter when the lakes are frozen," Dean said. "We could cut a hole in the lake and fish like your brothers do. Don't you think it would be fun, bundling up in warm jumpers and drinking hot cocoa?" Dean, like many Brits, loved all things American and was eager to try those activities weather and common sense rendered impossible in England.

"I doubt they'd be drinking cocoa," Matt said. "And you'd freeze—no matter how much cashmere you had on."

"Well, I'd still like to try it," Dean replied and looked over at me. "What's that blue ice cream you're eating?" Dean asked.

"She said it was Blue Moon—a Wisconsin specialty." The girl behind the counter had failed to tell me the flavor tasted of the sweet milk left at the bottom of a bowl of Fruit Loops. By the funny looks I was getting from the Blue Moon–licking children sharing the bench with me, no one past the age of puberty was taken seriously eating a Blue Moon ice cream cone.

"Is it any good?"

"It's great—very sweet."

My phone rang while I was licking my ice cream cone. I managed to retrieve it from the side pocket of my cargo shorts.

"Unknown Caller" meant it had to be a work-related call from London.

"Hello," I said. Notwithstanding the combination of bright sun and Blue Moon, my heart began to race, and I was taken thousands of miles away. The caller was a senior partner from a London law firm. They had reviewed the work of an internal investigation we had carried out of some infractions of U.K. securities trading regulations. The actions of the bank's traders were inadvertent rather than designed to rig the markets. The partner said that the U.K. authorities were unlikely to take any action that would result in monetary fines, but they could issue an embarrassing public rebuke.

"Really," I said. I fished for a pen in my other pocket but could not manage to hold my ice cream cone. I walked to the corner and tossed the unfinished cone in the trash. I scribbled some notes on an ice cream–stained napkin and hung up—so much for my holiday.

Dean and our friends were finishing their cones. Dean looked at me. After twelve years, he knew from the tone of my voice when something wasn't right.

"Bad news?"

"Could be better. I have to make some calls." I excused myself and walked to the car. At the corner, I looked up the street.

"I like the sign," I said, pointing to the nostalgic neon sign in the shape of an oversized waffle cone that hung from the building's corner.

While it did not seem very significant at the time, I wondered what would have happened if I had not received a phone call that day and had been able to enjoy the rest of my ice cream cone like anyone else on a brief break from his unfulfilling job. More than likely, I would have returned to the office, showed some photographs of me sticking out my blue-stained tongue, and planned my next holiday.

The months that followed were muddled, as though I were operating in a fog. Dean and I returned to London, where we made big decisions involving buying and selling property, signing contracts, and transferring large sums of money more by the seats of our pants than by my typical and rational decision-making process.

These events culminated on a cold London morning in mid-February. I was about to take the final step to a new life that, with luck, a low cholesterol diet, and moderate exercise, would last another forty years, provided my pounding heart did not give out on me before the lift doors opened.

I worked for one of the American financial giants in their London office. London was the headquarters for EMEA—Europe, Middle East, and Africa. Despite the United Nations–sounding name, we did not broker peace amongst nations or attempt to conquer hunger. Ours was the noblest of goals—*enhancing shareholder value.* I had been at the bank for over nine years and had just been promoted to the coveted position of managing director. I attributed my success to endurance, a well-groomed affability, and fear of crowded trains. Because I hated riding the Underground during rush hour, I arrived at the office before anyone else. My early starts were mistaken for some unbridled passion for my work and loyalty to the bank worthy of reward.

It was a very good job—worthy of a much better lawyer than I ever could be. It had been challenging, and there were colleagues who didn't live up to their Hollywood image of sharks and Gordon Gekkos. Many were smart, funny, well dressed, and a great source for hotel recommendations. But I no longer saw the point of it all. The long days, lost weekends, and job-related stress had manifested itself in a number of physical ailments that one normally associated with nursing homes and were too embarrassing to divulge. I feared I would die—if not by the massive and looming heart attack or exploding ulcers, then by some bizarre accident when the Aeron office chair adhered permanently to my behind and accidently rolled me into a double-decker bus off Piccadilly.

I alighted on the executive floor and walked toward my boss's office. My boss was the bank's general counsel for the region. He was a good guy—from St. Louis. He arrived at the office long before the business day as well, so I thought this would be a good time to catch him. From the end of the hall, I saw his door was open, but then I saw the back of the CEO for the region as he stepped into the office. This was my chance. I could turn and catch the same lift to the ground floor, walk across the atrium to the bank's second tower, return to my office, and no one would know the difference.

I had heard about adventure seekers who flung themselves from steep cliffs wearing only a small parachute and a winged spandex suit. Adrenaline surged through my veins as though I were one of those spandex-clad cliff jumpers, but there was one difference between them and me: I *had* to jump. I could put off the decision for a week or two, but I knew the actions Dean and I had taken meant I could not turn back.

I walked along the hallway toward my boss's office. I looked over the glass wall to an unusual interior open space whose sole purpose was to permit all occupants of the executive floor a large windowed office. I fell into one of the tub chairs in the hallway, wiped my palms discreetly on the cloth sides of the chair, and looked down into the atrium as though it were a cliff.

My boss's door was ajar, and I knew the conversation with the CEO would not take long. Perhaps my boss was updating the CEO on a pending case or a regulatory dispute. More likely, they were sharing bits of information on the recent shakeup among the management team in New York or, as they were both basketball fans, the upcoming NCAA championships.

I nodded to the CEO when he left the room. I pushed myself off the tub chair and approached the open office, tapped lightly, and peeked around the door.

SPRING

The Handover

It was the first day of spring, and daffodils bloomed in the window boxes of the home we had left in London. In northern Wisconsin, an Arctic wind blew in from Canada, frost clung to the bare trees, and the calendar seemed discarded below a foot of snow. Dean and I soared across this tundra from our cabin toward Hayward.

It was twenty miles to Hayward along Highway 77. In this part of the state, the pleasant hills and productive farmland of southern Wisconsin give way to a very different landscape. Farms grow smaller, and hardwood forests turn to the birch groves and pine forests of the central highlands.

Unlike the manicured forests of England framed in hedgerows and country lanes, the dark walls of pine in northern Wisconsin encroach on fields and engulf entire towns. At one small wooden home along the highway, the evergreen limb of a white pine appeared to knock on the front door. A blanket of snow still lay on the forest floor and in the sporadic fields where yellow and withered cornstalks had been left exposed to the winter. Dean scanned the sides of the road in search of deer that might make a kamikaze run across the highway.

We passed the Spider Lake Town Hall, the administrative center for our local township. Sawyer County was divided into roughly equal-sized townships. Each township had an elected body of geriatrics who drank coffee, collected property taxes from residents and second-home owners, and organized the annual pancake breakfast to raise money for the fire department, during which the township's only fire truck was parked outside the town hall garage to make room for long tables.

Nearby, the Spider Lake Church, a small, white clapboard structure, sat in postcard position surrounded by tall pines. A bell tower rose above the arched entrance. A sign in front of the Spider Lake Church promoted its Sunday service. The church was loosely Protestant, but its affiliation fluctuated according to the prevailing fervor of its congregants. At the moment, it was a member of the United Church of Christ, but there were rumors that zealotry was on the rise.

If we continued on Highway 77 and its successor road on the Minnesota side for another two hundred miles, we would come to Browerville, where I was born. I suspected the area around Browerville was flatter with fewer trees, but I couldn't remember. My family moved when I was still a toddler after an attempt at farming in north-central Minnesota had not worked out as planned. I was told it was because the soil was rocky and poor. I guessed the soil around Hayward also made for poor farming.

Even though it was a first day of a life-changing period for us, it wasn't the first time Dean and I had packed everything to start over on the other side the world. About six months after our eyes met across the smoke-filled Queen's Head Pub in Chelsea, I was asked to move to my law firm's Hong Kong office. Dean arranged a transfer with the company he worked for at the time. I had just turned thirty, Dean was only in his late twenties, and we didn't have much stuff. Asia was booming, and Hong Kong was in its waning days as a British colony. We traveled everywhere, knowing we could return to London at some point. But this was different—we were older and hopefully wiser, and returning to London would be difficult. And we had a lot more stuff.

"This is fun," I said to Dean. "Driving to work together—you never drove me to work in London."

"Well, I did work from home." Dean laughed. He had been an overachieving sales executive for a software company. When he wasn't traveling, he worked from home or drove to his offices near Heathrow

Airport, whereas my bank's offices were in the opposite direction in Canary Wharf, the modern financial district east of London.

"Anyway, soon you'll be driving us to work, Miss Daisy." Dean referred to the awkward fact that I had not driven a car in nearly twenty years. I had always lived in large cities and relied on public transportation. In England, I had enough anxiety as a pedestrian weighing the risks of crossing the street. I was never a very confident driver, and according to my high school driving instructor, Mr. Frogman, I wasn't very good either. When we finished the lessons, he wished me luck on the exam and added, "Miller, you'll need it."

"Would you like me to drive?" I asked.

"No, we can save that for another day. You just prepare yourself for the meeting with Bruce." I looked out the window and thought of the road to Browerville.

In the general counsel's office, after I told my boss I was leaving the bank to move to Wisconsin, he initially smirked and asked a number of questions before it dawned on him: "Say, aren't you from up there— Wisconsin or Minnesota?" He raised his hand and waved generally. I nodded. "So, you're going home. That makes sense," he said as though he was convincing himself.

This time I wanted to smirk. What was he suggesting? I hadn't lived in the Upper Midwest in twenty-five years. This move was about a new and great opportunity, for a more balanced and meaningful existence. It was not some sort of homecoming. If anything, London was my home, and I would miss it more than anything. I knew the city— at least the central bits—like the back of my hand. Thanks to Dean, I had family in the Ribble Valley and could spot the best cockle stand at the Blackburn Market. My accent was neither here nor there, and Britishisms were ensnared in my vernacular. I even became a citizen, swearing an oath to the Queen and her heirs—especially the cute ones—and made a promise not to take the mickey out of Her Majesty's hat collection.

As we approached Hayward, we crossed the Namekagon River near the town's bowling alley. *Was my boss right?* I wondered. Dean and I could have gone anywhere in the world to buy a business or take advantage of some opportunity. Was it purely coincidental we had chosen a spot only a few hours from my home?

To the west, the river flowed into Lake Hayward, more of a widening of the river than a true lake. Back in 1882, this section of the river provided lumber barons A. J. Hayward, who named the town after himself, and Robert McCormick the perfect site for the mill for the Northern Wisconsin Lumber Company. Lumberjacks lived in small encampments spread throughout the area from November to early spring. As the ice cleared on the rivers to the north, the logs were strewn into the water and maneuvered toward the mill on Lake Hayward, which served as the holding pond for the virgin timber awaiting the mill's blades. At the mill, the huge logs were trimmed, cut, and loaded onto railroad cars headed south to St. Paul or Chicago or north to Ashland, where the timber was shipped through the Great Lakes to the urban centers in the East or across the Atlantic to European markets.

Hayward quickly grew to accommodate the hundreds, if not thousands, who came to profit from the logging boom. It was difficult to imagine Hayward at the peak of its logging days in the late nineteenth century. At that time, lumber was the equivalent of today's oil and technology industries. Not only was Hayward key to the area's lumber industry, but northern Wisconsin was also producing more lumber than any other region in the country, if not the world.

In fact, it was difficult to imagine Hayward as the center of anything. Today little remains of Hayward's logging era. After the virgin timber had been harvested in the early 1900s, the lumber barons moved to new markets, and the landscape was scarred for generations. The business of the Northern Wisconsin Lumber Company slowed, and in 1922 the mill mysteriously burned and was never rebuilt.

We turned right onto Main Street, which had been the primary artery north to Lake Superior until, several years before, the highway had been rerouted east of town. Main Street was now a one-way, single-lane street with diagonal parking on either side.

"Where do I look?" Dean asked. It was an odd pattern, as parked cars from either side of the street inched out into the oncoming lane of traffic. We drove past Angler's Bar & Grill, a landmark restaurant and bar and four-lane bowling alley. Inside was a veritable natural history museum, its walls lined with mounted fish, deer, bear, and any other creature one might hook, shoot, trap, or run over with the truck. Next to Angler's was the Packer Store, a squat, box structure made of cinder blocks with large front windows displaying bright green and yellow jerseys, T-shirts, pajamas, hats, underwear, and a plethora of other accessories essential to any fan of the Green Bay Packers, pride of Wisconsin.

We made a left at Second Street. At the end of the block, the familiar kitschy blue and yellow neon sign for West's Premium Ice Cream welcomed us back to town. The sign's painted background had faded and chipped with time, but we could make out the waffle cone with a scoop of yellowed vanilla and faded pink strawberry ice cream. The sign extended from the corner of the building so it might catch the attention of drivers and passersby along both Second Street and Dakota Avenue, which ran parallel to Main Street and was the busy route preferred by those in a rush to the Catholic church at the end of the street.

"It's a great sign," Dean said. "You don't see those anymore."

"We'll definitely keep it," I said. "It may need some work." A few pieces of neon were broken, and another section blinked and twinkled. There were holes in the painted wooden backing, and it appeared that a family of sparrows or starlings called the sign home.

Built in the 1920s, the shop once housed a car dealership, and one could imagine a Model T on display behind the large plate-glass windows. The dealership had either closed or moved at the beginning of the Great Depression, and the Hayward City Dairy took over the premises. At some point, the faux barn façade had been painted across the entire building, including the outline of a hexagonal barn roof and blue sky. An oversized fiberglass head of a cow greeted visitors to the shop. An aged fiberglass canopy extended over the front of the building and protected the cow's head from the elements.

"I'm not so sure about the cow," I said.

"Oh, I think it's cute, but it could use a wash," Dean noted as he turned the corner onto Dakota Avenue.

We parked on the side of the building by the service entrance across from the municipal parking lot. The service entrance was not so much a loading dock or garage door as it was a simple metal door with chipped red paint that opened onto the sidewalk and the busy street. To the side of the door, a stack of sturdy plastic milk crates was waiting to be picked up or perhaps stolen to create bookshelves in a college dorm room.

The closing for the purchase of the dairy was not scheduled until the end of the week, but we were keen to begin the handover and training process. I had phoned Bruce West, the seller, to schedule a time.

"Oh, so you can hit the ground running," Bruce said.

"Exactly," I agreed.

"Well, hell, come around anytime. We're usually here," Bruce proposed without suggesting a specific day or time.

As we walked around to the front door, it wasn't clear whether the dairy was even open. There was a light, but we couldn't see anyone. What would have happened if I had received that fateful call from London not in front of this ice cream shop but outside a tattoo parlor in Glasgow or an off-sale liquor store on the outskirts of Topeka?

Life has always been about fate and timing—alignment of opportunities and decisions made in light of those opportunities. The cabin gave us refuge from the stress of our corporate lives. Dean had always dreamed of living in America. In our case, however, our friend Matt, who dabbled in real estate, proved to be the crucial link to our fate.

Dean leaned to avoid the cow's head and pulled at the door. "I guess they're open."

Back in September, Matt had noticed a "For Sale" sign in the window of the ice cream shop. He took it upon himself to speak with the owner about the sale of the business and then told me about this amazing opportunity to acquire a local institution. Dean and I were returning to Hayward in October and agreed to tour the business. It was a warm autumn Saturday. Happy customers lined up to purchase cones and shakes. People used the sunny day as an excuse to buy a last ice cream of the season. Bruce showed us the plant room where he made the ice cream and described how the business had become a local mainstay. It didn't take much to convince us that we had found the perfect opportunity to leave behind our bitter corporate world for a new and, with any luck, fulfilling life as entrepreneurs in the sweet world of ice cream.

Perhaps it was the sun and crowd of ice cream–licking customers, or perhaps I had been just an overworked lawyer looking through rose-colored glasses, but the dairy looked very different now on this gloomy, cold day. There were no customers—in fact, the place looked deserted. My eyes were drawn to things I hadn't noticed—the cracked and uneven red linoleum floor, the makeshift wooden shelves display-ing an endless supply of wild rice, a dozen or so dust-coated jars of Wisconsin maple syrup, and some crystallized honey in plastic, bear-shaped containers. Moisture had stained the wall near the glass doors of the walk-in cooler. Some of the cooler doors had been sealed shut and covered with Milk Promotion Board posters of milk-mustached athletes and celebrities. Behind the glass door to the cooler were a few gallons of milk and a lonely block of white cheese.

Oh, God, what have we done? Was it really that bad—my corporate life? Sure, being a lawyer had turned dull and tedious over the years. It was not just the "oh, this is a bit dull" kind of boredom but the mind-numbing boredom that required a fork in the eyeball to keep you awake. After fifteen years, my body and psyche had adjusted to very minor levels of stimulation. *But can life get any better trying to sell cheese?* I thought.

Dean tapped my shoulder and pointed to the sealed cooler doors. "Who's that?" He gestured at one of the milk promotion posters. The man on the poster was clearly a football player—American football— with a green and yellow Green Bay Packer uniform and milk mustache. I looked at the signature in the corner.

"Brett something," I said. "Never heard of him."

"What about that?" Dean pointed above the door. "Does that come with the building?" he asked, referring to a large mounted head of a deer adorned with a huge rack of antlers. Its mouth was blackened and cracked around the edges. Its eyes were made of bright brown marbles that gave life to the figure. A small note card wrapped in cellophane revealed that a man named Buck had shot the deer some fifteen years ago.

"I guess it's Buck's buck. I'm sure he'll want to take it with him," I said.

Near the cooler, an old door hung askew from its hinges and creaked as someone on the other side maneuvered it open.

"Howdy!" Bruce said. "Come in the office where it's warm."

The office was no more than ten by eight feet. A large window faced Second Street, but apart from a small square in the middle, the window consisted of thick glass blocks that permitted into the room only a bit of light and the shadow and muffled voices of people passing by on the street. Bruce stood by an old, gray steel desk.

"Do you know Buck?" Bruce asked. He pointed to the old man facing the television in an orange vinyl chair with narrow wooden arms, the type found in a hospital waiting room. Buck must have been in his late seventies. His soiled red baseball cap emblazoned with *West's Ice Cream* covered what could be only a few long strands of gray hair.

Buck's eyes sparkled as he managed to raise himself out of his chair to shake our hands in the doorway to the office. His round face framed a tombstone smile that took one aback at first sight.

"We were just about to watch *The Price Is Right*," Buck said. The large television was perched on a wooden box no more than three feet from his chair. The office was crowded with a second desk facing the window as well as a filing cabinet piled with boxes of old papers, invoices, and a few unidentified spare parts. There was another chair next to a small, blazing space heater that sounded like a small jet engine.

Dean and I stood in the doorway, not sure where we should go for our meeting with Bruce about the handover, or if we should stay to watch *The Price Is Right*.

"Come on in." Bruce pointed to an open spot in the middle of the floor behind his desk. There were a few upturned milk crates that served as stools for us to sit on. We maneuvered ourselves between the television and Buck, who was sporting a bright white pair of high-top basketball shoes.

We heard a flushing sound from what I thought was a broom closet. The door at the end of the office opened to reveal the tiny toilet. Out came an old man, smaller than Buck, with a walking stick. He wore khaki trousers, a red-checked hunting jacket, and a matching cap with earflaps. His high-top leather basketball shoes were similar to Buck's. I imagined a geriatric game of pickup at the senior center.

"This is Little Bob," Bruce said. "Bob, these are the guys buying the dairy." Bruce raised his voice as though Bob had a hearing issue.

"Oh, hi. How are you?" Little Bob nervously rattled, looking down at the ground to make sure he didn't trip on his way to the empty chair. Bob sat carefully so as not to touch the heater.

"Bob was over in your country during the war," Buck said. "Yep, Bob was stationed in England during World War II."

"Oh, really. Whereabouts?" Dean asked.

"Oh, it was Norwich," Bob said. "We watched the airport over there." He scratched the top of his head. "Yeah, that's what we did."

"He drank that strong English beer is what he did!" Buck said. Bob paid no attention to his friend's attempt to embarrass him as he became quickly engrossed in the pricing game on TV.

"My dad was in World War II—the Pacific," I said.

"I was stationed in the Pacific as well," Buck said.

"Bucky, you had a desk job in Hawaii," Bruce said and had a laugh at his friend's wartime experience.

"Well, we were getting ready to invade the island of Japan!" Buck replied, implying he could have died if it hadn't been for the atom bomb.

"What does your dad do now?" Buck asked. It seemed an odd question given that my father, if he had lived, would be over ninety years old.

"Well, he died when I was five."

"Oh, that's a shame," Buck said and returned to the TV. Dean was distracted by the game on the screen. Bob provided a helpful explanation. He was clearly an expert when it came to all things *The Price Is Right*, although Buck chimed in to correct him on key nuances of the game.

"Oh, you gotta watch this one. No one ever wins this one—the dumb bastards." Buck waved his hand with added flourish.

Bruce fingered through a pile of papers and computer printouts piled high in something vaguely resembling an in-tray. At sixty-five, Bruce still had a thick head of unruly hair and a wind-burned complexion. His manner was folksy. If you put a worn cowboy hat on him, you might mistake him for a rancher out west.

Bruce's parents had bought the dairy in 1951. Bruce had worked the family business nearly his entire life. In the early years of the dairy, he collected large pails of raw milk from nearby farms for processing, bottling, and delivery to most of the homes in Hayward. Over time, though, people began to buy their milk at the supermarket, and West's had discontinued its bottling operations over twenty years ago. Although West's no longer produced its own milk product and there was never a farm associated with the business, everyone in town still referred to West's as "the dairy."

Based on our original tour and follow-up conversations, we understood there were two components to the dairy's business. The wholesale milk business operated pretty steadily, even in the winter months. West's purchased milk from a large supplier to resell to local schools, convenience stores, and restaurants. Bruce acknowledged that the margins were small, but the business covered much of the overhead during the off-season. The other and larger component was the ice cream business. The ice cream was produced in the back of the building for sale in the shop as well as to local restaurants and other ice cream parlors. We had seen how busy the shop could be in the hot summer, and we had convinced ourselves this quaint ice cream business with its loyal following was poised for greatness.

Although neither of us had run a business, Dean and I had a cocky self-confidence that comes with achieving any sort of success in a tough corporate job. We discussed how we would divide responsibilities. Dean, with a background in sales, had been looking into the potential for rebranding and marketing the ice cream to a broader market. I would manage the dairy's operations, including the accounting and production. I also had some thoughts of my own as to how to take cookie dough to the next level.

Bruce stood cautiously holding onto the desk to support his large frame. In the corner between the desk and the wall stood a plastic body brace. Bruce had described to me over the phone his encounter while hunting in Colorado late in the autumn. He had shot and killed an elk and was dragging the animal down the side of a mountain when he lost his footing and slipped nearly one hundred feet down the hill, the elk landing on top of him. Although he must have been in excruciating pain, rather than seek medical treatment straightaway, he popped a few aspirin, got into his pickup truck, and drove for twenty hours back to Wisconsin—with a broken back.

"Shouldn't you be wearing that?" I asked.

"Oh, it gets so dang uncomfortable. I'll put it on before I go home to the wife," Bruce said.

Buck gave Bruce a scornful glance to suggest he should take better care of himself. "He's a crazy man, this one," Buck said.

"Oh, go back to your game, Bucky!" Bruce chuckled.

"So, where should we begin?" I said. I rolled up my sleeves, ready to get into the details of the dairy's business and for some relief from the heat in the room. I had been looking forward to this—as a way to get a head start on better understanding the day-to-day operations of the business before the closing.

Bruce looked at a partially crumpled computer printout. He explained that the dairy's milk supplier had left such printouts with each delivery itemizing the products delivered, such as gallons, half gallons, and so forth. He suggested it was important, although not essential, that we keep hold of these because we might wish to compare them with the statements the supplier sent. "Every once in a while, they make a mistake—sometimes in your favor but not always," Bruce said.

"Okay. That's good to know," I said. I wanted to move onto something more substantive, such as the schedule for ice cream production or any current research on new flavors. Bruce placed the printout on top of an overflowing basket of similar printouts that resembled a tray of crispy papadums at an Indian restaurant.

Dean saw that the handover was focusing on "back office" issues and turned his attention to *The Price Is Right*. After all, it was leading up to the game's dramatic pricing showdown. He asked why I had not shared this American gem of a game show with him. "Well, I gotta go over to my lawyer's," Bruce said. "Perhaps I'll see you guys later."

"Oh, sure . . . later," I said. I looked at Dean. *Is that it?* I thought. *That's the handover?* I had imagined this process taking days. This was going to be our livelihood, after all. *What about ice cream formulations and the process for developing new ice cream flavors? What about pricing strategies? And how could we get our hands on some of the dairy subsidies the government handed out?* I wanted to ask Bruce if he had any useful inside information that could be used to play the milk futures.

"Before I forget"—Bruce turned as he was going through the office door—"Tom is going on vacation next week, so you guys will have to do the milk route with me. I'll drive, but I can't do any heavy lifting because of my back." Bruce pointed to his brace still in the corner.

"Sure, that's great. That will give us some firsthand knowledge of the business," I said and raised my fist.

When Bruce left, Buck looked at us and gave a mischievous smile, as if to say, *You fools don't know what you're getting into.*

"Oh, I forgot," Bruce shouted from the front door. "The city called. They're going to begin resurfacing Dakota Avenue next week." He pointed to the street. "They're tearing up sidewalks and widening the road. It's gonna be a real mess, but they say they should be done by Memorial Day." He smiled and left the building.

"Oh, that's gonna hurt business," Buck said. He shook his head.

Dean and I looked at each other, not sure what to do. Should we watch the rest of the game show or leave?

"You know," Buck said, "when I first saw you guys walking up here, I thought you were a couple of preachers. *Them is preachers,* I said to myself. You were all in black and clean-cut looking. I knew you weren't from around here." Dean and I laughed at the impression we had given the old man. "Remember, I showed you around the shop. You said you might be interested in buying the dairy. So I called Bruce." Buck pointed a bent finger toward us. "I told Bruce, 'You won't believe it, but there are these two guys from London who want to buy the dairy.' He said, 'Bullshit.'" Buck lowered his voice to imitate Bruce. "I said, 'I think they're the best prospects we've had yet.'" Buck seemed to be suggesting a knack for understanding the situation and his significant role in our decision to purchase the dairy.

The Price Is Right was over. Little Bob got up, shuffled to the doorway, and was about to leave without even saying good-bye.

"I'll see you later at the co-op for some lunch," Buck shouted. Bob raised his hand to acknowledge the luncheon meeting as he left the building.

"Say, I bet you guys would like an ice cream cone," Buck said. It was only 10:30, but we had no other plans.

Buck got out of his chair. His right shoulder dropped and he hit the door jamb, catching his balance. Behind the ice cream display freezer, or dipping cabinet, Buck picked a favorite scoop out of the well of water and gave it a big shake to remove any excess liquid.

"So, what color can I get you?" Buck asked, referring to the dozen flavors on display in the dipping cabinet. A second cabinet used in the summer had been shut down. I scanned the options—from maple walnut and butter pecan to mint chocolate chip, which had been my favorite as a child. My mother used to buy it in large, five-quart containers. I ate it after school before she returned from work. I rarely ate any dinner.

"Do you still have that Blue Moon?" I asked.

"Oh, for sure. The little ones love that blue stuff," Buck said. "You should see them with their faces filled with the ice cream. It's really quite comical, you know."

I asked Buck for his expert opinion as to which was the most popular flavor.

"Well, that would be our Almost Sinful. Bruce's dad came up with that one—it's vanilla and walnuts, chocolate peanuts, and"—Buck bowed his head to remember all of the ingredients—"oh, and fudge."

"Sounds great. Two of those, please."

Despite his years and some apparent arthritis in his bent fingers, Buck mastered two beautiful cones piled high with no fewer than three scoops of Almost Sinful. Dean and I took our cones to one of the benches in the window.

"Cheers," Dean said as he raised his cone as he might a pint of beer.

"Cheers." We began to work on the cones. Buck stood behind the counter, watching us and waiting for a reaction.

It was actually really good. The ice cream was better than I remembered, and despite it being a cool spring day, the smoothness of the vanilla ice cream was refreshing, as was the crunch of thick chocolate around the salty peanuts.

"So, will you be taking your deer home?" Dean asked, pointing to Buck's buck above the door.

"Well," Buck laughed, "he doesn't really fit in my trailer, so I could leave him here if you like. You know, people love seeing the old buck when they come in for ice cream."

"Gee," I said, "thanks. We may have to take him down when we paint," I added, thinking the animal could get lost in the process.

"Oh, you gonna paint the place, are you?"

It's going to take more than a bit of paint, I thought. Dean and I scanned the dairy to see what would be needed—new floor, ceiling, signage, and lighting. *It will add up.* I returned to my ice cream cone. The phone rang.

"Hayward Dairy," Buck answered. He listened for a moment.

"One poly—no problem. I'll be right there." Buck put down the phone.

"Karb's needs a poly," Buck announced, referring to Karibalis Restaurant on Main Street. He walked through the swinging doors toward the walk-in cooler at the back of the building. In a few minutes, the doors swung in the other direction, and Buck reappeared with a red dolly carrying a single milk crate containing a five-gallon bag of milk, a poly, to take to the restaurant. "I'll be right back. You don't mind watching the place, do you?" Buck said.

"What if a customer comes in? Do we need to know how the cash register works or anything?" I asked.

Buck laughed. "Don't worry—there won't be any customers this time of year."

We finished our cones and looked outside. Buck was right. The street was empty. Across the road at the Hayward Fly Fishing Shop, the owner waited for the ice to melt and sat in the window constructing fishing flies with feathers and bells at a small worktable. Next door, at a handmade pottery shop, the clerk quietly unlocked the door, looking up and down the street to see if anyone had seen her arrive so late in the morning.

Although the handover was brief and I learned little apart from some tips on effective bidding on *The Price Is Right,* I was not particularly concerned. Bruce had agreed to stay on for a month free of charge after the closing and would be on retainer for the summer to help make ice cream.

I was more concerned about the business prospects. We had never seen the dairy in the off-season, and it looked bleak. Closing of the primary road to our business for two months would not help. On top of it, this closer look at the physical state of the dairy revealed that the renovations needed before the summer would take more time and money than we thought.

"Well, at least the road should be done before the summer," Dean offered, sensing my unease after the meeting. "We can start on the new logo so it's ready when we've finished the renovations. I found some graphic designers in Minneapolis," he said.

"That would be great," I said. "I like the idea of using an image based on the neon sign."

"Let's see what's new on Main Street," Dean suggested.

When Buck returned we told him we would see him soon and walked toward Main Street. Patches of blue sky appeared above. People maneuvered around the remaining piles of dry and dirty snow. They seemed cheerful knowing winter was near its end.

"So, what do you think the deal is with Buck? Does he work there?" Dean asked.

"Perhaps he comes with the building."

A Walk Up Main Street

In the winter of 1892, a young English evangelist, Charles Hamilton, joined a YMCA missionary on a tour of the lumber camps of northern Wisconsin to spread the word of God. Hamilton had been a student at the Moody Bible Institute in Chicago and welcomed the challenge. He knew the camps were notorious for vice—alcohol, swearing, and worse. The towns that had risen out of the lumber boom catered to these vices with saloons, opera houses, and other establishments of ill repute.

In his diary, Hamilton wrote that his first stop that winter of 1892 was Hayward. Even though he had spent his childhood in India and knew cities such as London and Chicago, he had never seen a boom-town the likes of Hayward. It was hard to imagine, he wrote, that in only ten years, this town had sprung from the forest. The streets were lined with taverns, hotels, and even an opera house—more of a watering hole than a house of Mozart. Although he knew vice and sin lurked behind these walls, the young Mr. Hamilton was impressed with the vitality he saw in Hayward.

Dean and I turned the corner onto Main Street. Most of the buildings on this section of the street featured a log exterior built over the original brick, and many had balconies extending from the second floor over the sidewalk. This design feature had been favored by the City of Hayward a few decades back to reinforce the logging town image. One must give them credit for such a plan, even if the effect—to the outsider—was more Dodge City than lumberjack village. One imagined Miss Kitty appearing on the balcony above the bakery, flirting with a passing cowboy before breaking into a cancan.

The taverns and music halls from the logging era had disappeared, but with the rise of tourism in the area, so had any grocery store, drug store, or other purveyor of life's necessities. Main Street's focus was on tourism, with competing T-shirt shops, Tremblay's (a fudge and "olde tyme" sweets emporium), Sophie's Dog Bakery, and Legend of the Celts, a shop featuring imported Irish clothing and whistles. We might have assumed the good people of Hayward lived on a diet of fudge and dog biscuits and wore brightly colored T-shirts with clever messages under thick tweed jackets from Donegal. One would have better luck finding a pair of pants and ingredients for a salad in a Tibetan village. Of course, we knew Hayward's residents shopped at the Wal-Mart Supercenter and the suburban-style grocery store with its own olive bar, both built on the edge of town.

Like the Bible-thumping Charles Hamilton, Dean and I arrived in Hayward in the middle of an economic boom that many thought would transform the town. Demand for lake homes by the recreation-seeking classes in the region had turned Hayward into one of the hottest property markets in the state. Second homes drove much of the local economy. Everyone was trying to get into the market of selling a piece of heaven on the area lakes—builders, contractors, building supply firms, law firms, mortgage providers, and home décor specialists.

Since we had last been in Hayward, the hardware store had been replaced by an upscale furniture and home accessories store catering to second-home owners. A woman with a dark bob hairstyle and a smart suit was instructing a man about something on the roof. You could tell he was a contractor by the way he scratched his head in hope that a solution to an apparent problem would rise to the surface of his brain. This shop joined another on Main Street specializing in high-end cabin kitsch for the "up north" lifestyle, including antler chandeliers, antler end tables, chairs cobbled together from sticks found on the forest floor, and, of course, cushions embroidered with a bear or moose.

Dean and I welcomed the changes in Hayward. In fact, we were part of a wave of people who had come to the area to start their own business or take over an existing one. We figured anything that brought more people to town would be good for business.

We learned, though, that some people tended to overstate the potential for change. It started with the realtors, who put pressure on prospective buyers to act quickly or lose their piece of heaven to the couple from Eden Prairie, Minnesota, who had scheduled a visit the following weekend. While Dean and I were looking at a squalid, damp, chalet-style home on a weed-infested bay of one of the less desirable lakes in the area, a realtor dropped the "O" word. He casually threw out, "Did you hear that Oprah was looking at property out on the flowage?"

"Oh, really?" we said in unison to hide our disbelief.

"Yeah. You know, she's in Chicago, so it's a short flight in her jet to the Hayward airport," he said, referring to the small, weed-lined strip of tarmac on the edge of town.

The implication, of course, was that once Oprah acquired a property in the Hayward area, all of Hollywood would follow, and then only the super-wealthy would be able to afford lake property here.

"Hayward is changing," a member of the local chamber of commerce told us on one of our exploratory visits to the area. He then looked up and down the street to see if anyone was in earshot and lowered his voice. "They say Hayward could become another Aspen."

Dean and I looked at each other and then up and down the street. For as far as the eye could see, there were no mountains or even challenging hills. While nearby Cable had a ski resort, its chairlift had been condemned after the place had fallen into bankruptcy, and the resort offered only "tubing" down the hill.

Now, I had to admit I liked the prospect of Hayward becoming the Aspen of the north woods and "getting in on the ground floor," so to speak. And seeing Oprah or Tom Cruise in the checkout line at Wal-Mart would be fantastic. However, I somehow doubted that Oprah, no matter how glamorous the après-tubing scene might be, would be attracted to the delights of sitting in the inner tube of a tractor tire and slipping down the side of a small hill in Cable, Wisconsin.

Main Street inclined up a small hill, giving the Congregational church an overwhelming presence at the top. One of the oldest buildings in town, the church had been built in the Queen Anne style and was painted canary yellow. Its single shingled turret rose above the entrance on the corner of the street. The Congregational church was not typical of small towns in Wisconsin, which were dominated by Lutherans. It was, however, the church of the city's founders, and the sign at the front suggested Charles Hamilton had had some lasting effect on the community as it announced, or rather warned, that the scripture was "God breathed."

Shall We Go Inside?

We walked north on Fourth Street along the side of the Sawyer County Courthouse to Kansas Avenue. On the corner, a woman in a chenille bathrobe used a broom to chase a black cat from a chair on her front porch. Her tone suggested this was not the cat's first offense. It may have been that she was not much of a cat person and had an ongoing issue with her neighbor. When she saw us around the corner, she merely looked up from her sweeping.

"Damn cats!" she said.

Across from her home was a city park with a small body of water known as Shue's Pond. The ice was cracked and open near a culvert on the northwest corner from which water streamed into the pond. Footprints in the snow revealed that some children had been playing on the overgrown island in the middle of the pond. A small wooden gazebo of no structural or historical significance sat precariously on its foundation. Cigarette butts littered the floor of the gazebo under a picnic table. Nearby, a small playground lay quiet for the winter; the ice-covered swings swung gently in the breeze.

A big old house overlooked Shue's Pond from the other side of Fourth Street. A pink granite hitching post rested by the curb in case any visitors still arrived on horseback. Three sets of steps interrupted a cement path leading to the covered veranda in front of the house. Two ancient maples occupied the front lawn on either side of the path, their branches twisted with age like a witch's broom. A giant Norway pine extended upward over one hundred feet, and its broad limbs provided a wide canopy over much of the lawn. A giant wound inflicted by a lightning bolt had left a wide scar on the tree's trunk.

On its own hill, the imposing house stood isolated and seemingly vacant. Architecture buffs would call it folk Victorian, with a no-fuss clapboard style and simple trim with some Shingle or even Queen Anne assets such as a large turret stretching to the third floor, much in the style of the Congregational church a block away, and the protruding bay windows and decorative balcony. The house had been painted green and magenta in the painted lady style of refurbished Victorian homes in San Francisco or other large cities, but this lady was in desperate need of a bit of makeup or even a complete makeover.

Water dripped from the veranda's roof over the front steps. The house could have been the home of one of Wisconsin's more psychopathic serial killers.

The small wooden sign at the corner of the property said *Lumberman's Mansion*. The house had been the home of lumber baron Robert Laird McCormick. McCormick was a lawyer from Pennsylvania who had become a Minnesota state senator. In the early 1880s, with a young family, McCormick gave up his comfortable life in politics for the wilds of northern Wisconsin. Perhaps he did it for the adventure but more likely the money. The logging business was booming, with demand for virgin timber at record levels in the growing cities in the East and in Europe, and Wisconsin was about to become the center of the trade.

As our young missionary friend discovered, Hayward was a rough place in those days, and it would take some effort for Mr. McCormick to convince Mrs. McCormick to leave the comforts of St. Paul for Hayward, with its taverns, loose women, and wooden shanties clogging the streets. Fortunately for McCormick, the Congregational church with its graceful bell tower lent an air of civility worthy of Mrs. McCormick and her young children. With the promise of a grand home, Mrs. McCormick, Laird, Blanche, and Amelia moved to Hayward in 1887.

After the virgin timber in the area had been harvested by the early twentieth century and the treeless landscape resembled a deserted battlefield, McCormick and his business partner, Frederick Weyerhaeuser, moved to the new state of Washington, where the logging industry was taking off. Subsequent heads of the Northern Wisconsin Lumber Company lived in McCormick's Hayward mansion until the mill burned. The home then went from family to family, was at one time broken up into apartments, and generally fell into disrepair.

"Shall we go inside?" Dean asked.

"Do you have the key?"

Dean pulled a tiny latchkey from his pocket and opened one of the double doors.

"I've decided we should call it McCormick House, a Small Inn of Distinction," Dean said in the form of an announcement. "We will furnish it with a combination of antiques and modern furniture, just as the McCormick family would have done if they lived here today."

"I like it," I said as I followed Dean into the house.

We had first seen the property back in November. Given the distance of our cabin from town, we thought we would look at homes in Hayward. We enlisted the services of the realtor who had sold us our cabin. Matt also joined us. He had obtained his realtor's license in Minnesota and was buying up rental properties in the city. We all jumped into our realtor's car for the tour of a few homes around Lake Hayward. After looking at a colonial requiring a new roof and kitchen, our realtor pulled out details for her most expensive property in Hayward.

"It's a bit bigger than you might be looking for, but it is unique. It was a bed and breakfast," she said. "And it will require a bit more work than the others." The full disclosure was not necessary.

"Oh my God!" Dean shouted as he read a one-page summary of property particulars. "I cannot believe this is on the market! It would make a great hotel. And look at the price! It costs no more than a one-bedroom in Tooting!"

While neither the realtor nor Matt would have understood the reference to London real estate prices, they sensed Dean was a serious buyer. Matt glanced at the agent, who was near realtor orgasm thinking she was about to make the easiest sale of her life. The first thing they learned in real estate school was how to detect a serious buyer. Then Matt looked at me as if to suggest I should control Dean, who was giving away any room for negotiation on the price. By the time we reached the property, Dean had decided on the drapery fabrics, the color of the interior halls, the thread count for the guest room linens, and the brand of complimentary toiletries. The realtor staggered out of the car.

Now, Dean's early enthusiasm for the B&B was not surprising, and one could ask, if Jeff and Dean had been together for twelve years, why did it take them so long to buy their first B&B? The world knows only two types of gay couples—those who own B&Bs and those who haven't found the right property. Dean and I had previously discussed how wonderful life would be to run a beautiful inn or hotel. Dean relished the prospect of renovating an old property. For me, the motivation was always the same—to give up my legal career. We never advanced beyond drooling over advertisements for chateaux in Normandy or Provence, but once we did a drive-by of an ancient stone inn in the Cotswolds. The issue was always the cost of entry as gay couples from around the world drove up the prices of any property with potential charm. Of course, we hadn't looked in Hayward.

Like Mrs. McCormick, Dean fell in love with the house at first sight. As the realtor showed us the property, Dean gushed at its potential as a boutique hotel. I was not convinced. While the sales of shares in bank stock I received as bonuses over the years and of our home in London would generate enough money to fund the purchase of the dairy and could be stretched to purchase this house, the cost of refurbishing the property would burn through any cushion we hoped to save. In addition, to the extent Dean's attention was diverted to running a B&B, he would not be able to focus on the expansion of West's ice cream brand.

The realtor sensed a potential problem in me, and while we considered the remains of the kitchen, she said, "I heard the county was thinking of making an offer to buy the property."

"What would the county want with such a beautiful house?" Dean asked.

"Well, they would tear it down to provide more parking for the courthouse," the realtor explained, pointing to the building across the street.

"Jeff, did you hear that?" Dean exclaimed. "We can't let them tear it down."

If I hadn't known better, I would have thought Dean and the realtor had teamed up. Dean knew I hated to see old buildings, especially ones with the slightest historical significance, demolished. I knew from that moment that Dean and I were destined to become innkeepers.

We entered a cramped foyer, and Dean closed the front door. A handsome oak staircase wound its way to the second floor. To the left of the foyer was a large pocket door. It was missing a panel, but it opened to the lounge. A wood-burning fireplace filled a corner of the room at a forty-five-degree angle and faced a bay window. The blue Victorian tiles forming the hearth and surround were cracked, broken, or missing. The basket held the ashes of the last fire. The room was bright even as the light struggled through the large, unwashed windows that looked onto the courthouse across the street.

In the early 1990s, two sisters had raised funds to purchase the house and had converted it to a bed and breakfast. They tore out the shag carpet, patched the original wood floor, removed the wood paneling and the walls dividing the apartments, and added necessary washrooms in the guest rooms.

After operating as Lumberman's Mansion for ten years, the property was put on the market. We were not sure why it closed. Perhaps business was not good, although we heard the owners sometimes entertained guests in Victorian costumes on the veranda. Perhaps the house required further renovations that were beyond the owners' budget. We heard rumors of ghosts and bats disturbing guests in their sleep, but they may have been village myths.

As we moved into the library to the right of the foyer, I touched the stone-cold radiator coated in several layers of dust and paint. I felt a draft blowing through the thin panes of glass in the window overlooking the front porch.

"Oh, it's going to be beautiful!" Dean's enthusiasm for the project poured out of him. With the eye of a professional, he overlooked the odd pieces of Victorian furniture—straight-backed wooden chairs without a table, a horsehair daybed, and a solicitor's bookcase—that had been left behind as though the moving van had been too full or someone had forgotten them altogether. His eyes scanned every corner, assessing every need.

He pointed to the wall and began, "We'll put built-in mahogany bookcases there and a new hearth and surround, of course, for the fireplace. Low-voltage lighting here, there," he said, pointing to the ceiling. "Oh, there will be so much low-voltage, directed lighting everywhere." He raised both hands in a flourish. "Oh, and I think we'll serve Wilkins jams with breakfast—very British." Dean added these details as they popped into his head.

Much like my reaction to the cracked linoleum at the dairy, Dean noticed as we walked around the house every crack in the wall and every floral wallpaper border that would have to be removed. Some of his initial excitement about the project melted away, and I could see he was becoming overwhelmed by the job it would take to convert the house to the inn of his dreams.

"It's going to take a lot of work, isn't it?" Dean asked.

"Oh, no," I said. "It's going to be great," I assured him. I hated to see him discouraged.

"So, what do you think of an oversized-lampshade-style chandelier in the center?" he asked, relieved. Over the years and after many building and renovation projects, I had learned to defer to Dean's judgment as to all aspects of design and interiors. I agreed politely, if not convincingly, even if I was not exactly sure what he meant. Dean was in charge of lighting and soft furnishings.

With its grand size and authentic Victorian features, it was not difficult, even for me, to look beyond the warped and patched floorboards and obsolete heating system to imagine how beautiful the home had been when it was built. It had even made the news. A Chicago newspaper in 1887 described how a "palace" had been built with all the modern features of the day among the lumber camps of northwest Wisconsin.

In the library, a large painted desk with ornate claw feet sat in front of the bay window. The library, even in its forgotten state, was inviting. A fireplace similar to the one in the lounge dominated the back wall. One could almost make out the smell of Mr. McCormick's stale cigar from a century ago as he met with Hayward businesspeople who wished to build their homes across from this mansion overlooking what was originally known as Park Lake. Mrs. McCormick may have sat at the desk writing a note while she watched young Laird, Blanche, and Amelia playing on the hitching post at the front of the house.

"What will you do with these?" I picked up a dust-covered knit slipper from a basket at the bottom of the staircase. The message on the basket invited guests to wear the slippers to protect the floor or possibly their feet from slivers.

"Burn 'em." Dean laughed.

We climbed the oak staircase. Dean paused and looked up at even more wallpaper that would require removing. He sighed as though he were peering at a floral-bordered mountaintop.

There were two large bedrooms at the front of the house, a large room at the back, and three much smaller rooms along the connecting hallway. Each room had an antique bed with a bulbous and equally aged mattress that sagged in the middle and leaned in some uncomfortable direction, a cheap and often miniature armoire, a portable television, and in some rooms a giant Jacuzzi bathtub. An oversized tub took up a third of one room's floor space and sat next to the bed. Given the tilt of the bed, it was conceivable that a guest could roll off it into the hot tub and drown, his poor wife finding him when she woke in the morning.

"Oh, they gotta go!" Dean pointed to the tub in the middle of a room.

"Are you sure?" I asked. "The realtor made it sound as though Americans like hot tubs in their rooms."

"Well, they are one freaky people, then."

"What about the rubber ducky?" I asked, pointing to the small yellow duck on the edge of the hot tub.

"They can stay—for now."

We inspected the bathrooms for any redeeming qualities—fixtures, sinks, toilets—but found none. The sinks were small, chipped, and discolored. The shower and bath tiles were yellow or, worse, covered in mold or mildew. As we moved through the house, the findings took a toll on Dean's enthusiasm.

Finally, we reached the back of the house. The room had potential, with four long windows looking out the back on each side and a nice-sized shower room. The room was quiet and, as the midday sun approached, bright and airy.

"Oh my God!" Dean looked out one of the back windows.

What he saw was the aerial view of the "garden." We knew it was bad, but from this height, it resembled a railroad yard. At one time, a beer distributor had owned the property and had erected a large cinder-block building to house large beer trucks. At another time, the owner also owned a fleet of school buses and had built what might have been a storage facility, small office building, or brothel containing a number of little rooms. These buildings surrounded a very old yet large garage filled with miscellaneous construction equipment, wood, and garbage. The grounds were covered in snow, but muddy patches revealed no grass or even visible driveway.

"Perhaps we bit off more than we can chew with this house," Dean said. I agreed with the thought. The original estimate we had received for the renovation was reasonable, but we feared it might fall short of the actual costs. Dean looked forlorn. I knew he was seeking encouragement, some air to fill his sails.

"Nah, it'll be fine—it's going to be fantastic," I said, trying to sound convincing. "Look, we even have our own back staircase!" I opened a door outside the back bedroom that provided a narrow, dark path to the ground floor.

We had hired a local, well-regarded contractor to undertake the renovations of McCormick House. However, his schedule would permit him and his crew to begin only in the summer. Apart from disposing of the contents, there was little else we could do with the house for the next few months. The contractor assured us the house would be ready for opening in the autumn. "So, what should we do now?" Dean asked.

It was only 11:30 AM. We thought the handover at the dairy would have gone at least through lunch. We could return to the ice cream shop, but there was not much happening there.

"Let's go back to the cabin," I said.

A Cup of Tea on the Edge of the World

On the way to the cabin, we drove by Hayward's most famous landmark—the equivalent of the Eiffel Tower for Paris or Big Ben for London. The Big Fish was located on the grounds of the Fresh Water Fishing Hall of Fame and Museum, an army barracks disguised as a fish museum. The Big Fish was just that—a giant fiberglass fish.

The Shrine to Anglers was a giant musky constructed of concrete, steel, and fiberglass. We saw the fish from the highway before turning into the museum parking lot. It wasn't a Disney-style creation with a big smile and bright eyes, nor was the musky the panda or koala bear of its species. In fact, its name stems from the Ojibwe word for "ugly fish." The military-green replica had a long, protruding face and a serious underbite, revealing its sharp teeth. Nevertheless, this ugly fish attracted over fifty thousand visitors each year.

After browsing through extensive displays of lures and fishing line in the museum, visitors entered the shrine through the fish's posterior that sat near the ground and climbed a gentle staircase to the open mouth. Here, the creature's extended lower jaw doubled as a natural viewing platform for up to twenty people at a time. From the elevated position, visitors could see almost all of the museum grounds and, on a clear day, the supermarket down the road.

The concept of the Big Fish was the dream of Bob and Fannie Kutz, both local anglers. In the 1960s, with the help of other Hayward fishing enthusiasts, they put together a plan for a fishing museum and an eye-catching attraction. The structure was completed by the mid-1970s and has been a hit ever since it opened.

I took comfort from the Big Fish. Building a giant fiberglass fish must have seemed a crazy idea. Surely everyone said, "Fannie Kutz, you are nuts! Who would want to climb into the ass of a giant, ugly fish?" Fannie and the other founders of the Shrine to Anglers proved the naysayers wrong.

Many people—friends in London and colleagues—found our move to Hayward courageous if not enviable. Others thought Dean and I were crazy to give up careers with pensions and a home in a comfortable London neighborhood for an uncertain life in Hayward. We knew little about making ice cream and no more about innkeeping than anyone else who had stayed in a hotel, and we had spent no more than a few weeks in Hayward, Wisconsin.

When we obtained financial data on West's business, I sent the information to a friend, a former investment banker. I did not hear from him. He had moved back to his family's home in Dubai and for all I knew was lost in an oversized shopping mall built in the shape of a camel. A few weeks before leaving London, after we had sold our home, after I had notified the bank I was quitting, and while I was living in a service apartment, I received an e-mail from my banker friend with an ominous warning: "Whatever you do, do not buy that business!"

I was not so surprised by his assessment. The ice cream business was highly seasonal, the cost of goods represented a higher-than-expected percentage of revenue, the margins on the wholesale milk business were negligible, and the historic revenues produced little more than a basic return on investment before we paid ourselves any salary or considered the aging state of the equipment, including the twenty-two-year-old step van that we had not even seen.

The men and women who built the Big Fish may not have crunched all the numbers or conducted any market analysis of the likely success of their efforts before constructing a giant musky on the shores of Lake Hayward, but they must have had a hunch that the Big Fish could be a big hit. Perhaps they believed the Big Fish would attract visitors to the Fresh Water Fishing Hall of Fame and Museum. Dad could dawdle around the tackle box exhibits while Mom and the kids climbed the rear end of the fish to stand under the teeth of its open mouth. The kids could drop candy on unsuspecting museum visitors below them.

I explained to my friend that we had a hunch about West's and the potential for the ice cream business. There was a lot of history and character associated with West's Hayward Dairy that provided the basis for a great marketing campaign, and the ice cream was good. Surely, Almost Sinful could compete with something as silly as Ben & Jerry's Chubby Hubby, and, if Dean's research on the need for upscale accommodations proved correct, McCormick House would be well situated to take advantage of such a market and would be the perfect overflow guesthouse when all the rooms at Oprah's lake home were full. These floundering or nonexistent businesses provided a blank spreadsheet on which we had managed to imagine all our dreams—independence, the ability to call our own shots, make something a huge success.

More importantly, as I tried to explain to my friend in Dubai, what price would we place on missed opportunity? Once we discovered the ice cream shop was for sale, once we found the big empty house waiting to be revitalized, it made us sick to think that someone else would come along and snatch them from under us. We would watch as they turned them into successful businesses and enjoyed a comfortable life in Hayward. In the end, the price of the businesses did not seem very relevant.

The museum was still closed for the season. We saw a maintenance person enter the building, perhaps dusting the exhibits for the spring opener. We sat in the parking lot and gazed up at the fish's open mouth. From this distance, we could see the handrail around the inside of the mouth.

"It looks as though the fish has braces," I said.

Dean looked up but was not in the mood for joking. "Do you think we did the right thing?" he asked. "That house is going to take so much work—and money. What if we sink all this money into it and no one comes?"

"It's going to be the nicest hotel in the area—possibly the state by the time we're done with it." I tried to persuade Dean that even with the renovations and expense we had yet to incur in rebuilding both West's Hayward Dairy and McCormick House, we would be okay. "Clearly, our projects are not as crazy as building a giant plastic fish. Perhaps Hayward was the perfect place for us," I said.

We left the Big Fish and our new ventures in town. The springtime sun cast long shadows as we headed east. Across from a small, snow-capped pond, a rustic sign on a stone base erected by the U.S. Forest Service announced that we were entering the Chequamegon (pronounced she-WAH-me-gan) National Forest. The Chequamegon is the largest national forest in Wisconsin, comprising nearly 900,000 acres, or 2,000 square miles across six counties. The forest stretches from Sawyer County all the way to Lake Superior sixty miles away.

Twenty miles from Hayward and four thousand miles from London, a white sign pointed down a gravel driveway toward Sunset Lodge. A wall of pine trees lined the narrow drive. Snow lay thick and undisturbed on the forest floor apart from the occasional deer or fox tracks.

After a third of a mile, there was a fork in the road. We veered to the left toward an old log cabin. Nestled in nearly three feet of snow at the back of a forest clearing, the one-story log structure with small, square-paned windows sat low to the ground as in a nursery rhyme. Snow hung from the eaves; a wisp of smoke trickled from a metal chimney.

In front of the house, a log garage sat precariously. Large crevices had formed between the horizontal logs where the chinking that bound the logs had cracked and fallen through. The roof sagged with heavy snow. I had only peeked into the garage after the realtor told us it provided refuge to a large segment of the local bat population. Today, the garage sat silently as its hibernating occupants enjoyed the final days of their winter slumber.

Dean turned off the engine. We sat for a moment, unable to move or speak, almost transfixed by the silence and stillness around us. When my mother died a few years ago, she had left some money to each of her children. Dean and I decided to put it toward a down payment on the house. It was an L-shaped home, built out of tamarack logs that may have been harvested to make way for the foundation itself. It was built in 1927, the same year my mother was born.

In the manner in which someone close can read your thoughts, Dean asked, "What would your mother think of this?"

I laughed. "Well, I think she must be turning over in her grave—after twenty-five years of making those short visits, I move home only after she's gone." I shook my head. "She would ask what in the world could have possessed her son to give up being a lawyer," I added. She was proud of her lawyer son, and I didn't know what she would think. She would worry that I was giving up any financial security—perhaps I worried about that as well.

Dean smiled. "I don't think so. I think she'd be happy you've come home, and if she had any idea how miserable you were as a lawyer, she would be happy you gave it up."

"Maybe," I said. "I'd like to think that."

"Did your mom like ice cream?" Dean asked. "I don't remember," I said. "She may have been lactose intolerant."

Outside the car, the sun was blinding as it reflected off the snow in the clearing between the driveway and the cabin. The only sounds were the trickle of melting snow off the cabin roof and a light breeze through the branches of the tall oaks surrounding the property.

After being cooped up all morning, the dogs were anxious to get out and explore. Freddie, our pint-sized Norfolk terrier, held her head high to catch as much of the unusual scents as she could muster. Her paws slipped as she walked across the ice-covered path. Spike, a scruffy West Highland terrier, jumped onto the ice-covered snowbank as he might a comfortable sofa. He stepped gingerly; a thin coating of ice on the snow supported his weight. As his confidence surged, he took a short run, but after only a few seconds the ice cracked and his white body sank into the snow. Apart from his charcoal nose, he was undetectable. After a few shakes, he managed to look up, awaiting Dean's rescuing hand. Freddie shivered and scampered around my feet; she had had enough of the cold.

Dean had to duck his six-foot-plus frame through the Hansel and Gretel–proportioned door that opened to a new kitchen we had installed in what had been an old porch. As a true log structure, the interior walls were made of the rough log, presenting a challenge to picture hanging. A coat of varnish gave them a satin sheen that complemented the new wide-planked oak floor.

I unpacked some groceries we had picked up in town. The kitchen was small, having only a few cupboards and some open shelves to hold pots and pans. Even with just a few bags of groceries, the pantry was full.

Through a low, timber-framed archway painted a traditional forest green was the living room. In the log mansions being built today, this room would be called a great room, with high vaulted ceilings over a cathedral-sized lounge. Here, the ceiling was high enough not to bump your head, and a small chandelier made of deer antlers hung over a rustic bench that served as a coffee table. In the oversized fieldstone fireplace, the scent of burnt timbers from months ago lingered.

Dean hooked up the new television we had bought in Minneapolis in the corner of the room where a jack to the new satellite dish was installed. This was a priority. Dean had been fretting over the fact that he would not have access to *Coronation Street,* but he had recently discovered *Law and Order* and was excited to hear that it had been airing in the United States for decades and could be seen on some channel most every moment of the day.

"Do you think we should have bought the larger TV?" Dean asked.

It looked fine to me, but as he had asked the question, I knew we would be returning it soon. "Well, let's see how it feels when we're watching it," I said.

It was only their second day at the cabin, and the dogs were still getting used to their new home. They seemed exhausted after what must have been a day of sniffing and running from room to room. They might have detected evidence of mice and possibly a red squirrel inside the house. Freddie ran to the window, which was a perfect height, permitting her to stand on her back legs while supporting herself on the windowsill with her front paws. She let out her piercing bark at the squirrel standing on the deck only a few feet in front of her. Spike quickly ran to the window to provide backup even though he was not sure what his friend had seen. He let out a bark that was much deeper than one would expect from a small dog.

"They're going to love it here," Dean said.

I unpacked a few remaining suitcases and filled the small closets in both of the cabin's bedrooms. The cabin was less than half the size of our terraced house on Limerston Street. We knew space would be tight. We rationalized that we would not need room for suits and dress shirts.

Dean hauled logs into the living room from a pile of wood that had been sitting in the snow behind the garage.

"I think I'll build a fire," he said. He dripped and tracked mud through the kitchen to the fireplace. The house was cold. The log walls provided great insulation from the heat in the summer, but the structure had the effect of an igloo in winter.

The dogs stood in the window of the sunroom off the living room. I called it a sunroom given the expanse of windows, but due to its northern exposure, it caught only a glimpse of the sun as it set to the west in the peak of summer. The room was an addition to the original structure and provided space for dining, board games, and sitting.

More than anything else, however, the room provided a panoramic view of Teal Lake. Through the branches of a few aspen and boughs of a giant Norway pine was an expanse of ice that spread as far to the east as to the west, and only a few islands obscured the view of the distant shore on the north side of the lake. A lone deer crossed to Raspberry Island on the bridge provided by the frozen lake. I grabbed a pair of binoculars sitting on the table. The deer was being watched by a bald eagle perched high above in its island nest. Apart from traces of the homes set back from the shore on the other side, the frozen lake appeared uninhabited and looked as it must have for centuries.

We had seen the view for the first time a little more than a year ago. Although it was snowing hard that day and the distant shore was only a muted shadow, we knew it would be difficult to find a more impressive view of the north woods. When we returned in the summer, the lake shimmered, and the forest abounded in the deepest green. Loons, eagles, and even some prehistoric-looking herons went about their summer business. On our last visit in the autumn, the forest delivered a blazing splendor of color. That seemed so long ago.

Only a few days ago—on St. Patrick's Day—we were in the middle of our leaving party at a Chelsea pub. It was more of a tasteful gastropub than the smoke-filled Queen's Head down the street. Close friends as well as many of Dean's colleagues had come to the party. A few friends from the legal department at the bank had made the long trek across London from Canary Wharf. It was a last hurrah with champagne for all.

"You won't see much of this in Wisconsin," a drunken friend said and waved a bottle of Veuve Clicquot over his head. Young men and women in black vests thrust trays of tasteful canapés along with a few sausage rolls, a tribute to Dean's northern heritage, at our guests. Glasses were raised to our decision to leave the rat race behind.

"If only I had the courage to do what you guys are doing," a colleague whispered into my ear. "But I would have to leave the wife." He chuckled and slapped my back.

They left cards, well wishes, and some cheesy gifts, including an engraved ice cream scoop—"Jeff & Dean: The World's Best Scoopers." Everyone said they would visit, but I knew that with the nine-hour flight, three-hour drive, and no guaranteed sun, theme park, or Saks Fifth Avenue, few would make the trip.

I liked to think it was a mutual decision to leave London—the house, the walks with the dogs in Kensington Gardens, the fantastic restaurants, shopping at Harvey Nichols, and holidays in Europe and Asia. But when I thought back, it was really my decision, or at least I was the one who had first put the idea before Dean after Matt told me the ice cream shop was for sale. I didn't have to twist Dean's arm or anything—he wanted to live in America and welcomed the chance to run our own businesses. I didn't have to ply him with alcohol and Thai food, but there may have been some of each. If I hadn't suggested it, though, we wouldn't be here.

We had spent no more than a week at a time and several weeks altogether in Hayward. We knew only a few people—real estate agents, bankers, lawyers, builders—who all seemed very friendly, but as our friend Dave reminded us, they were also very happy to be taking our money. For all we knew, the others were all gun-toting, banjo-playing types not so accustomed to welcoming outsiders—especially a couple of "fellers" from London. For us, the decision to leave the corporate life—even with its trappings—became very easy when we thought of this view of Teal Lake.

After I told my boss I was leaving a career in law to run an ice cream business and renovate a small inn, he asked, "What are you looking for?" I was surprised by the question, but then, for him, the decision didn't make sense—all I had to do was stick it out another ten years and then enjoy a retirement in France or Tuscany. But I couldn't do it for another ten years. Even if I survived, by then I would be as old as my father had been when he died. I was afraid any answer I gave might offend him or come across as ungrateful. Telling him about this view of Teal Lake would come across as crazy.

"I'm not sure," I said. "Perhaps I'm looking for adventure."

On this first day of spring on our first day in the north woods, the view of Teal Lake appeared completely different from our previous visits. The lake was still a glacial plate that began to glow in the light of the setting sun. Opposite the lake began a thick pine forest, represented only by a dark smudge between the frozen lake and a giant, endless white sky. There appeared a vastness that had not been apparent when we had visited as mere tourists and when London was just a few days on the other side of this view, when London provided a lifeline back to a comfortable world.

Now our sunroom, some fifty feet above the lake, sat on the edge of the world, or at least a timeless wilderness that spread over the curvature of the Earth. And it was true—if you drew a line from the sunroom to the North Pole, it was possible that you would not encounter a city, town, or even settlement. This timeless wilderness of lakes and forests extended some fifteen hundred miles to the shores of Hudson Bay, and while I had lived and traveled around the world, I had never in all my life encountered anything so vast as the view before me.

From that moment, I was no longer an observer or mere visitor to this wilderness. I was now part of this landscape—small and insignificant, if not completely out of place, and wholly unprepared for what I was about to face. I knew there would be challenges, failures, and hopefully a few triumphs. I realized I was frightened of that wilderness more than anything I encountered in the city. If you dropped me in some crime-ridden slum, I could at least get a taxi. I'd be helpless in the wilderness and probably be wearing the wrong shoes. No matter what I had done in my nearly forty-two years, I realized I had never done anything to prepare me for this. It was unlikely that I could ever go back to the life I had just left in London. I would never see many of the friends and colleagues I had left only a few days before.

The sun was setting on the lake and the islands; pine-covered shore and sky disappeared into gray and then blackness. This would be my great adventure.

In the room behind me, Dean's fire was already a raging inferno. A bit of a pyro, he glowed with pride and the fiery light of the furnace he created. The dogs, tired from their long day of surveillance, lay on the floor a warm yet safe distance from the sparks and ashes spewing from the fire.

I admired Dean's ability to live in the moment—happy with his fire rather than concerned about anything unknown on the fringes of the Arctic Circle. But he was prone to restlessness. In London, if he was bored, he might pop out to visit friends in the shops on Bond Street or suggest we try a new Asian fusion restaurant in Soho. Would he be content with the twenty-mile drive from the cabin to the Wal-Mart in Hayward or the new menu at the Norske Nook? At our going-away party, an American friend gave us a DVD of the *Green Acres* television show, the joke being I was lawyer Oliver Wendell Douglas while Dean was the accented one who adored a penthouse view.

Now, Dean was as eager as I to move to Hayward, but it was all new to him. I could at least scour the recesses of my memory for a connection—my school in Chaska looked much like the red brick high school on the edge of Hayward. I was certain the interior walls were cinder block and there was a tough kid they called "Kitten" ready to shove you against the metal lockers that lined the hall. The people we met in town looked, spoke, hunted, fished, and fretted about the weather like members of my own family. In other words, I knew better. I knew we had come to a remote, Prada-free, and sushiless place with long winters and harpoon-wielding mosquitoes.

And there were times when, for Dean's sake, I may have glossed over some of the details of what life might be like in the north woods. For example, when Dean was surprised to see snow on the ground in late March, I told him it was probably a fluke. I certainly did not mention that the snow he saw could still be there in May.

"Not bad, if I say so myself, especially as these logs were really damp," Dean said as he sat back in the nearest easy chair with the poker at hand.

I remembered the box of PG Tips tea I had brought from London. "Would you like a tea?" I asked.

"Oh, yes, please!" Dean exclaimed. "I would love one!" As he always did when I offered tea, he expressed incredible relief and gratitude, as though I had just offered him a new kidney.

What About the Ambassador?

The closing for the purchase of West's took place at the office of our lawyer, Mr. Thomas Duffy, Sr. His office sat across from the post office at the top of Main Street and had the appearance of a Swiss Alps ski chalet with shingled siding and a small balcony off the second floor. On the front of the building, a local artist had painted a mural of an apparent Alpine scene. From a distance, you could make out only the jagged, snow-covered peaks and a lake in the foreground. As you approached the building, you could see a single wooden dock in the lake. Just as on the lakes of the north woods, a boat was moored to the dock. On the back of the boat was the name *Duffy.*

I was no stranger to closings. At one stage of my illustrious career as an international lawyer, I worked in my law firm's Hong Kong office under a Korean American who had managed to attract much of the Korean banking business in town. Every other week, it seemed a different Korean bank issued debt or established a syndicated loan. As a junior associate, my task, for which I was vastly overpaid and provided a comfortable housing allowance, was to ensure our standard documents reflected any changes from the previous deal and to supervise the photocopying and binding of such documents with special attention paid to the signature pages, as those were the only pages anyone ever saw. I could have replaced the others with pages from the Hong Kong phone book.

These closings took place at a conference room of one of the large Hong Kong hotels. A table was set up with a chair for each of the signing banks in the syndicate. After a few words by the bank issuer or lead manager, I ceremoniously opened the documents to the signature pages and went down the line, pointing out where each person was to sign, after which he passed the document to his, or occasionally her, left and received the next document for signing from his right. Each signatory was presented with a pen—a nice pen, either a Waterman or Montblanc—as a gift. On occasion, there was a spare pen that made a nice souvenir for an overworked associate.

The focus of such closings was always the lunch. The Korean bankers loved nothing more than a Chinese-style banquet with as many as nine courses, including shark's fin or abalone soup and numerous pots of tea. The lunches dragged on, and after the usual banter about how I was enjoying life as a single man in Hong Kong I hauled myself back to the office along with my box of signed documents and occasionally a nice pen.

I was not familiar with the protocol for closings in Hayward, but I doubted there would be a banquet lunch at the local Canton Garden. And without shark's fin soup, was there really any point?

Mr. Duffy's assistant, Pat, met us when we walked into the small lobby. The walls were lined with wood veneer paneling popular in the 1970s, especially for converting basements into cocktail bars with pool tables. The furniture reminded me of Buck's orange chair at the dairy. Behind a counter was a large room in which Pat maintained at least three desks by herself and several neatly labeled filing cabinets.

"They're all here," Pat said. "Let me show you to the room." She was trim and wore a smart suit. I wondered whether she dressed so professionally every day or only on those days when there was a closing or other meeting in the office.

Pat ushered us down a long and narrow hall with no room for any artwork. On the left, we could see the offices of our lawyer's son, Mr. Thomas J. Duffy, Jr., who was also the mayor of Hayward. Pat passed an open door, turned around, and held her hand out as if to offer us the room. The small, windowless room was stark white. Several people were already squeezed around the table in the center, but two chairs had been reserved for Dean and me.

Bruce and his wife, Jan, sat across from us with their lawyer. Bruce wore a checked dress shirt for the occasion and seemed quieter than usual, if not a bit anxious as he fiddled with a paper clip lying on the table. Jan, pen in hand, was eager to sign.

According to Buck, Jan had come down to the dairy one day, announced the place was on the market, and put "For Sale" signs in all the windows. "Oh, she had them in every window," Buck said. "When I called her to say she forgot a window, she was back in minutes with another sign. Jan's wanted to sell the place for some time now." Buck did not believe Bruce was as keen to sell the business. "What's he going to do with himself?" Buck asked.

Bruce's lawyer, a middle-aged woman with hassled light-brown hair and an old black trouser suit, sat quietly. We heard she was also an urban transplant who had left a good job and the rat race of Minneapolis or Chicago to hang a shingle in Hayward.

As Dean and I squeezed into our chairs around the table, the size of which was more appropriate for a bridge game, Mr. Thomas Duffy, Sr., burst into the room with a pile of documents. Pat followed with the signature pages that had been removed for easy signing. I recognized and appreciated her efficient style. Mr. Duffy wore a thick wool shirt and trousers with a sportsman's vest. An active skier and cyclist, he looked decades younger than his seventies. This was all the more impressive considering Tom Sr., in addition to being a descendant of one of Hayward's first families and one of the leading lawyers in Sawyer County, was the patriarch of a clan of a dozen or so children.

Most of the offspring had remained in the area, and they popped up when you least expected it. In addition to the mayor, another son was a dentist, another installed fireplaces, and a daughter ran the video store/tanning salon. Another son was the district attorney in nearby Ashland, and many said he could be governor of Wisconsin someday. They were all very attractive, Catholic, and Republican and had bright smiles and a healthy glow that looked as though they had just been on a beach holiday.

Tom Sr. was in a jovial mood and spoke to everyone rapid-fire as though he was in a great hurry or had had too much coffee that morning.

"So, how's everyone today? What do we have here? Oh, the dairy—a great business, I say." When he saw us sitting at the table, he turned to say, "So, how you guys enjoying Hayward? Have you hit the trails yet? There is still some good snow, you know." Before we could respond, he was out the door because he had forgotten some documents in his office.

Pat was parsing through the signature pages with the help of Bruce's lawyer, who said, "I think Bruce has something he would like to say."

"Oh, yeah. Well, we've got some good news. Garcia was able to get the van running," Bruce announced. "It was the carburetor."

"That's great news," I said.

Bruce's lawyer seemed relieved given that the van was part of the property subject to the documents. I vaguely recalled a rather high figure associated with the vehicle and had told myself I should look into the value of the step van before signing anything. We had not raised any concerns about it, but I now saw by the lawyer's reaction that perhaps we should have at least asked to see the vehicle.

"Oh, I forgot the pens," Pat called out and darted from the room again. I was not expecting Watermans, and she returned with an assortment of pens she may have found in the bottom of her purse amid tissues and old mints.

Others joined us and stood in the back of the room, including Tom Sr.'s cousin, who ran the local title company, and someone from the bank.

The various signature pages were passed from Bruce to Jan to Dean and to me. With all the documents signed, Tom Sr. said, "There's just one more thing." He looked at Dean and me. "The check?" he added.

"Oh, yes," Dean said. The others laughed as Dean handed Bruce the envelope containing the cashier's check.

Bruce took the check, but his hand trembled and it looked as though he might be overcome with emotion. He had given his life to help his parents and then had committed himself to the business that had given him and his family a nice life in the only place he had known. I sensed this closing was more than an exercise in pushing paper, more than some bricks, mortar, and revived carburetors changing hands. Bruce quickly handed the envelope to Jan, who safely deposited it in her handbag, which she held with both hands.

The mood lightened, and people began to ask questions about our plans for West's and how we liked Hayward so far. We assured them that we planned on leaving the dairy pretty much as we had found it and that everyone had been great to us so far.

"So, what will happen to the ambassador?" Tom Sr.'s cousin asked.

Dean and I looked at each other, thinking we should know to whom he was referring.

"Oh, you mean Bucky," Bruce clarified. "Well, maybe the guys will keep him on—he knows the place pretty well."

Although it had not been discussed and there was no mention of an opinionated, game show–watching septuagenarian in the inventory of purchased items, I got the feeling that in addition to a twenty-two-year-old step van with a dodgy carburetor I had never seen, we had just bought ourselves an old man.

When we gathered our things to leave the room—there was no mention of lunch—I looked at the pens left on the table. They may not have been Watermans or Montblancs, but I thought for the first time that a pen could have sentimental value someday when I looked back at the day my life forever changed. I picked one and examined it. It was from a local septic firm. It had the name and telephone number along the barrel of the pen with the slogan, "We take crap from everyone."

I thought for a moment and then returned the pen to the table, wiped my hand with a tissue from my pocket, and left the room.

Did You Have a Milk Route in England?

The alarm sounded at 5:00 AM. I shook Dean, who lay comatose and oblivious to the alarm.

"I don't wanna deliver milk," he mumbled into his pillow.

"Too bad. You're now a milkman," I said without sympathy. I stepped onto the cold wood floor. While the cabin's windows were of vintage charm, their panes had the repellent effect of cheesecloth.

Spike and Freddie waited anxiously at the door as they once did in London. This was the time I woke to get ready for work at the bank. I would have walked downstairs and opened the back door to a small garden enclosed by a ten-foot brick wall separating us from the hospital grounds behind us. After a few minutes—longer if there had been evidence of the neighbor's cat on the wall—the dogs would have returned to the house.

I looked out the window toward the garage. There was no enclosed yard. It was still dark, but the last of the moon's light left the snow-covered ground aglow. The garage, with its resting occupants, was caught in the shadows of the looming oaks and pines behind a retired out-house. I knew it would take only a scent of a rabbit and Spike would be halfway to Ontario before I could find a pair of slippers. I grabbed the leads from the kitchen counter and wrestled them onto the excited dogs.

A strong wind sounded like a freight train as it swept down the drive and pushed against the front door. The dogs pulled in every direction, dodging remaining snowbanks and enticed by a myriad of new and unusual forest smells far more interesting than the exhaust and leaking fumes of cars parked on Limerston Street.

Apart from a few deer that darted into the forest at the sight of the dogs, the coast seemed clear. *Nothing to fear,* I told myself. Or was there? Perhaps a bear had heard the dogs and decided it was time to wake from his winter nap and have a bit of breakfast. I didn't know what bears ate for breakfast. I heard eagles could spot their prey from three miles and snatch an animal up to ten pounds in weight. I looked at little Freddie; she might want to add a few pounds.

"Come on, Freddie, inside," I called, but she was engrossed by a mound of dirt and snow. "We'll go out later when it's light," I reasoned with the dogs as though they were toddlers. Once I suggested breakfast, they darted back to the kitchen. I closed the door behind us and took one last glance at whatever was lurking in the woods.

While the car was warming, Dean extinguished the remaining glowing embers in the fire with a few pokes. I scraped the frost from the windshield. It was cold for late March, below twenty degrees Fahrenheit, but it was due to warm up nicely by afternoon.

Bruce greeted us at the back door of the dairy. It was still dark. The van was idling at the curb, emitting plumes of strong exhaust over the street. Perhaps Bruce was afraid it wouldn't start if he shut it off. At some point in its career, the van could have delivered parcels for UPS. Painted white and rust, the vehicle sported a peeling decal depicting an arrangement of dairy products—milk, cheese, and cups of colorful ice cream—under the words *America's Dairyland*. A large crack streaked across the passenger side of the windshield.

"So, are you ready to work?" Bruce said. "First, we need to check the hospital, then the convenience stores to make out the orders." Bruce handed me a small metal notebook. Inside were lists of the desired stock levels for each customer.

Dean and I jumped into the van, unsure where to sit. There was a seat only for the driver. Dean stood by the open door of the vehicle, and I took what I thought might be a safer seat on an upturned milk crate next to the driver. In either case, we were both at risk of flying through the expansive and already cracked windshield in the event of a sudden stop.

"You all set?" Bruce asked. "Hold on!" He jumped off the curb and into the street. The van coughed and bucked as he changed gears.

After we checked inventory for each customer, we returned to the dairy to prepare handwritten invoices and load the van. With Bruce's broken back, Dean and I did the hauling.

The milk products came in standard heavy-duty plastic crates. Each crate held four gallons of milk yet nine half gallons, which struck me as odd. They weighed between thirty-five and forty pounds apiece. Bruce instructed me to stack six crates, or approximately two hundred pounds of milk, on a dolly. After he gave me advice on proper angle and maneuvering, I tilted the dolly but my foot slipped, and the stack would have toppled over had it not been for Bruce's timely intervention.

"Whoa," Bruce said as he took control of the dolly and reminded me to keep the load as vertical as possible. I tried again, but this time with only four crates. I figured I was younger and quicker than Bruce and could make up the difference in speed.

Once the van was loaded, we set off. This time, Dean rested on the metal bar with his hand on the side door for support. I took a seat on an upturned milk crate next to a stack of two percent milk. Bruce demonstrated the trick of putting the van in gear. Dean, who would be doing the driving, looked over to the old dash with the broken windshield as he might have looked at a time machine. A stack of milk rocked precariously as Bruce drove off the sidewalk and jerked the van into the street; I reached out, but the stack stabilized.

"It'll be all right," Bruce said. "But you gotta be careful on those turns or you'll have a real mess."

"And no sharp braking, either." Bruce glanced at Dean.

For the good part of four hours, we hauled milk from customer to customer and returned to the dairy only to reload the van. Because of his broken back, Bruce directed us through the maze of kitchens and convenience store coolers, often stepping over boxes and supplies left by other vendors. Dean and I took turns hauling and stocking the shelves, rotating the products when necessary to ensure those with the closest sell-by dates appeared on top. While we did this, Bruce chatted with the customer, keeping watch on us out of the corner of his eye to ensure we didn't screw up or place the chocolate milk where the two percent should be stored.

At each stop on the milk route, in addition to describing the stock required and the direction to the walk-in cooler or freezer, Bruce introduced Dean and me as the new owners of the dairy.

"And they came all the way from England," he said. This usually elicited at least an "Oh my gosh . . . that's a long way."

"Did you have a milk route in England?" an old dear in a hairnet asked. The latter elicited a great guffaw from Dean, who had never imagined donning a white cap and zipping around the countryside in one of the electric-powered milk floats that clogged the British roadways at their maximum speed of twenty miles per hour.

Dean, his sales manager's hat on, went out of his way to assure West's customers that we would continue to provide the same service levels they were used to over the years, just as he might have told one of his million-dollar software clients. The dairy's customers seemed more interested in how he said it. At the kitchen of a local hotel, the cook stood transfixed by Dean and finally said, "My, what a beautiful accent you have." She then shouted to her colleague, "Hey, Peg! Come over and listen to our new milkman talk. He's all the way from London, England!"

By the time we returned to the dairy, I was exhausted. My arms ached from lifting the crates out of the van and onto the dolly. My lower legs throbbed from trying to steer the heavy dolly up curbs, down ramps, and around corners on slick kitchen floors. Calluses erupted on my soft lawyer's hands. It was only 10:00 AM, but it felt like 4:00 in the afternoon.

"So, what the hell do we have here?" Buck said when he heard us enter the dairy. "Have you made dairy men out of these two guys yet, Bruce?" he asked.

"Oh, they're getting there."

Although Bruce was happy for us to acquire the dairy and had never expressed any doubts about how we would run the business, I could tell he wondered how two office types would manage the manual work. After the morning's deliveries, I thought he was impressed with how we took to the work, hauling the milk into tight corners of restaurant coolers and rotating the stock, all without much complaining or crying.

We unloaded the empty milk crates from the van and stacked them next to the building by the service entrance.

"Guys," Bruce said when we finished, "I have a doctor's appointment Wednesday morning. Do you think you can handle the route on your own?"

Dean and I looked at each other, each masking the horror we knew the other felt.

"Sure, no problem," Dean said.

I looked at my sore hands. I had my doubts.

Dream Catchers

On Wednesday morning, I woke at the crack of dawn. Dean was already up and dressed.

"Come on," he said. "There's milk to be delivered."

An icy fog floated just above the ground, and all around us the limbs of trees wore delicate crystal sleeves. We made the rounds to obtain orders. I wrote up the invoices. We had a few debates over the interpretation of Bruce's chicken-scratch instructions as to the desired inventory levels for each customer, but we erred on the side of leaving more rather than less as it would help the bottom line.

At the dairy, I found a pair of old gloves. They smelled of stale milk but would keep my hands warm and protect them from further damage. The van was parked in the municipal parking lot. Dean worked to turn over the engine and then moved the van to the dairy, reversing onto the sidewalk. He inadvertently shut it off whereas Bruce always allowed it to idle while loading.

With gloves protecting my healing hands and remembering Bruce's hauling tips, I quickly loaded the van. We double-checked the orders and took our positions. Dean turned the ignition. After several attempts, the old van coughed, whimpered, and finally succumbed to another day's work. Dean raised his hands in praise.

"Just like the Porsche?" I said. Dean had a penchant for high-performance sports cars and changed them like one might buy a new umbrella.

"No, the Aston Martin." He laughed.

The van jumped the curb as we left the dairy. We popped up like a pair of jacks-in-the-box and squealed.

"Whoa!" Dean shouted. "Hold on."

Our first stop after loading the van was the LCO Reservation, home of the Lac Courte Oreilles Band of Ojibwe, on the outskirts of Hayward. LCO is one of the largest reservations in northern Wisconsin and one of West's largest milk accounts.

With approximately 100,000 in the United States and another 80,000 in Canada, the Ojibwe constitute the largest group of Native Americans in North America, with bands living across the entire Great Lakes region.

The Ojibwe are Algonquian people, related to other nations of the northeast, who moved westward across the Great Lakes from New York and lower Quebec in the 1700s. Eventually, a band of Ojibwe settled on Madeline Island off the coast of Wisconsin in Lake Superior, seventy miles north of Hayward. By the mid-eighteenth century, a group of Ojibwe had established a village along the shores of the lake now known as Lac Courte Oreilles just outside what is now Hayward, where a community of Dakota Indians had lived for many years. Legend had it that during the first winter, a young Ojibwe child died. The grieving parents refused to leave the burial site, and soon the better-armed Ojibwe forced the Dakota west into what would become Minnesota.

With the migration of the Ojibwe across the Great Lakes, a legend grew and was visible all across the LCO Reservation. Because Spider Woman, protector of the Ojibwe, was unable to watch over the Ojibwe children as they dispersed westward, mothers and grandmothers helped her out. They took a small willow branch, shaped it into a circle, and wove a sinew web within it. This instrument was then hung over the cradles of young children, where it caught any bad dreams and allowed only pleasant dreams to pass through. The bad dreams perished as dawn broke each day. The "dream catcher" has remained a prominent symbol in the Ojibwe culture, often hanging from the rearview mirrors of cars and vans in the area to bring the driver good luck.

The van hemmed, hawed, and hesitated to make a hill east of Hayward. From the top of the hill, we could see the valley below, a few frosty fields as fog cloaked the pine groves in the distance. It was a serene, picture-perfect countryside view but for the massive fortress in the foreground trimmed in neon and bright lights. The LCO Casino, Lodge and Convention Center stood as a beacon for slot-starved geriatrics and fans of the near-dead in the world of country music. The sign at the entrance displayed a profile of an Indian man with the band's slogan, "Lac Courte Oreilles—Pride of the Ojibwe," and the flashing sign "Bingo Every Night—Doors Open at 6:00."

We checked in at the security entrance at the back of the bingo hall. As the kitchen had not opened, a young security guard with a badge, shaved head, and tattoo of a snake running up his neck from his open shirt escorted us through the casino to the kitchen area. Much like the fog in the trees behind the casino, a cloud of cigarette smoke filled the room at 6:30 in the morning as insomniacs puffed and pulled at the slot machines that lined the football field–sized room.

The casino was open twenty-four hours a day for the gamblers staying at the adjacent hotel. Here, time was not a factor. Even the doors at the front of the room to the parking lot were tinted to withstand any natural light. A few retirees who may have woken up with a lucky streak fed nickels in robotic fashion to the machines in front of them.

Although Dean and I had been at the casino with Bruce only two days ago, we were confused. The other day, we had entered from the back of the building, but today we seemed lost in a maze of storage rooms and food preparation areas. It did not help that some milk products were stored in the walk-in cooler next to vegetables, peeled potatoes, and the daily lunch specials, while other milk was designated for refrigerators in another part of the restaurant.

As I opened the refrigerator door, I realized . . . "Damn."

"What is it?" Dean asked quietly so the young waitress making coffee nearby would not hear us.

"I forgot the chocolate milk."

"You are bloody kidding me," Dean said, to the amusement of the waitress. Her long black hair was pulled neatly behind her and swung loosely.

I blamed it on my subconscious and the image I had of the Rat Pack or the casinos depicted in the Bond films. I could not imagine a svelte cocktail waitress with a hiked-up skirt and plunging neckline mincing up to a gentleman at the poker table and seductively whispering, "Your chocolate milk, sir," to which he would look her up and down and with a wink respond, "Keep 'em coming, sweetheart." Even at the LCO, a glass of Metamucil would have been more appropriate than a glass of chocolate milk. We unloaded the products we remembered to bring and told a cook we would return before lunch with the chocolate milk.

After a few more stops, we found our rhythm. Dean cleared the display space while I loaded the dolly with milk. We maneuvered around stacks of soda and bottled water in the cramped coolers at the convenience stores. Dean checked the dates and rotated stock as necessary. Many customers even remembered our names; only one commented she didn't think she would see us again.

"I think we're getting the hang of this," I said as I handed Dean gallons of milk over a tower of caffeinated energy drinks.

"This is clearly our calling in life. We should go to the Norske Nook for breakfast when we're done," Dean replied.

The final stop was the LCO Ojibwe School a few miles down the road from the casino and near tribal headquarters. The fog was lifting, and the sun emerged from the forests in the east. Days of melting snow exposed stalks of last year's corn harvest in muddy fields.

We turned onto a narrow road heading south. On the left, a field was home to some rusting farm equipment, including a plow and tractor. Near the top of a lone and leafless tree, a robust owl looked toward the oncoming van like a sentry granting us permission to enter the LCO nation.

At the end of the lane guarded by the owl sentry, there was a sharp turn to the left. A water tower, painted deep blue with the band's logo, the Indian-head profile, stood near the road. The van only reluctantly switched gears in order to make the turn. I grabbed the frame of the windshield with one hand to hold myself and used the other hand to steady a stack of milk crates holding half pints of milk for the school.

After making the corner, Dean hit the brakes with such intensity that I could barely keep from flying toward the windshield. My instinct was to prevent the milk from toppling, but I could reach only a single stack of crates. The rest—nearly thirty stacks of milk, four crates high—toppled like dominoes. Each case held fifty half-pint containers of school milk; hundreds of little cartons of milk lay scattered around the back of the van.

"Did you see that?" Dean shouted. I was too busy assessing the damage at the back of the van to glance out the window. When I looked, all I saw was a small bungalow on the left and a development of modest tract homes on the right. Not until I opened the door of the van did I see what was out there. Lying in the middle of the road, not more than fifteen feet from the front of the van, was a dog—a very large dog, part Rottweiler and part black bear by his size—resting and oblivious to the chaos he had just caused.

Dean got out of the van, and the dog—a seemingly happy old guy— slowly rose from his nap and swaggered off toward the bungalow's driveway.

"Any casualties?" Dean asked as he peered toward the mountain of milk cartons and crates in the back.

"Well, nothing worth crying over," I said. "We can probably salvage most of it at the school."

The LCO Ojibwe School is a modern, handsome stone building with a jagged roofline resembling a cliff with a carved eagle extending from the roof. The school had been built in the 1980s to permit children on the reservation an alternative to the Hayward schools. About a hundred students attend the school from kindergarten through twelfth grade. In addition to the standard public school curriculum, the school emphasizes tribal history and customs and the Ojibwe language.

We parked by the kitchen door. Dean and I sorted through the wreckage, examining every carton for leaks by holding it up and tipping it upside down before restacking it in the milk crates. When we finished a stack of crates, I rolled it into the lunchroom to the milk dispenser. It was already late in the morning, and the youngest children had begun to gather for lunch. The girls had long, straight black hair tied in pigtails, and most of the boys had closely cropped hair as though there was a lone local barber with clippers and one style. They waited in a wiggly line, waving their plastic lunch trays, distracted by the new milkman.

A small child approached. He stood next to me and put his hands on his hips. "Hey, mister!" he yelled into my right ear. "You're late!" he admonished me.

I had spent my adult life avoiding the unpredictable nature of children and was unsure how to address my new critic. *No milk for you,* I thought.

"Well, I am very sorry, sir," I apologized. "How would you like a chocolate milk today?" I held out a fresh carton for the boy and checked for leaks.

"Thanks, mister." He smiled, took the milk, and retreated.

I returned to the van to load more school milk. Dean had nearly finished examining and restacking the milk. He piled the crates four high outside the van. An instructor leaving the building watched us as we examined each of the spilled milk cartons for leaks. "Perhaps you guys need one of these in your van?" he said, pointing to the large dream catcher hanging from the rearview mirror of a parked car.

Welcome to Turk's

Dean and I had not given much thought to the sacrifices we might be making in moving from London to Hayward. There was one exception—food. Typically, when I got home from the office at 8:00 or 9:00, we headed to our local Indian, Thai, or sushi restaurant. It seemed the perfect way to unwind. For special occasions, assuming we had booked a table months in advance, we made a pilgrimage to the latest restaurant creation from Britain's rude celebrity chef. If we were lucky, the bad boy chef may have been in the restaurant that week to slap around some of his staff involved in the plating of our reinvented fish and chips. It wasn't that we were snobs about food. In fact, we both grew up on basic meat-and-potato diets, except my mother served hers with a canned vegetable while Dean's mother boiled vegetables northern style, until translucent. While Hayward had many fine restaurants with some of the freshest pickled herring relish trays, we knew within weeks we would be craving some pad Thai. We had already marked our calendars for May 17 and looked forward to some Scandinavian specialties at the Norske Nook's *Syttende Mai* (Norwegian Constitution Day) celebrations.

Our favorite Hayward restaurant was the Ranch Supper Club. It had been around forever. On the wall near the entrance was a photograph of Vivian, a former owner from the 1950s, sitting on a swaybacked horse. There was a long cocktail bar that reminded Dean of the bars on American television, and it was not long before everyone knew our name.

Cheryl, the bartender, was in her mid-fifties and the eldest of a large Norwegian family in Hayward. She owned the restaurant with her sister and brother-in-law and was known for her mean cocktails and repartee. She took a shine to Dean, who made it his goal to work through her arsenal of cocktails. Cheryl started him on the Wisconsin supper club favorites, the Old Fashioned and Manhattan, both of which Dean spat out and, to the amusement of the others around the bar, described as undrinkable. For the time being, he settled on the Tom Collins, which strangely had the color of powdered orange drink and, due to its sugar content, kept Dean awake at night.

The bar had an ornate top of pieces of granite and other stones covered in a thick lacquer. The smooth surface compelled people to rub it as a form of stress release in case Cheryl's cocktails did not do the trick. The best spot at the bar was at the end where a horseshoe-shaped appendage was conducive to conversation.

The cast of characters around the bar included Cheryl's adoring boyfriend, who sat at the end and helped retrieve ice or clean glasses from the kitchen when necessary. There were some patrons who were clearly missing from dinner at home, two women who ran a local antique business and another Jeff, who was in the throes of opening an upscale kitchen shop catering to Hayward's new economy. We heard he had written a pamphlet on the proper cleaning and cooking of road kill—rabbits, squirrels, deer, and other creatures flattened by oncoming traffic. Chef Jeff downplayed such delicacies as he described his new line of rich salsas and dipping sauces.

Dean and I usually had one of the Ranch steaks and ate at the bar so we could continue chatting with Cheryl. After a few visits, the entire serving staff knew to bring Dijon mustard with our steaks, to replicate how we had eaten them at La Brasserie on the Brompton Road. We had to admit the steaks were better than La Brasserie's French cut, and the wild rice blend was a nice alternative to French fries.

We survived our first weeks in Hayward. We completed the purchase of West's Hayward Dairy and learned the ins and outs of the milk route. Our milkman, Tom, returned from his time away, and we immediately gave him a sizable pay raise on the condition that he never took another vacation. Rock-throwing evangelicals had not chased us to the edge of town, and it was my forty-second birthday.

To celebrate these milestones, we asked our friends at the Ranch where we should go, and they all said, "Turk's." So we booked a table for dinner at the Turk's Inn. Billboards coming into town from every direction promised "excellent food and cocktails since 1934." They said not only that the steaks were excellent but also that dining at Turk's was a true "Hayward experience" not to be missed.

It had been a warm spring day. The sun stretched later into the evening and set aglow the tall pines that surrounded Turk's Inn, located on the banks of the Namekagon River a few miles upstream from Lake Hayward. When George Gogian, an Armenian immigrant, found himself in northern Wisconsin, he built a restaurant in a clearing along the river. It was said he planted each of the pine trees himself.

The restaurant, serving Chicago-style steaks, became a destination for the well-heeled traveler. No visit to the area was complete without a steak at Turk's. Time may have dimmed the reputation of the restaurant, but George would certainly be proud of the forest he planted. The trees, over eighty feet tall, dwarfed the low-rise building with its red Turkish-style canopy over the front door.

The musty odor hit hard when we entered the windowless foyer. Sectional sofas dating back to a time when you would expect a long wait for a table at Turk's were covered with unopened boxes of restaurant supplies, table linens in their plastic laundry bags, and other paraphernalia that either did not have another home or no one had bothered to put in their proper place.

The hostess was watching *Wheel of Fortune* on a small TV suspended from the ceiling corner. She squinted to make out the letters on the TV, and Vanna White was nearly impossible to see on the small screen. Somewhat startled, the hostess rose slowly from the sofa and turned to look at us. She was elderly, tall, and pale with short gray hair. I wondered what the deal was with the old people of Hayward and game shows in the workplace.

"Hello. Welcome to Turk's," she said.

We told her about the reservation. She insisted we have a drink in the Souk's Lounge before moving into the dining room, and she led us to the bar. She was also the bartender.

The lounge was Turk's version of a 1950s-style cocktail bar. A red Formica bar curved to a point in the manner of a Turkish slipper. Heavy, red, cracked vinyl barstools were fixed permanently to the floor, leaving an uncomfortable distance between my body and the bar. A matching red vinyl banquette wrapped around the entire exterior wall. Framed black-and-white photographs of the political figures and celebrities who had visited Turk's over the years hung below large windows overlooking the Namekagon River.

Many of the photographs featured a small man—he could not have been more than five feet tall. This must have been George. Any sporting star, news anchor, or political figure of standing would have his or her photo taken with George to appear on the wall. I imagined George waiting at the door every evening for the trophy shot—a Frank Sinatra or Rosemary Clooney.

In a prime position above the bar was a painting of an elegant woman in a contemporary Turkish gown. This was George's wife, and the portrait may have been painted on one of many trips back to Turkey during which family and friends listened to stories of George's success in America. Near the painting of Mrs. Gogian was a photograph of a beautiful young woman with penetrating brown eyes and sultry dark hair.

"Is that Marge?" I asked our hostess-turned-barmaid.

"Oh, yes. That was when she was in New York," she said. "You know, she was in the fashion industry for many years, even attended the inauguration of President Kennedy."

"Really," I said.

"But, you know, her dad needed her here. He was getting old, and there were no other children to help with the business. It's the Turkish way, I guess," she said of the sacrifice a young woman made for her family. "And she has been running the restaurant ever since. You know, she cuts her own beef in the basement." This was a fact most often associated with Marge and Turk's. I pictured a young Turkish beauty in flowing robes hacking away at a side of beef in the basement of this dated restaurant.

"Is Marge working tonight?"

"Of course! Marge never lets anyone else cook."

I had heard much of Marge's story earlier that day when I told Buck we were heading to Turk's. As it turned out, Marge had been a classmate of Buck's at school in Hayward.

"Oh, she was a beast, she was!" Buck said. "She'd go into a rage at the drop of a hat. The whole family was like that—real hotheads. They were from Turkey, you know," Buck said, as though rage was a genetic or national trait. Buck smiled, reflecting on the past. "The old man and his wife were always fighting in the kitchen. It was really quite comical," he added, using the only term he applied to anything funny or amusing. He leaned toward me and lowered his voice as if to reveal a secret. "You know, though, Marge was very beautiful. I think she was even a model in New York but came back to help her dad."

After only a few minutes in the bar, our hostess/barmaid-turned-waitress decided it was time to eat and asked us to follow her to the dining room. The room was crowded with tables covered in pink linen and plump, white, wood-framed chairs with mint green vinyl seats. An artificial fig tree dominated the center of the room under a small dome in the ceiling. It could have been Tavern on the Green circa 1960.

"It's like a museum," Dean said, glancing about. We immediately felt fortunate to be here, as though it could soon disappear.

Our friend and now waitress scanned the room for the perfect table. The restaurant was empty apart from a family of four at the far end of the room. She looked over to the kitchen door and then led us to the table furthest from the kitchen, next to the family. We awkwardly sat and nodded as though we had been asked to join the other group of diners in a private celebration. They politely smiled and returned to their conversation.

I scanned the menu for Turkish items. Amidst a number of steak dishes, I found shish kebab, an appetizer made of filo pastry and cheese called *borek,* and another appetizer, Turkish pickles.

We waited a long while for our waitress to reemerge. We assumed she was washing dishes as well. She came through from the Souk's Lounge with more cocktails for the family, who were finishing their meal. Based on the volume and degree of giddiness of their conversation, this must have been the latest of many rounds of cocktails. The mother was the center of attention. With a loud, gravelly voice and smoker's cough, she appeared to be celebrating a birthday or maybe the news that her iron lung had arrived.

"I said I would quit before I turned seventy—so this will be my last cigarette," she told her family as she got up, grabbed her cocktail, a brandy Old Fashioned, and headed to the bar. In Wisconsin, it was prohibited to smoke in the dining room of a restaurant, but you could still smoke at the bar. "I'll be in the Souk's Lounge," she announced with special emphasis on *Sooouk.*

With a pad in her hand, our hostess/barmaid/waitress returned to take our order. We asked for some recommendations.

"Oh, the porterhouse," she said, without equivocation. The porterhouse was the largest steak on the menu—twenty-nine ounces. And it was also the most expensive item.

We ordered the borek, some Turkish pickles, and two porterhouse steaks. She asked Dean how he would like his steak prepared.

"Medium-well, please," he said.

"Oh, no. You can't do that," she admonished Dean as though he were about to throw a child in front of a moving bus.

"Why?"

"Marge doesn't like that. She thinks overcooking meat is a travesty. I could ask her, but she won't be very happy."

Dean thought about it. He was from the north of England and preferred his meat dark brown. At the same time, it suddenly mattered to him what Marge would think, and he did not wish to make her unhappy.

"Okay, would medium be all right?"

Our waitress remained unimpressed but accepted his order. "Baked potato or fries?"

"Which do you recommend?" I asked

"Oh, the fries. Marge cooks them in lard," she said as though it was the superior method.

After taking our order, our waitress disappeared. She was gone for a very long time considering we ordered pickles.

We heard the birthday girl coughing up a storm in the Souk's Lounge. Only the shouting emanating from the kitchen drowned out the sound of her constant hacking. There was a man's voice, then a loud and steady shriek accompanied by the banging of pans.

"I hope Marge realizes you ordered the overcooked steak and not me," I said. "Do you really think that's it?"

We heard a thud, perhaps something falling. It could have been a quarter side of beef or a dead busboy hitting the floor. After a few minutes, our waitress reappeared through the swinging kitchen doors, carrying our appetizers—the borek and a plate of Turkish pickles.

"Is everything okay in there?" Dean asked.

"Oh, there's no problem," she reassured us with a wave of her very long arm.

"It sounded as though someone was unhappy." Dean really wanted assurance it was not about his steak.

"Oh, that's just Marge and Dave. It's the same thing every night. Marge would rather be in the kitchen alone, but she needs the help."

The pastry with cheese was tasty if a bit greasy, but after the long wait it hit the spot. The pickles were unusual, and I wondered about their provenance. They did not seem particularly Middle Eastern. They were crisp and sweet. I recalled the same pickles while I was growing up. Every year, a neighbor with an overflowing cucumber patch gave us a jar of sweet pickles she canned herself. My mother immediately opened them, tasted to her delight, and then put them in the refrigerator, where the pickles sat for a year until replaced with another jar.

With our fellow diners retiring to the Souk Lounge for a Kahlúa and cream, Dave emerged from the kitchen. He swung the doors so hard the wall of the kitchen shook. He wheeled a cart in order to clear the dishes from the table. He was young by Turk's standards but might have been as old as his late thirties. He looked familiar, as though we had seen him in another restaurant, but we could not place where. He mumbled under his breath—something about an "old rag" and a "dirty ditch," or so it sounded.

Our waitress wheeled in another cart laden with plates and accoutrements. It was meant to impress, and it did just that. She carefully placed two silver-domed platters in front of us and, despite a bit of arthritis in her hands, managed to remove both domes simultaneously thanks to her exceedingly long arms.

"Oh my God," Dean and I said in unison.

It was dinner for Fred Flintstone. The porterhouse was at least three inches thick and hung over the edge of the platter like Fred's brontosaurus chop. On a separate tray was a mound of golden, thick-cut fries for us to share. The blood in my arteries stopped for a moment to take it all in.

"Can I get you anything else?" our waitress asked.

"Perhaps an ambulance, or just skip the ambulance and get the coroner," I said.

She was not amused and walked away.

The fork-tender steak was delicious, and it must be said that lard made for a nice French fry. After dinner, we had Turkish coffee that was served in a traditional brass pot with a long wooden handle from which our waitress poured into a demitasse. It was a fine touch, and, as I maneuvered my tongue around some coffee grounds, I was for a moment taken to another place. I wanted to hop on a plane to visit the Blue Mosque in Istanbul. I had been there on business, saw the sights, bought a carpet, and ate the coffee. But then I would miss the chance to see Marge, our celebrity chef.

As we finished our coffee and picked the bitter grounds from our tongues, Marge appeared from her lair in the kitchen. No more than five feet tall, she looked nothing like her youthful portrait but wore her jet-black hair shoulder length, suggesting she retained a sense of style. In a soft, grandmotherly voice and nothing like the shrieking mad-woman we had heard through the doors earlier, she asked how we had enjoyed the dinner. I wanted to ask if she had any regrets about giving up a life in New York to run Turk's, but I could tell there were none. After our enthusiastic appreciation, she asked, "Would you like me to read your coffee grounds?"

She took Dean's coffee cup and turned it over onto the saucer. She slowly lifted the cup to examine the patterns left by the grounds on the inside. Her eyes squinted to distinguish a hidden meaning. "I see some legs—beautiful legs." She looked at Dean and grinned slyly. "Perhaps a woman will enter your life," she said.

Dean grimaced and shook his head to say that probably was not going to happen.

"Perhaps they are children's legs." She changed her prediction, but the response was pretty much the same. If she had said they were the legs of a puppy, we would have been thrilled.

Marge put down the cup and sighed. "You know, I don't really know much about this. I just listened to what my father used to say," she confessed. She smiled and held out her arms to thank us again for coming to her restaurant. We promised to return.

"We should bring Matt and Dave. They'd like it here," Dean said.

We said farewell to Marge and her staff, then fell into the car for the journey home. I held a juicy cocktail napkin with pieces of porterhouse for Spike and Freddie.

"They're going to love Turk's," Dean said.

Ice Out

Although the calendar said spring had arrived nearly a month ago, there was little evidence of it on the ground. Temperatures rose above freezing during the day, melting much of the snow, but they dipped below freezing in the evening, and no one was surprised when, in the second week of April, we woke to two inches of fresh snow. Teal Lake remained trapped in a glacial time warp. Even the dogs wondered what was happening. Through the windows, they surveyed the land around the house for life other than the occasional squirrel or deer. Outside, they dug through mounds of fragrant forest decay revealed by melting snow. They must have wondered when the fresh green shrubs and bushes, their new toilets, would appear.

I looked everywhere for signs of spring—a delicate crocus, a bright daffodil, or a plump robin. Given the state of affairs, I struggled to imagine how summer could begin in six weeks. I should have remembered how late spring arrived in the region. As a kid, I was an amateur weather watcher. I was a fan of Barry ZeVan, a television weatherman who resorted to humor as the only way of conveying the sad state of Minnesota weather. I recorded the high and low temperatures for the day and envied those folks in Cleveland with a high of sixty-five degrees in April, but then I had never been to Cleveland. Now and then, I recalled an image—watching April floodwaters rise along the Minnesota River against the bare trees on the opposite shore near my home, or picking lilacs and violets for Mother's Day in mid-May—that would remind me I had to wait a little longer.

Finally, however, there was a sign that spring was in the air. It was about 6:00 AM on April 14.

"What was that?" Dean shot up from bed. There had been a loud cracking sound or a muffled thunder and a frightening thud. It was surely too early in the season for a thunderstorm. When I parted the curtain, I saw only a gray sky in the faint light of dawn. As I looked closer, however, it became clear. Gone was the yellowed and slushy sheet of ice that had covered Teal Lake. In the distance, I saw a large chunk break up and sink before my eyes. The sound must have been the cracking of the ice. The dark water just released from its icy coffin seemed to gush to the surface with the vengeance of a much larger body of water.

"The ice is out!" I shouted. Dean came over to the window.

"That's amazing."

This glorious news of the arrival of spring to Teal Lake had not reached the trees and shrubs on the drive into town. They remained brown, bare, and lifeless and knew not to succumb to the tempting rays of April—too risky. Daffodils and tulips would take another month before they breached the Wisconsin tundra.

Without worrying about the hospital, casino, or any other milk deliveries, I strolled into the dairy at 9:00 AM. I was excited to tell Buck the news about the ice going out on our lake.

"Oh, yeah, most lakes are now open," he said as though he had toured the area himself. He was either guessing or was repeating something he had heard at breakfast at the co-op. "Whitefish is always one of the last to go," Buck said. "It's the deepest lake in the area. Teal Lake is average or a bit on the shallow side, so this is about the time."

Buck was watching the morning news. Since we had told him we intended to keep him on the payroll, he had been less solicitous, not as eager to please as he was in the early days. He was more relaxed in front of the television. But of all the people who have worked for me, including young ambitious lawyers with six-figure salaries, I have never had a more enthusiastic or loyal employee. He opened the dairy by 7:30. When I arrived, the lights were on, the coffee was made, and Buck had a cheery hello ready for me. Occasionally he would lock the door shortly after that in order to accompany Tom on the milk route. He did not help deliver any milk, just rode along for something to do. He visited with the convenience store workers, kitchen staff, and other customers he knew.

Apart from his two years of wartime duty in Hawaii, Buck had spent his entire life in Hayward. He knew the town and its people like the back of his veiny, gnarly hand. He had lived most of his life on the family farm near Chippanazie Lake but didn't make a living off the farm. He had worked at a number of places over the years, including a local florist, but had retired about fifteen years earlier as a driver for a home fuel delivery service. About that time, his wife left him, and they sold the farm in order to divide their assets. She moved to a mobile home park on the south side of town while Buck moved to a similar park on the north side. It was then that Buck started helping Bruce at the dairy. He seemed to love being at West's, but I also got the impression he didn't like being alone.

Nevertheless, Buck had a reputation around town as a cantankerous old fart, and some people thought we made an odd pairing. He had his opinions on any subject, was prone to rant—usually about today's youth and the speed at which people drove down Dakota Avenue—and could be very ornery. Usually, he just liked to talk, and whenever his rant went on too long, I changed the subject—"So, what's going on at the senior center?" Buck would then begin a long story about people I didn't know. It reminded me of when I spoke to my mother from

London and she would update me on the ins and outs of Mrs. So-and-so's recovery from gallbladder surgery.

Little Bob arrived just in time for *The Price Is Right*. He and Buck compared notes and debated where ice had gone out on the area lakes. He mentioned my report from Teal Lake. He again reminded me about Bob's lackluster wartime experience in England. "He didn't even earn a single stripe!" Buck said. Bob ignored his friend and changed the channel on the television.

Since we had first met Bob, we learned he was a spry eighty-five years old. He had moved here twenty-five years ago after retiring from a janitor's position in Chicago. He never married and lived in a tiny rustic cabin in the woods thirty miles north of Hayward. It was rustic not in the sense of antler chandeliers and bear-embroidered cushions but in the sense of no running water or indoor toilet.

Every morning, Bob drove his small pickup truck to the co-op for coffee and a donut. As in many small towns, the co-op was Hayward's original grocery store and was owned by the members who shopped there. There was also an associated hardware store, feed mill, gas station, and perhaps a tanning salon. However, when anyone talked about the co-op, they usually were referring to the diner attached to the grocery store. It was a true greasy spoon, popular with builders and retirees. There was a bench in front of the co-op, usually lined with old men digesting their breakfast or lunch and contemplating their next move, which, given their age and what they had just consumed, could be their last. The bench had a nickname—"death row."

After spending some time on death row, Bob usually came to West's to watch *The Price Is Right* and chew the fat with Buck. Around lunchtime, Bob headed back to the co-op for a cup of soup. I hoped the co-op had a few customers with heartier appetites than Bob. He often returned to the dairy in the afternoon, where he gave Buck a single dollar for a small vanilla ice cream cone. I allowed this discretionary pricing for him to continue for the time being.

Business had been slow. The City of Hayward had blocked Dakota Avenue as Bruce had warned and had begun to remove the pavement and sidewalks. The closure meant anyone traveling to West's by car had to fight the traffic on Main Street, turn on Second Street, and drive toward the dead end. This was not so bad, but to leave, people had to make a three-point turn to exit in the same direction, usually while holding an ice cream cone. This type of motoring skill was far beyond the levels of convenience tolerated by most locals.

Buck turned up the volume on the TV to overcome the sound of jackhammers on the corner fighting through levels of blacktop and concrete to find the aging water pipes to be replaced. I wondered how long the project would really take. They had been at it for a week and had only dug a few holes, created a ton of dust, and annoyed everyone. They were progressing at a rate similar to that of spring in Hayward.

With summer around the corner, Dean and I turned our attention to sprucing up the dairy. The plan was to paint over the faux barn on the exterior, replace the linoleum floor, remove the posters of the young milk-mustached boys (or at least most of them), and paint the interior. This all seemed perfectly manageable. Upon closer examination, we decided to remove some of the aging cooler doors and install a retail display area of shirts, hats, and local maple syrup and wild rice.

The real problem was it was already the middle of April and we had no one to do the work. Due to the property boom in Hayward, most builders were in the throes of someone's dream home—cathedral ceilings, radiant in-floor heating, central air conditioning, and a game room with large patio doors through which they might see the lake while sitting in front of a fifty-two-inch television.

"I'm afraid you left it a bit late for this year," I was told many times. "Perhaps we could fit you in in September or October before hunting season." I looked at the chipped linoleum floor and park bench seating and could not wait.

One morning, the phone rang at the dairy. It was an aunt of a friend of a local acquaintance. She said she heard that we were new to town and were having trouble finding a builder. She told me about a great group of guys who recently did some work at her house. She said they were very nice fellows, always polite, and the quality of the work seemed great. "Nothing has fallen down—yet." She laughed.

I inquired further as to the nature of the work she had done. As it turned out, they had only built some window boxes and installed a new screen door. I looked around at the dairy—the chipped linoleum, stained walls, and broken display racks.

"They sound perfect. Can I have their number, please?" I asked.

After many attempts and messages left with the builder's mother or wife, he called. His name was Timmy, and he sounded very young and distracted, as though he was busy with Little League practice or a Boy Scout meeting. He assured me that he and his brother, with help from others, including an electrician who went by Sparky, would have no problem completing the desired renovations.

Days passed, and there was no further word from the builders.

By lunchtime, a few customers trickled into the shop from Main Street as well as some dust-coated customers who risked life and limb to cross the construction on Dakota Avenue. For two weeks, I had spent my afternoons working under Buck's tutelage to master my scooping technique. The goal was to roll a ball by pulling the scoop across the surface of the ice cream. After the third or fourth roll, you could shape the ball of ice cream to place on the cone. The trick, according to Buck, was to leave plenty of air between the layers of ice cream and inside the cone.

"This makes the cone look bigger than it is," he whispered so no one would hear this trade secret. "That way, you can save on ice cream." I appreciated his looking out for the business like that.

Even with Buck's technique, West's ice cream cones were large. A small cone was two and a half scoops, or at least eight ounces of ice cream. A large cone was the size of a grapefruit and possessed the caloric intake of a small African nation.

The other staple at West's was a shake or malt. In Britain, a milk shake is just that—a bit of flavor added to some milk that is then shaken. If there is any ice cream in the shake at all, it is undetectable. An old-fashioned American malt or shake is thick—the thicker the better. For many, the test of a good shake or malt is when you use all the power within you even at the risk of a collapsed lung in order to suck the drink through a straw.

A West's shake or malt started the same way—four or five scoops of vanilla ice cream to which you added chocolate, strawberry, pine-apple, blueberry, caramel, or hot fudge. For malts, Buck added a few heaping teaspoons of malt powder. We had on display a few vintage malt machines, one from the 1920s and another from the 1950s, a mint green unit that resembled something from an old-time dentist's office. The concept for the malt machine had not changed over the years, and the one we used was at least twenty years old. Normally, one mixed the ice cream in a stainless-steel canister and then trans-ferred the drink to a glass or paper cup. Buck did not believe in this method, as it meant you usually made too much and wasted ice cream and, as he pointed out, "then you have to wash the damn thing!"

Buck mixed the malt in the waxed paper cup. It would take only a slight slip or tilt of the cup and the tiny blade at the end of the wand could pierce the cup, spraying you, the machine, and anything within ten feet with ice cream or, worse, blood from your pierced finger.

I had been working all week perfecting my shakes and malts. Buck had been supervising my technique, but it seemed there was no pleas-ing him. "No, you need more ice cream," he said. Then it was, "Now you need more milk."

I didn't mind. Buck considered himself pretty much the best in the business, and most people in town agreed. Many customers were not content with anyone other than Buck making their malt. There was one customer in particular who sang praises to Buck's malt-making prowess. Al, a clerk from the post office, often took his lunch in the form of a chocolate malt at West's Dairy.

After a few days and several attempts, usually for me, as Buck said my work was not ready for the public, I believed I had mastered the craft and could be left alone to run the shop, so I told Buck to go to lunch.

"Are you sure you can handle it?" he asked.

"Of course," I said.

"Well, Al was in yesterday for his malt, and he usually doesn't come in two days in a row," Buck said. "So you'll probably be okay." The implication was that if his best customer came in, there would be a problem.

"I'll be fine," I said.

Of course, within minutes of Buck leaving for the senior center for his Salisbury steak lunch, who should come in for his chocolate malt lunch? Al! "Is Bucky around?" he asked.

When I told him the bad news, Al looked disappointed, as though someone had died or the government had cancelled Columbus Day and his day off from the post office. But he also looked uncomfortable, as though he was not sure what to do. I thought he might turn and run for the door.

"Would you like anything?" I asked. I knew exactly what he wanted.

"Nah, that's okay. I may go have some soup."

"Are you sure? How about a chocolate malt?"

"I don't know." He grimaced as though he didn't wish to take such a giant gamble. He was, after all, a federal employee.

"Look, Al," I said. I was getting a bit annoyed. After all, we were only talking about a blended ice cream drink, and I had a law degree! "If you don't like it, I'll refund your money."

I saw Al's mind working. He was the type who thought if it sounded too good to be true, it probably was. Nevertheless, he agreed to let me make his malt.

I scooped the ice cream and added the chocolate syrup, the milk, and an appropriate amount of malt powder. I was somewhat nervous. Al watched me as though he had seen my profile on the FBI's most-wanted list at the post office.

It went smoothly. The malt was a perfect consistency with no spraying of malt or torn cups or bloody hands. It looked great! It was perhaps my best work to date. I smiled and handed Al the finished product.

I watched him as he sat and tasted the malt. He tried the straw, but it was pretty thick, so he used the parfait spoon and took a taste. Al had a real poker face—no emotion, no sense of pleasure or disgust.

Finally, I couldn't take it anymore. "So, how is it?"

He hesitated. He took another spoonful, smiled, and gave me a thumbs-up. "But let's not tell Buck," he said.

"No problem."

What I Learned at
Ice Cream School

Finally, after a month, I was getting the chance to make ice cream in my own shop. Business had been slow or nonexistent for most of April. The dust clouds on Dakota Avenue had not helped. Although the mornings were warmer, by afternoon people were eager to peel off a layer of Packer gear even if they held it in their hands in case of a cool breeze. For local businesses, April was still considered a winter month, and typically Bruce made ice cream no more than once a month in the winter.

I was eager to make ice cream, and what Bruce didn't know was that I had been to ice cream school. I was certain he would be impressed. A few months before we moved to Hayward, I was doing some online research in my office—*How to get rich in the ice cream business*—when I came across a course at a nearby university that promised to teach you all you needed to know about the manufacturing of ice cream. And the course took only three days!

Under the guise of an extended Christmas break, I stole to Paddington Station to catch a train to Reading. I had enrolled in the University of Reading's School of Food Bioscience Ice Cream Course, taught by the U.K.'s leading experts in ice cream science and production. The course was going to give me a taste of the sweet life ahead of me.

I felt as though I was a man of international intrigue—from the spy novels I read—on a secret training mission. Because neither of us had resigned from our jobs, Dean and I had kept our plans more or less to ourselves. On the platform, I dodged the working hordes and kept my head down in case I was recognized by anyone from the bank. I could not tell a convincing lie to save my skin and would crumble at the sight of the tea lady. I would spill my entire plans for the ice cream business and impending move to America. She would tell my boss, and my annual bonus, due to be paid in a few weeks, would be axed.

At Reading Station, I hopped into a taxi for the campus on the outskirts of the city. Like many Americans, I had a fond image that all British universities looked like Oxford or Cambridge, grand gothic edifices protected by fierce gargoyles. Aging professors who looked like John Gielgud hovered across the grounds in black robes while handsome young men played cricket or punted down a shallow river, contemplating their sexual ambivalence and high treason.

This wasn't Oxford or Cambridge. It appeared the university had been built on a budget sometime between the last world war and the Falklands War. The university's very practical buildings were scattered around a treeless common crisscrossed by concrete trails. The university was closed for semester break; a few foreign students headed to the library or the lab.

The course was taught in a ten-story concrete tower with monotonous rows of windows on the edge of campus. The front door was propped open, and a handwritten sign directed attendees of the "51st Ice Cream Course" to the second floor at the end of a long cinder-block hall.

"Welcome to the Ice Cream Course," an elderly woman said. Her graying hair was pulled back in a bun. She smiled as she handed me a thick binder with course materials. "Please wear this badge at all times to identify yourself as a course participant." The oversized badge had my name typed in bold letters and a border of happy ice cream cones.

Some other participants gathered at the back of the small lecture hall around a table of tea and biscuits. *How civilized,* I thought. I managed to grab a cup and saucer, pour some tea, and snag a few chocolate-covered biscuits before we were asked to take our seats.

The course administrator, a thin and graying professor in a white lab coat, dryly introduced us to the course outline and set out the itinerary for the next three days. As there were no more than twenty students, he asked us to introduce ourselves and explain why we chose to attend the 51st Ice Cream Course. There were a few dairy farmers from Hampshire who looked to supplement their farm income with a small ice cream and sandwich shop on their farm. A young couple, he in dreadlocks and she with a pierced nose and exposed navel, dreamed of opening a homemade organic ice cream shop in Camden, North London, a place where hipsters visiting the market could sit and "chill."

At the back of the room sat a contingent from Unilever, the large British foods conglomerate. They were very coy as to why they were at the course; perhaps they were scouts looking for the next big untapped opportunity. Unilever had recently acquired Ben & Jerry's, leaving Ben and Jerry with a huge pile of cash.

With my Unilever friends in mind, when it came to my turn, I introduced myself as a lawyer fed up with the rat race who was leaving life in London to purchase a small ice cream business in the heart of America's dairyland. I looked over to see if any of the Unilever chaps had a curious *Oh, this could be interesting* expression, but all I saw were bored faces whose only interest appeared to be in the complimentary biscuits.

The principal lecture for the day was on the "science of ice cream." Of course, as every Wisconsin student learns in the first grade, I knew that ice cream began as a solution of whey proteins plus lactose and milk solids with some added sugars resulting in a colloidal dispersion of casein micelles that underwent a coalescence during the concomitant whipping and freezing processes as the fat globules trapped air molecules to produce a solid structure that we knew as ice cream.

However, I did not appreciate that ice cream was so much more than that. It may have had something to do with the instructor's enthusiasm. He unbuttoned the top of his lab coat to reveal a humorous cow print necktie. As he spoke, his hands became more animated in order to give energy and life to the topic. Of course, it may have been the slight sugar rush produced by a half dozen biscuits and the caffeine of a few cups of tea, but it suddenly dawned on me that ice cream was life itself.

The professor explained that while ice cream did not live and breathe, its components—fats, sugars, milk fat solids, stabilizers, and emulsifiers—existed in perfect balance. For example, if you increased the fat content of the ice cream, you must also adjust the sugar content and reduce the milk fat solids in order to maintain the desired flavor and consistency. If the composition became unbalanced—just as my life had become unglued by the stress of work commitments—you were left with an inferior and even distasteful product.

I listened to the professor and watched the cows on his tie seemingly dance around the chalkboard. It made perfect sense. Few foods other than ice cream rely on actual stabilizers, usually in the form of a seaweed extract such as carrageenan or locust bean gum. These stabilizers act like family and friends to bind with ice cream mix and interact with proteins and other components, increasing viscosity and inhibiting the growth of ice and lactose crystals and other harmful elements, thereby improving the body, texture, and shelf life of ice cream.

I felt a burst of energy and enlightenment, more than you can get from even the best of British biscuits. But as we got closer and closer to the move to the Midwest, I was feeling more and more anxious. On so many levels, the move to Wisconsin to make ice cream was a poorly conceived if not desperate attempt to address some midlife crisis. I realized now that my life had become out of balance. There were times when the stress and grind of work were like an overhomogenized soft serve. With any luck, the move and new life would allow me to restore balance between work and freedom, adventure and discovery.

In the classroom, my euphoria was short lived because the instructor turned to the freezing process, the specifics of freezing point depression, the physics surrounding the formation of ice crystals, and the devastating effects of overemulsification. I looked around the room. The guys from Unilever looked smug; the dairy farmers looked mystified. I recalled a painful year of college astrophysics and panicked.

My palms started to sweat. *What was I doing?* I was giving up everything to make this very fragile product that, with the wrong move, could turn to a pile of cold goop that would stick to the roofs of kids' mouths. The kids would cry "ick!" and spit it out, burst into tears, and run to their mother's arms. The parents would be angry; they had just paid three bucks for ice cream that made their child cry. And I could find only a course that lasted three days. Perhaps there was a course in Scotland that would take a week.

I took a deep breath and closed my eyes. By the end of the lecture, my panic had subsided. It was time for a break. The instructor pointed us to the back of the room where they had replenished the biscuit tray and announced that we would be moving to the plant room for the afternoon in order to make our ice cream mix. I grabbed a few biscuits. I ignored the guys from Unilever and walked over to talk to the farmers' wives.

That evening, at our local Chinese restaurant, I described for Dean my "life is ice cream" argument. I explained that our problem had been that the formulation our lives had taken was out of whack. We worked far too much and enjoyed ourselves too little. Over the years, our lives had become confined to moving from Chelsea in the morning to Canary Wharf for me or near Heathrow Airport for Dean and back again. It was as though there was too much fat in our formulation and not enough sugar, diversions, and amusement to give our lives more flavor.

Our waiter, whom we saw every week but did not know by name, delivered the crispy duck with the appropriate fanfare. He smiled as he shredded the duck. At the table behind us, a popular and aging actress known for her work in a James Bond film yelled into her phone, "Darling, I must go! Clive finally arrived." She blew kisses to her companion, who had arrived two gin and tonics late.

"You're overthinking this whole move, Jeff," Dean began as he gracefully plucked the sliced cucumber from the porcelain dish with his chopsticks and placed it on his shredded duck. "Half the people we know hate their jobs, but we are doing something about it. We might be crazy, but it could be the best thing that happened to us. I think we're pretty brave as well, taking a chance like this." Dean lowered his voice. Until now, any bravery on our part had been limited to the sartorial courage of wearing brown shoes with a charcoal gray suit. "Did you catch the names of those guys from Unilever?" he asked. I shook my head.

I busied myself by spreading plum sauce evenly on my pancake. Dean was right. I had to admit my metaphor lost some of its brilliance over the course of the afternoon. Perhaps it was the biscuits.

"You know . . . I am really going to miss crispy duck," Dean said.
"I know," I said. "So am I."

On my first day of making ice cream, there was a slight drizzle, and the sky was dark and gray. When I arrived at the dairy, Bruce was already at work using the back end of a wrench against a reluctant screw.

"Howdy!" he shouted. "You ready to make ice cream?"

"You betcha!" I caught myself saying.

At ice cream school in Reading, the plant room was spacious with gleaming white-tiled walls and equipped with modern self-cleaning machinery that hummed and purred as it churned out semi-frozen delights. The room smelled of nothing other than the sweet fruit purees and roasted nuts. Narrow windows at the top of the high walls permitted beams of natural light that illuminated the ice cream angels who wore long white lab coats and white hats.

In contrast, the plant room at West's Hayward Dairy was small and windowless. The room was not big enough to park a car and was formed at the back of the building by a wooden partition. There was the faint odor of dairy sanitizer. Two boilers rusted side by side. Bruce had told me that neither on its own provided sufficient hot water to clean the equipment, but together they worked fine. Cream-colored porcelain tiles ran halfway up the wall and fluorescent tubes suspended from the ceiling lit up something very different from the ice cream heaven in Reading.

Bruce wore a thick fleece under a frayed white coat and tucked his hair under a West's Dairy baseball cap. He stood in front of a stainless steel table with tubes, nuts, bolts, and gaskets arranged in some mysterious order.

"What are you doing?" I asked with just a bit too much alarm.

"Oh, we need to put the machine together." Bruce detected my concern. "Yeah, you need to take apart these old machines after each session to clean and sanitize them." He began to sort through the pieces and reassemble them as though he could do so blindfolded. I began to panic. My instructor in Reading had never said anything about auto mechanics. I did the only thing I could, grabbing the legal pad I carried in my bag for notes. I wasn't sure what to do, so I began to draw the pieces in the form of a diagram.

Bruce looked puzzled. I might have lost my chance to impress him with my knowledge of ice cream making when I pulled out the legal pad.

"Why don't you watch this time?" he said. "It'll come to you eventually. Anyway, I'll be here awhile." He chuckled.

I was assured by his presence but knew his confidence in my mechanical skills was misplaced. How one managed to view a movie from a little box next to the TV remained one of life's great mysteries to me.

As a graduate of the 51st Ice Cream Course, I knew ice cream could be made in a batch freezer the size of a small refrigerator that produced nine or ten gallons of ice cream at a time. The alternative, and what we used at West's, was a continuous freezer. It was like the freezers in Reading but much older. The advantage of the continuous freezer was that it produced large amounts of ice cream, provided you continued to fill the vat with ice cream mix. Bruce could produce up to eighty gallons of ice cream per hour.

The large stainless steel–lined vat sat in the very center of the room. The vat held fifty-five gallons of sweet cream that flowed from a spout near the floor through a short, opaque rubber tube to the freezer. Next to the vat was the dairy's vintage continuous freezer, which seemed to be Bruce's pride and joy. The freezer must have been as old as I was, was built of stainless steel, and was nearly five feet high and no more than three feet wide and deep. On the top were some controls, one to manage the freezing unit, another to adjust the pump. Each control had a red and black button and a red light. At one time, the unit would have looked modern and futuristic, something the Oompa-Loompas might have operated in Willy Wonka's chocolate factory.

Bruce cared for his freezer like a vintage car. With the enthusiasm of my ice cream professor, he described the process and order in which he assembled the unit. The freezer operated on a simple concept. The sweet cream was pumped from the vat through a transparent tube to the bottom of the freezer, where it entered a cylindrical chamber no more than six inches in diameter. The dasher consisted of a metal cylinder with two long, sharp blades that both incorporated air into the ice cream mix and scraped the frozen mixture from the sides of the chamber. The semi-frozen ice cream was then pumped out of the top of the chamber through a long tube.

"You don't want to tighten them too much or you'll strip the screws. This way, the bolts will last longer," Bruce said as he whipped his wrench swiftly from each bolt on the machine.

"That's a good idea," I said.

Just before 7:00 AM, Buck strolled in the back door. He had on the same loose jeans he had worn since we met. He attempted to brush the rain from the shoulders of his faded denim jacket.

"What the hell's going on here?" he bellowed. He lifted his cap and scratched his head. I looked around and saw one disposable white lab coat hanging in the corner. It had not been worn in a very long time.

"Where have you been, Bucky?" Bruce shouted to be heard over the banging of the wrench against a reluctant bolt.

"Oh, I was just bullshittin' with Little Bob at the co-op," Buck said.

"Well, wash up and get some gloves on so you can help," Bruce instructed.

"Now, once we sanitize, we're good to go," Bruce advised for my benefit and put aside a wire basket of gaskets and bolts that for some reason were not needed this time around. He poured the sanitizer liberally in the vat and around the equipment. He took a large white brush about the size of a broom and scrubbed the vat vigorously inside and out. I stood back as he splashed sanitized water around the room.

"Oh, he's a wild man with that water," Buck said but did not move, letting Bruce splash him.

Bruce switched on the freezer's pump, which banged with the rhythm of a steam engine as water moved through the system. Soon, sanitizer flowed from the vat through the freezing chamber and then to the extraction tubes. The frothy sanitizer began to gurgle out of the joints, prompting Bruce to tighten some of the bolts more than he had initially.

Once we were all soaked, the room wet, and my ears ringing, Bruce asked me to haul the mix from the cooler. He wrote in a plastic binder the flavors we planned on making for the day. We started with vanilla followed by flavors that relied on vanilla as the base, including chocolate chip and cookie crumble.

I hauled five cases of mix at a time from the cooler to the vat and opened each box. The bags were flimsy and awkward. Bruce watched my first attempt to open a bag.

"No! No! You gotta grab it by the neck," he said as I took off the lid and cream spouted up toward my face.

"Oh, yeah. I see," I said, embarrassed that I couldn't manage the simple task.

"You'll get the hang of those sons of bitches!" Buck laughed. I grabbed the bag by the cap and squeezed it below the cap to prevent the cream from escaping. I filled the vat with fifty-five gallons of sweet ice cream mix. Bruce added the natural vanilla extract. The vanilla came from Madagascar. The aroma was strong, sweet, and exotic.

"Are we ready?" Bruce asked. He turned on the freezer unit and then the dasher, each making distinct whirling and grinding sounds. The noise was deafening and at times painfully pitched as the blades scraped the ice cream from the walls of the chamber. Bruce and Buck appeared immune to the racket and raised their voices over it as Buck continued with his tales of the morning at the co-op.

We waited a few minutes. The freezer pumped and whirled in a sound similar to agony.

"Is it working all right?" I asked out of concern the machine was about to break down.

"Perfect," Bruce replied. "That's the sound it makes when it's freezing."

The mix flowed from the vat into the chamber. After only minutes, a semi-frozen mass inched its way through the extracting tubes.

"Get ready, Bucky!" Bruce shouted in order to be heard over the roar of the freezing ice cream. He hoisted the extracting tube over his right shoulder like a fireman ready to battle a raging blaze as he directed Buck and me to back him. We began by filling one hundred half-gallon containers of vanilla ice cream that were sold in the shop and local convenience stores.

"Buck, you stand here and put the lids on the containers."

"All right," Buck said, struggling to place the latex gloves over his arthritic hands.

"Jeff, I want you to stand next to Buck. When he passes you the ice cream, put three tubs in each of those cardboard sleeves." Bruce pointed to a stack of cardboard at the end of the table. "Once you have two or three sleeves, you need to haul them into the freezer—as fast as you can."

"I guess that's why I got this job," I said.

"Oh, I've hauled plenty of ice cream to the freezer in my day," Buck quipped, sensitive to his age.

"Let's go!" Bruce shouted as the finished product reached the mouth of the extracting tube. He filled the first half-gallon container and shoved it with his free hand to Buck. Buck's hands wavered as he secured the lid. I filled two cardboard sleeves each with three containers and carried them to the walk-in freezer. By the time I returned, there were three tubs waiting for me. Buck smiled in a *not so funny now, is it?* kind of way.

It took only twelve to fifteen seconds to fill each container. Soon I was behind as I juggled to hold the awkward sleeves while opening the oversized freezer door handle and then climbed over large tubs of ice cream in a dark freezer to put the sleeves on an empty shelf. Not to be defeated, I picked up the pace and managed to keep up even if I was out of breath in the process.

"How you doin', kiddo?" Bruce laughed as he hoisted the extraction tube higher onto his shoulder. I wanted to ask if I would be able to fill the containers, but perhaps it was too early for me to handle such responsibility.

"Kenny!" Bruce yelled to the hefty man who entered through the back door.

Kenny was slightly younger than me, with a brown beard and a stomach protruding through his open green and yellow Packer jacket. He stood in the doorway shuffling from foot to foot, a bit reluctant to enter.

"Come in here, Kenny," Bruce said. "I asked Kenny to help because we'll need him to make Almost Sinful." He may have been seeking my approval.

"Fine," I said. I introduced myself to Kenny. I was getting the impression that making ice cream was like organizing a barn-raising. The local elders, Bruce and Buck, determined that Jeff and Dean needed ice cream, so they organized all the menfolk, or Kenny, to help. I was expecting someone to drop off a bowl of homemade potato salad for lunch.

"Say, I picked up some donuts at the bakery—they're in the front," Buck said.

"Don't mind if I do," Kenny said as he went into the store in search of breakfast.

While he was out of earshot, Buck filled me in on Kenny. He lived in his parents' basement. His father was a self-proclaimed evangelical preacher who had billboards on either end of town in the shape of a lighthouse and the slogan *Have you seen the light?* followed by a toll-free telephone number. Kenny washed dishes at a few restaurants in town and held other odd jobs, including helping Bruce and working in the bogs during the cranberry harvest. I began to suspect that Kenny was another fixture at West's when additional help was required.

As Buck finished his story, Dean arrived. He had been at a meeting with representatives from the visitors and convention bureau about marketing the B&B.

"Look! Now the whole crew is here!" Buck shouted when he saw Dean.

"I figured you'd need help, Buck," Dean teased.

"Oh, I've done this a few times in my life," Buck said in his own defense and directed Dean to the donuts.

In preparing to make Almost Sinful, I tidied up the plant room, and Dean prepared a mix of walnuts and chocolate-covered peanuts. Bruce poured the fudge into the small vat attached to the variegator that would produce a ribbon of fudge throughout the Almost Sinful. I kept an eye on the double doors to the store in case any customers came in for ice cream. No one did.

Bruce announced that we were ready. Buck and Kenny came through, finishing the last of the donuts. Bruce made some final adjustment that involved a bit of banging and connected the variegator tube to the main extraction tube.

"Are you ready for Sinful?" Bruce asked as he re-sanitized the machine.

"It's quite an operation," Buck added.

"Okay, Bucky, you come over here and hold the containers."

"Kenny, Jeff, you stand downwind from Buck," Bruce laughed.

Buck moved ahead of Kenny in the assembly line, giving Bruce a free hand.

"Dean, why don't you come over here to add the nuts to the mixture?" Bruce directed as though he were moving actors around a stage. Dean came to stand on the other side of Buck. Kenny was given Buck's task of placing the lids on the containers, and I was tasked with running containers to the freezer. I was convinced it was the worst job. *I should talk to the owner,* I thought.

While I ran back and forth from the freezer, Buck updated us on the news from the senior center. Kenny stuffed his mouth with chocolate-covered peanuts and walnuts that Dean scattered on the table as he filled the containers of ice cream. Dean inquired about the mechanics of the machine and the funny noises it made as well as Buck's stories from the senior center.

It had been a long morning—nearly five hours of making ice cream—and we were nearly done. We had practically a barnful of fresh ice cream that would last most of May. It had been a good day, even if I wasn't able to impress anyone with my ice cream credentials. We finished the half gallons of Almost Sinful. Bruce carried on filling three-gallon containers. There wasn't really anything for Kenny to do, but he stayed to help Bruce clean up when we finished.

I noticed ice cream oozing out of the seam of the extractor portion of the freezer. I hesitated, not sure if I should say something that might appear dumb. Just as I was about to ask Bruce, pressure built up on the top piece, and it broke away from the freezer, releasing a geyser of ice cream that sprayed as high as the ceiling. "There she blows!" Buck yelled.

"Oh, crap!" Bruce cried.

Dean laughed as, with his finger, he scooped up ice cream that had landed on the table and ate it. Most surfaces in the plant room were hit with some ice cream splatter.

Bruce quickly shut down the freezer and pump and explained that this happened sometimes after a long session. "I should have tightened those bolts some more. Kenny, get the hose."

Before I got caught in the deluge as Bruce sprayed down the ceiling, walls, and freezer, I managed to use my finger and taste a bit that landed on my shirtsleeve.

"Well, what do you think?" Buck asked.

"It's good—really good," I said.

"That's Sinful!"

Classic Bowling in the Ladies' Room

By the end of April, I felt as though I had made some progress. I mastered scooping ice cream and running the shop by myself. I learned the ropes of managing the milk route and even transferred Bruce's manual accounting system to a web-based accounting tool to simplify the process. With any luck and clever planning of Tom's vacations, Dean and I would never have to deliver milk again. And while my initial foray into ice cream production raised some concerns as to my own ability to control the old thing—the freezer, not Buck—I figured I would eventually get there, and in the meantime, I could rely on Bruce and others to help me.

The numbers for the month of April, however, told another story. Our shop sales barely exceeded nineteen hundred dollars—for the entire month! In other words, I probably ate more in ice cream, malts, and shakes than I sold. Everyone said, "It's April. You can't expect much." Nonetheless, the electricity bill for the dairy building was fifty percent of our takings for the month. I did not want to calculate the cost of heating, insurance, or any other overhead.

I couldn't see any improvement outside. A few weeks of sunshine and above-average temperatures gave way to cold, wet days. As I looked out the large window, heavy winds blew sheets of rain across the dirt lot that was the main road outside West's. The large digging equipment and tractors sat quietly, further delaying the project. The whole town was quiet. But for the rain, I am certain there would have been tumbleweeds blowing down Main Street. To top matters, I had not heard from the young builders I lined up to carry out the renovations since our initial conversation.

Buck sat in the office in his orange chair watching TV. He was gripped by another nail-biting episode of *Classic Bowling*. The hero of the program was a mullet head with a thick mustache worthy of the Village People. Notwithstanding his Tootsie-framed glasses and skin-tight red polyester trousers, he was nearing a perfect game in the Wichita Open.

"So, what time do you think the boys will get here to start your fancy remodeling?" Buck asked, slipping in some sarcasm. Buck didn't believe the dairy needed any improvements. He loved it the way it was. He didn't go as far as saying we were making a mistake, but he reminded me that people came here for only one thing—that ice cream cone.

"They should be here today."

For nearly two weeks, I had been calling the builders. I begged, I pleaded. I reminded them that they had less than a month to complete the work. I hated confrontation—in all those years as a lawyer, I had never seen the inside of a courtroom and was a pushover in any heated negotiations. Finally, I asked Dean to phone them.

"Look, if you cannot do this job for us, that is perfectly all right. We've found someone who can start tomorrow. Please let us know," Dean told Timmy over the phone. His voice was calm, his accent crisp, and what he said was a lie.

"Why did you say that?" I yelled. "There is no one else."

"They're all the same, these builders. They push it as far as they can, but they don't want to lose the work. It always does the trick," Dean assured me. "Anyway, they'll be here tomorrow."

"So, where do you think we can put the TV?" Buck asked. I had not shared with Buck the detailed plans for the renovations, but he may have suspected the first task would be to remove the contents of the office to begin constructing the new restrooms.

"Well, . . ." I paused, looking for a way to explain this delicate situation. "I thought, . . ." I hesitated. "We could store the TV at the B&B

while the work is being done . . . you know, so it doesn't get full of sawdust and dirt." I looked to see if Buck was buying it, but he gazed straight ahead as mullet head bowled another strike and pumped his fist into the air. I had planned the design shortly after we had seen the dairy and before I had become aware of the central role the television played in the life of the place. The new restrooms would take up most of the old office space. But now I felt bad. Maybe I needed to have Dean smooth things over with Buck.

"Anyway," I said, "you'll need to keep an eye on the workers to make sure they aren't screwing up."

Mullet head got a perfect score and claimed his ten-thousand-dollar prize and a sloppy kiss from a bleached blond bowling groupie who may have been his wife. Buck stood up, turned off the TV, put the remote on the desk, and quietly left the room. It was as though he were at a wake saying good-bye to an old friend.

I followed Buck into the other room. He sat looking out the window at the parked equipment on Dakota Avenue. To cheer him up, I tried one of my favorite games—"Who's that?" The game tested Buck's claim to know everyone in town. So on quiet days—most every day so far— I looked out the window, picked a random person, and asked, "Who's that?" Usually he knew not just their name but also where they lived and most of the details of their lives, or at least made up a convincing story.

I pointed to two old ladies walking across the construction zone. "Who's that, Buck?"

"Oh, that's the Olson twins," he said as though I should know that. He described how the sisters had moved to the same apartment building after their husbands died within months of each other. He assured me there was no foul play—one had cancer and the other a bad "ticker." He said they were heading to the co-op for lunch. The short one, he said, would have tuna salad on wheat while the other usually had the daily special.

The Olson sisters maneuvered their way through the abandoned equipment in the construction zone known as Dakota Avenue. Buck got up and said he had some business to take care of, which meant he had to use the restroom. My attempt to distract him had failed.

While he was away, an old pickup truck pulled up to the dairy. It was my builders. I was so excited, I almost jumped out of my chair, but, remembering I had been angry, I remained in my seat.

They pulled a small horse trailer behind the truck that held the equipment they required. The pickup had a rear seat. I figured Timmy was driving. When he got out of the truck, he smoothed his blond hair and grabbed a notebook from the seat. It might have contained notes from our phone conversation or been his algebra homework. He had the appearance of a high school junior. Another man, possibly his brother, opened the rear door of the truck for another passenger. Timmy, still holding the notebook, pulled equipment out of the trailer, including a hand-painted sign to stand in front of the building to advertise their business.

They entered the dairy a bit sheepishly. We exchanged pleasantries about the weather and their drive to Hayward and began to discuss logistics about where they would park to unload materials. Timmy's brother, Tommy, was in desperate need of a comb, a shower, and a clean shirt, yet he possessed Marlboro Man good looks. An older man, Pete, finished off a glazed donut they had found at the bakery and brought in a table saw, electric drills, and some sawhorses that he set up in front of the dipping cabinet. No attempt was made to allow for customers who might come in during the day to buy an ice cream cone.

It looked promising. Their newfound enthusiasm almost made me regret the last two messages I had left for them. I really had not wished to drag their mother into it. I decided to start fresh. I would give them plenty of room to carry out the assignment and would not question their work ethic again. The important thing was that they were there to begin the project, yet I wanted them to know I was serious. I expected the work to be completed by the end of the month as originally planned. There would be no time to sit around eating ice cream.

"Well, look who the cat dragged in!" Buck shouted to the builders as he came through from the toilet. "I thought Jeff was going to blow his top waiting for you guys to turn up. Hey, would anyone like an ice cream?" Buck asked as he took his position behind the counter. Well, so much for my plan.

"Maybe when we're done today," Timmy said.

I waited until Buck left for lunch to tell the builders they could remove the contents of the office—desks, chairs, furniture, filing cabinets, Buck's orange chair, and, of course, the television. I wished to avoid a situation where I had an old man chaining himself to a file cabinet or spreading his arms across the doorframe to prevent removal of the office's contents.

The boys worked like a synchronized drill team, effortlessly picking up furniture and avoiding each other going through the small space. Within thirty minutes, the room was empty—almost made me think they were familiar with emptying homes and offices quickly. The contents would be stored in one of the garages behind the B&B until we figured out what to do with them.

The office already looked much larger, and before Buck was back from lunch, the crew had begun to mark and erect the stud walls to form the new restrooms and small office space. In the front, Pete nailed to the ceiling wooden trim to which tin tiles would be secured.

When Buck returned, he glanced over to the empty office but didn't say anything. He shuffled behind the counter, washed the ice cream scoops, and checked on the hot fudge levels. He leaned against the dipping cabinet and folded his arms as if to say, *This is my new position.* He watched Pete for a few minutes, trying to figure out why he was nailing wood to the ceiling. "What in Sam Hill are you doing up there?"

Pete explained he was preparing the surface for the new tin ceiling. "Tin ceiling!" Buck exclaimed. "Now I've heard it all!" I took this as my sign to leave.

When I returned at the end of the afternoon, I was impressed with the progress. The stud walls had been erected, defining the new men's and ladies' restrooms and my new office. I entered the framed space for the men's room and crouched as though I were in a wheelchair and twirled. The law required that if you undertook any changes to restrooms, they must be made accessible to people in wheelchairs. *Yes, I think it must meet code.*

My office would be pinched between the men's room and the ladies' room. Only three feet wide, it had the massive window onto West Second Street. I'd had better office views. In New York, my first office was in what was then known as the Pan Am Building, looking south over Grand Central Station and Park Avenue. In Hong Kong, my office had a view of the Governor's Mansion until another office tower was built to block it. The firm called in the services of the *feng shui* expert on retainer to rearrange my furniture. In London, my office at Canary Wharf looked east toward not much at all, and I spent a good deal of time and political capital angling for a corner office. As a lawyer, if I had been given something the size of my new dairy office next to the toilet, I would have stomped my feet and run immediately to the office manager to complain. Of course, I wouldn't be spending all day and night in my new office. There would be no endless conference calls. It didn't look like I'd have room for an adjustable office chair with additional lumbar support, but that would be okay.

"I don't think you'll have enough room here," Buck said, standing in what would become the ladies' toilet and pointing into my office.

"It will be perfect," I said. "It'll be the nicest office I ever had." And I meant it.

Buck looked up at the ceiling as though he could not believe the change. "I hope you know what you're doing," he said.

"It will be great, Buck. Just you see," I said. "Now, get out of the ladies' room!" I yelled at him behind the stud wall.

He laughed. "Well, we never had one of those here."

A Woman in a Long Green Dress

The new month did not bring great fortune in the weather. The sky had been gray for days, and rain came in several forms, from foggy mist and drizzle to showers and thunderous downpours. The dogs did not mind. Even delicate Freddie enjoyed a romp in the muddy puddles on the driveway while Spike devoured the scents released from the wet earth. New friends or potential enemies visited every day, including small voles, chipmunks, red and gray squirrels, and others in the big-tail rodent family. An old fox crossed the deck almost every morning back to his den. This set off a tirade of barks, yelps, and cries warning us of unusual dog-type invaders.

On warmer and drier evenings, Dean and I sat on the bench attached to the dock with a beer or glass of wine. With binoculars, we spied on the bald eagle couple on Raspberry Island. After a scrape with extinction, eagles now thrived in the tall trees of northern Wisconsin, home of one of the largest bald eagle populations in the country. Our feathered neighbors were in the midst of some major renovations to their nest home—perhaps even an extension given the size of tree branches the male eagle carried to the construction site like a remote mechanical crane.

The loons from last summer were back at the lake. Loons are monogamous birds who mate for life. Most lakes in the region have at least one or two loon families who return to the same lake every year.

We saw the male loon swimming, his body low in the water and his black and white head darting from side to side and occasionally plunging into the water in search of food. We suspected the female was nesting and anticipating a new arrival. Although they lacked the majesty of their treetop cousins, their haunting cry was heard across the lake every morning or evening. The sound leaves the listener with the sense of melancholy and woe, although experts say loons are merely communicating with their cohorts on nearby lakes, saying something along the lines of *Hey, what's going on over there? Are the fish biting?*

As I anticipated, the construction work at West's provided Buck with more than sufficient entertainment. It was not classic bowling entertainment but just as good. In no time, he took on the persona of a host of a home improvement show, following every move the crew made and questioning the merit of a tool or technique or the length of their break. Timmy did not mind Buck's constant questions and suggestions and usually humored him or simply laughed. Tommy teased Buck about his age and potential sexual exploits with the ladies at the senior center.

"Oh, I don't want nothing to do with those money-grubbing women," Buck shot back.

Scruffy Pete was most annoyed by Buck, who questioned Pete's every move. Pete usually responded by making more noise to drown out Buck's voice. When Pete carried a nail gun in his hand, Buck held back for his own safety.

All those brave or desperate enough to enter the shop were asked if they would like a topping of sawdust on their sundae or cone. Buck gave each customer a rundown of the status of the project, the scope of the renovations, and the anticipated completion date. "Well, that depends on how fast these boys finish," he added to incite the builders. Pete raised his nail gun to Buck's head, mock execution style.

Every day, as the builders began to put away their tools and sweep the floor of wood shavings and sawdust, Buck would open the dipping cabinets. "So, what will it be today, boys?" The builders had been working their way through the selection of West's ice cream and would try a new flavor most afternoons, although Timmy was stuck on Blue Moon. Even Pete enjoyed his treat from Buck.

"I don't know, Buck. Timmy got a bigger scoop than me. You're losing your touch," Tommy teased.

"Oh, if I had a nickel for every cone I scooped here, I'd be a rich man," Buck replied to what he thought was a serious challenge to his experience.

By the end of the second week of May, the office and restrooms were complete, including new plumbing, so Buck would not have to bother the people at the coffee shop down the street anymore. Timmy was finishing my new display shelves that replaced three of the four glass doors that opened to the walk-in cooler.

Pete completed the tin ceiling, and the stamped metal tiles gave an odd new focus to the room. When people walked in, their eyes were drawn to the ceiling. "Was that always here?" they asked, pointing up. The great debate was whether to paint the ceiling or leave it the original gunmetal color. "I think you should leave it as it is," Pete said as though he had an interest in the decision as he had nailed the tiles himself one at a time. I decided to paint it.

So far I had not seen Sparky, the builders' electrician friend, or the guy who was doing the floors. Timmy dismissed my concerns and assured me that it was best to leave those jobs until last. As I looked at the paint-speckled red linoleum, I could see his point. However, the old fluorescent lights had been removed to allow for the new ceiling, and the sun provided the only light in the building. I hoped Timmy was right. Business wasn't very good during this period. There was little improvement in the weather, and the ongoing roadwork on the streets by West's kept traffic to a minimum. Even those who came by had to be coaxed in around the construction going on inside the shop. They gingerly opened the door, peered inside, and examined the building work. "You're not open, are you?"

"Hell yes, we are," Buck replied and waved his arm as though he were swooping them past the builders. A hardy few customers took up his offer. I was tempted to provide complimentary hard hats to them to ease any anxiety and potentially reduce my own liability in case of a flying hammer or misdirected nail gun.

The only hope was that the work would be finished before the crowds arrived for the Memorial Day weekend at the end of the month, less than two weeks away. Although progress had been steady, days of rain meant the exterior painting was largely unfinished. When Sparky graced us with his presence and expertise at all things electrical, he had managed only to hang my new schoolhouse pendant lamps. They looked great with the tin ceiling and fresh paint finish. The only problem was that they didn't work. He gave Timmy some explanation and then said he had to finish wiring a new car wash in Cable. That had been over a week ago.

New ceramic floor tiles and wood flooring planks sat neatly in boxes in the corner next to pails of grout and wood glue. I had not even met the man who was lined up to install the floors. I had been given many excuses for his absence ranging from illness in the family to girlfriend issues and previous work commitments. Notwithstanding my intention to just let them get along with things, I repeatedly asked for updates on the status of the floors, or at least on the man's relationship with his girlfriend.

At McCormick House, Dean tried to find a way to dispose of the furniture and the assorted items that had been left behind. We thought of giving it away or donating the contents to the Salvation Army, but we'd have to pay someone to pack and transport everything. A friend suggested a better way, one in which people would come to the property and pay us money for the privilege of taking away at no expense to us the unwanted crap that had been left by the previous owners. In fact, we could even engage someone who would organize it, market it, and deal with the people who came to buy the stuff.

"Oh, yeah, auctions are a big deal," Buck confirmed. "Everyone will come to the auction at the mansion."

We engaged the services of Hayward's premier—and only—auction house. It was a family business. The wife had moved to the area from Florida in order to follow her passion for logrolling, not otherwise a popular activity in Florida due in part to the alligator issue. After a good run as a five-year world champion logroller as determined at the Lumberjack World Championships held in Hayward each summer, she had retired but still possessed the energy of someone about to fall off a rolling log. In no time, she had catalogued every item for sale, not only furniture and kitchen items but also bathtubs, sinks, kitchen cabinets— anything we intended to remove from the house was for sale. She even insisted on pulling out old light fixtures that we would have replaced.

"What about this carpet?" she asked regarding a threadbare specimen adhered to the floor of one of the guest rooms.

"You think someone will want that?" Dean asked incredulously.

"Oh, for sure," the auctioneer said. "It would be great in an ice fishing house."

The poster promoting the auction was impressive, with color photos of some of the finer pieces for sale and enticing people to view for the last time Hayward's Lumberman's Mansion before it closed for complete renovation. The auctioneer suggested we agree to donate a portion of the proceeds to a charity to increase interest in the auction.

Dean decided we should give something to the Northwoods Humane Society. We had met Deanna, the president of the humane society, one morning while we were standing in front of the dairy looking at the old canopy. She drove up to the corner and asked if we'd mind helping her with a "situation" on Highway 27. While driving into town she had seen a large turtle trying to cross the highway, and she asked Dean and me to hop in her car to help her coax the old guy across the road before it got squashed. When we returned to the spot on the highway, we couldn't see the turtle, so we assumed it made it safely to the ditch—or that Chef Jeff was preparing soup for dinner.

We learned that Deanna was part of a group of people in town who, like us and our log-rolling auctioneer, came to Hayward in search of their dreams. There was also a couple from the airlines who bought an antique store with very well-marked exits, and a radio sports announcer who owned a restaurant and bar where the favorite drink was always a "double." Deanna had come to Hayward from Chicago years before when she and her husband purchased a petting zoo south of town. They had sold the zoo and built the art gallery across from the dairy, where there were fewer rogue raccoon and obstinate opossums to deal with. In addition to helping the animals at the shelter, we heard she turned her own home into a haven for the older, blind, deaf, incontinent, or otherwise less-adoptable pets.

There was no improvement in the weather by the weekend before the Memorial Day holiday. On Saturday, the day of the auction, cold winds gusted amid scattered rain. When Dean and I arrived, cars lined both sides of Kansas Avenue and the streets around Shue's Pond. Many of the furnishings, kitchen appliances, cabinets, and bathroom fixtures had been removed and organized outside the house. Furniture that could be damaged in the rain was moved under cover of the front porch or in the large rooms on the ground floor. People walked up and down the paths the goods created in the yard, examining the items for sale.

Our auctioneer was anxious. She wore a Bluetooth headpiece to communicate with someone while she set up the items on the agenda for later in the morning. It was possible she was talking to her babysitter or her mother in Florida. "Yeah, it's a bit wet this morning but a good crowd so far," she said by all appearances to the tree she was standing near.

Her husband, who served as auctioneer, stood on a platform in front of a small travel trailer that doubled as command central for the auction. "Going once, going twice." He paused for any holdouts. "Sold to the woman in the Packers windbreaker," he said as the women in the crowd wearing Packers windbreakers looked around to ensure they had not just bought something. A young woman with a laptop and an anxious demeanor attempted to record the details for each sale.

"Remember, please," the auctioneer reminded people, "if you're a successful bidder, please see Lucy, who will take your details and payment."

The auction began in the back house because the contents of the outbuildings, primarily old building materials and rusted tools, were being sold for cheap, and much of the buildings themselves were being sold for scrap if possible. I noticed Buck, Bruce, and a few men from the co-op's death row in the audience.

The auctioneer then moved to the side of the house to auction the rusted hot tubs that had been removed from the guest rooms. These took on considerable interest by some farmers, who bid up the price. I noticed Bruce checking out the tubs with Buck. I couldn't hear him but could imagine Buck saying, "Why in Sam Hill would you want one of those things? You got a bathtub."

At the front of the house, the humane society had set up a snack bar complete with sloppy joes, a sandwich made of ground beef in a tangy barbeque sauce and served on a hamburger bun. Deanna stood behind a long table with two young helpers.

"Would you like a sloppy joe?" she asked. Deanna was a tall, striking woman with a brilliant and seemingly permanent smile. She stood out even more in the official bright pink humane society sweatshirt featuring a giant black paw on the front. Her curly salt-and-pepper hair blew freely in the damp breeze.

The two girls, who helped with the kittens at the shelter, assisted in preparing the sandwiches—one held open the bun while the other spooned the juicy meaty concoction without dripping, as the gray-haired lunch ladies from my elementary school did. It was early, but the sandwich had always been one of my favorite school lunches, and I had not had one in years. Deanna refused my two dollars for the sandwich, so I placed them in a plastic cup for tips, earning me an extra handful of potato chips.

"Great turnout," Deanna said. "This is so kind of you."

"You're welcome. Do you have a stand at other auctions?" I asked.

"No, but this is special—it's the mansion. Anyway, you and Dean must come to the shelter someday." I agreed to do that.

A crowd gathered on the porch as the auctioneer was coming around to begin the sale of six armoires that had been removed from the guest rooms. The cabinets were anywhere between fifty and seventy years old, cheap and worn, but women with their eyes on them had big plans to refinish them.

"This will be great in the guest room at the cabin," a woman said to her husband. "I can't believe we bought a house without closets," she reminded him as he stood in silence.

As the auctioneer began, interest soared, and the first two cabinets garnered nearly two hundred dollars. The auctioneer smiled and, when she saw me, gave a positive signal with her hand before returning to her headpiece. She entered the house to clear a room for the next round of the auction. I followed her, but the rooms were crowded as people stood near the items that interested them the most and waited for their turn to bid.

Dean was in the corner of the library speaking to a reporter from the *Sawyer County Record*. The reporter took detailed notes as Dean described the plans for the bed and breakfast. The reporter sensed this would be a big story and was careful to include all of the facts.

"So, you said the thread count on the Egyptian cotton sheets was what?" he asked Dean to confirm.

"No less than four hundred, of course," Dean said.

Others were taking a self-guided tour. Upstairs, the rooms had been largely stripped bare. The bedrooms looked larger without the big hot tubs in the corner. The bathrooms looked bare and miserable with stained walls and chipped tile.

"It's going to take a lot of work," I heard a woman tell her husband as they inspected the rooms.

"And money!" he replied.

"Oh, I hear they have a lot of money—came all the way from England," the wife replied. I ducked into an open room at the front of the house so as not to be seen as they came out into the hallway.

A woman sitting on a windowsill looking into the empty room startled me. "Oh, I'm sorry," I said before realizing I shouldn't have to apologize for surprising a stranger in my own house—especially one who was smoking a cigarette.

"It's okay." She looked through me in deep thought, turning only to blow smoke out the cracked window. She stubbed out the cigarette on the stripped floor with her shoe. Her hair was straight, blond with gray streaks. She wore a long, winter-style wool coat and white sneakers.

"Are you one of the new owners?" she asked. I nodded. "I used to live here—right here in this room." She spread her arms to encompass the entire space. "My bathroom and kitchenette would have been in the room next door." She explained it had been her first home in Hayward when she had moved here nearly thirty years ago. She must have been quite young, as she seemed only a few years older than me.

"Have you seen anything strange in the house?" she asked.

"Strange?"

"Like a woman in a long green dress?"

"A ghost!" I shot back in disbelief. She nodded to acknowledge that was exactly what she meant.

My visitor described how on more than one occasion, she had felt a presence in the room, usually while she slept. Once, she turned on the light by the bed and saw a tall woman standing near the door. She wore a long green dress with her hair in a tight bun.

"I wasn't dreaming," she said, as though she read my mind. "I got up and lit a cigarette. I watched her. She just stood there in the corner. She wasn't mean or anything, no slamming of doors or knocking things over." The woman again waved her hands to describe the chaos one gets with other ghosts. "But when I turned my head, she was gone," she concluded. "Oh, and I wasn't drinking, either," she said, reading my mind again. "At least then," she added.

She told me others had seen her as well, but no one knew who she might be. She may have been the wife of one of the lumber barons.

"This is the first time I've been in the house since I lived here all those years ago," she said before getting up and walking toward the door. She thanked me and left. When she was gone, I felt a chill run down my spine. I had a sudden urge to leave the room, but I was also interested in what might be there. She said the ghost wasn't mean, yet she didn't exactly sound very friendly, either. Perhaps there were other ghosts. *Should I tell Dean?* We always made fun of the ghost hunter shows on television where they walked around in the dark with terrified expressions on their faces, but that was before we had an apparition in our own house.

Notwithstanding the wet and the cold that may have dampened turnout for the event, the auctioneer was very pleased as she helped tally the sales on the laptop. The humane society collected a nice donation, and we made nearly enough to pay for the fence we were having built around the yard at the rear of the house.

Dean and I looked around the empty structure. "This will make it easier when they start the work next week," I said.

"Wasn't it funny—how many people came just to see the house? A lot of them said they lived here or played here when they were kids," Dean said. "We should have a big party when we're done with the work so they can all see how it turns out."

The auctioneers were finishing some cleanup work in the back. Everyone else had gone. I looked around and decided to share with Dean the details of my encounter with the ghost whisperer.

"She wore a green dress, you said."

"That's what she told me."

"Perhaps it's your mother." Dean laughed.

"Hey, that's not funny," I said. "But green was her favorite color," I added.

SUMMER

Don't Worry, They'll Come

At the end of May, most trees were just beginning to leaf out to their fullest. Springtime flowers, daffodils, and tulips still bloomed across town, and the lilac bushes featured in every lawn were heavy with purple cone-shaped bulbs ready to explode. For the people of Hayward who had endured over six months of frostbite, frozen pipes, and icy roads, the last weekend in May was the beginning of the summer season. For those residents who operated restaurants and other winter-starved tourist businesses, the three-day Memorial Day weekend felt more like a late Christmas.

Folks from all over the region got in their cars for the three-, five-, or eight-hour drive to Hayward. For many, it was a chance for a getaway at a local resort or hotel. The extra day justified the drive. Others came to reopen their cabin for the summer season. They arrived prepared with a list of chores, including putting the dock in the lake, taking the boat or pontoon out of storage, changing the winter storm windows for wire-screened windows in anticipation of cool evening breezes, and uncovering the barbeque grill for the first dose of heavily charred carcinogens of the season. They would also find time to check out what was new in Hayward for the summer.

Although there were a few new shops downtown this year, the buzz was already about the new owners of West's Hayward Dairy and the changes to the town's ice cream shop. On Wednesday, the painters finished the clean creamy beige exterior. On Thursday, the new chocolate awning was installed at the front of the building on Second Street and on the side facing Dakota Avenue. Large white letters spelled the words

Homemade Ice Cream, Malts, Shakes, Sundaes, Coffee. The large cow's head at the front door had been washed and touched up with some enamel paint.

Inside, the changes were more dramatic. After much hand-wringing and many unreturned phone calls, Timmy, Tommy, Scruffy Pete, and their floor guy managed to lay the new wood and tile floor on Thursday evening. On Friday, the painters finished touching up the skirting boards near the floor. Dean adhered the large stickers with West's bright new logo to the windows that framed the front door. New shelves displayed not only shiny bottles of locally produced maple syrup and honey but also trendy T-shirts, coffee mugs, and travel thermoses sporting the new logo. Old black-and-white photos Bruce had given me had been enlarged and framed. They told the history of West's Hayward Dairy—at least when Buck wasn't around to tell it himself.

On Saturday morning, Buck sat on the stool of a new bar-style seating area near the front door. He rubbed his hand on the smooth surface of the polished fir countertop. He looked comfortable and even pleased with the changes. Behind him hung a large vinyl mural based on an old photograph showing four girls in white waitress uniforms standing at attention behind the counter. He turned to look at the image of the women on the wall.

"What do you think of the photo?" I asked.

"Well, I think it was from 1939. I went to high school with those girls, you know. They were seniors when I was a freshman," he said to remind me of his relative youth. "The first is a Wittwer girl. Of course, her dad owned the dairy back then. She was a pretty girl, she was." Buck knew or at least told me with sufficient confidence the stories of each of the girls in the photograph.

"No, you did good, Jeff," Buck said. "It looks real nice in here—even smells good." Buck sniffed the lingering paint fumes. I was glad. I was going to remind him how at first he was against the planned changes, but I decided not to ruffle his feathers. Through all of his moaning and second-guessing the work and questioning the merits of each of the improvements and expense, it was important to me that he liked it. After all, he was the ambassador, and if Buck liked it, I figured most visitors would like it, too.

"Here, I think you should wear this, Buck," I said. I picked a new baseball cap from the shelves of assorted gifts. It was denim blue with an embroidered logo of an ice cream cone and *West's* in a red oval. Buck peeled from his head the soiled cap he had been wearing since Dean and I had arrived. He managed to place the new cap on his head at exactly the same cockeyed slant as he wore his old cap.

"There you go, Buck—you're our official greeter!"

My ambassador smiled and returned to his newspaper.

The tin ceiling gleamed with the morning sun while the pendant schoolhouse-style lamps and the halogen spotlights directed on the dipping cabinets looked smart. One problem—the lights didn't work. Notwithstanding more pleading, cajoling, and threats, Sparky failed for over two weeks to show up to finish the work and literally left us in the dark. The equipment was all wired and worked properly, but there were no ceiling lights—anywhere. I prayed for a sunny weekend.

"Do you think we'll have enough light, Buck?" I asked.

"Well, you know, Jeff"—he lowered his voice in a manner that told me to expect a doomsday prediction—"it's going to get dark." I chuckled at his nightfall prophecy.

Perhaps my favorite feature of the new West's Dairy was in the front window—six rounded leather club chairs. During my twelve years in London, I had spent many relaxing hours reading and sipping coffee in a comfortable leather chair at my favorite coffee shop in South Kensington. It was in those brief moments when I was not at work or worrying about the office that I fantasized about what it would be like to run such a place. So when it came to customer seating at West's, I wanted to create something similar. I searched all over the country for similar chairs. None of the coffee shops in America had anything like them, and furniture stores carried only oversized chairs meant for holding oversized American bottoms in oversized living rooms in front of supersized television screens.

After a few phone calls to London, I was directed to the supplier in Surrey, who advised me the chairs in question came from Spain. By the time they added the cost of shipping—"*Donde es* Wisconsin?"—the chairs were without a doubt the most luxurious chairs of any ice cream shop in the country. The leather was as smooth as caramel sauce.

I sank into a chair facing the recently reopened and paved Dakota Avenue. *This feels good,* I thought. I knew they would be covered with ice cream, cone crumbs, and the feet of small children in a matter of hours. At some point, however, a customer—perhaps a dad or mom with a high-pressure job—might take a moment to touch the leather and consider, however briefly, his or her own dreams.

"Where is everyone?" I shouted to Buck and pointed to the street. "This should be our big weekend."

"Don't you worry, they'll come—like clockwork," Buck said. "You'll see." He bent his finger and head toward me as he did when he was about to impart some wisdom. "They're all having breakfast now— some in their cabin, some at the co-op or the Norske Nook. The menfolk may go fishing—the fish will be biting this time of day. Later they'll come into town," he said. "You just wait 'n' see."

Behind the counter, one of my new employees, Liz, leaned back against the center island that held the malt machines and hot fudge dispenser, her arms folded in a picture of teenage ennui. After much pleading from me, she had tied her shoulder-length brown hair into a ponytail but kept a long fringe over her eye.

"We haven't had any customers since we opened an hour ago," Liz said.

"I can't believe you hired this one," Buck yelled to me as though Liz had left the room. "She doesn't even eat ice cream—she's a vegetarian!" he shouted in disbelief.

"Vegan," Liz corrected. "I'm a vegan. Vegetarians can eat ice cream."

"Well, I have never heard of anything so crazy in all my life!" Buck grumbled.

"Perhaps you could make me a cappuccino, Liz?" I asked to break up the two of them.

So far, I was confident in the young staff I had lined up for the summer. A few had helped Bruce in previous years. Jennifer was sixteen and had worked two years at West's. Bruce considered her one of his best employees, and I asked her to help train the new hires. She approached the job with the maturity of a much older woman. She was busy cleaning the island counter and wiping the inside of the ice cream display.

Stephanie also worked for Bruce, had just gotten her driver's license, and was moving her car after she had parked it in one of the four spots outside the dairy building. She took my request that she move her vehicle to the municipal parking lot so customers had priority to the few spots as an affront to her independence and suggested this country was not as free as we all thought. Jennifer said Steph was in a bad mood because her foreign exchange student boyfriend had just gone back to the Czech Republic.

Michael was a new hire. He was only fifteen but nearly six feet tall with a small head and curly brown hair. It was unclear whether it was due to his height or other developmental issues, but at times his limbs seemed to move without coordination or purpose as though he were dancing to music he alone could hear.

"I don't know what you're going to do with that tall drink of water," Buck warned. "We don't hire boys at the dairy. They're all lazy."

I told Buck I thought we should at least give him a try. As Michael stood there this morning watching Jennifer clean the counter, his arm swung out to tap the wall for no apparent reason. Perhaps Buck was right.

I turned to Liz, who was pulling a shot of espresso. She wore flip-flops, denim cutoff shorts—real Daisy Duke style—and a new West's

T-shirt she had managed to shrink so that when she reached for a coffee cup, you could see the small of her back. I made a mental note to work on a dress code.

I had opened the new coffee bar the previous weekend. Business was still slow. I attempted to train the staff in the art of espresso. The veterans such as Jennifer and Stephanie were suspicious of the machine and thought it would take too much time to make coffee drinks and scoop ice cream. Liz was reluctant to warm to the machine given her issues with milk. Michael liked playing with the knobs and making experimental drinks. I doubted the peanut butter latte would take off, but I didn't wish to discourage the lad for his initiative.

Michael stood behind Liz, critiquing her performance. As she poured the steaming milk over the espresso, Liz grimaced at the sight of the bovine secretion. However, she forced a courteous smile when she handed the mug to me.

"Would you like anything else, sir?" she mocked.

The phone rang. Liz jumped to answer, as kids do at home when there's nothing else to do.

"Karb's needs a poly of milk," she said.

Buck was engrossed in his paper, so I said I would take it myself.

Some dark clouds appeared in the western sky, but by 10:00 AM it was already a warm day, and my T-shirt stuck to my back. I balanced my coffee on the handle of the dolly holding the crate of milk and headed for Main Street. Other shopkeepers were out doing some last-minute tidying up. At the art gallery, Deanna vacuumed a strip of outdoor carpet and waved. "Are you ready for the deluge?" she yelled from across the street and smiled.

"Hope so."

A jeweler sat on the bench outside his shop and smirked as though he knew something I didn't.

Inside Karb's, the owner sat on a stool at the end of the bar. It was early, but he was braced for a busy lunch. I rolled my dolly and crate of milk to a corner of the dining room outside the kitchen where a rectangular cooler with a vinyl wood-grain door rested on a Formica counter. When I looked at the mysterious milk-squirting box for the first time back in April, I had one of many *what am I doing here?* moments. I opened the door to find a deflated intravenous bag of milk. I self-consciously looked around to see if anyone in the dining room knew me before I asked the owner for help with inserting the full bag of milk into the cooler and feeding the squirting udder through the slot at the bottom of the door. By now I was quite proficient and in no time replaced the milk bag, deftly fed the udder into position, wheeled my dolly through the restaurant, and wished the owner a good weekend—all part of the service.

Across the street from Karb's, on the bench in front of the bakery, a young couple attempted to train their two toddlers the trick to eating a jelly donut without getting a shirt full of jam. Their patience was admirable, but they should have known it was impossible to eat a jelly donut without dripping on your shirt. Next door, tourists gathered in front of the fudge shop. Cameras were aimed at a frail old woman stirring a sugary concoction in a large copper kettle. She wore a long red-checked skirt, a white blouse, and a vintage white bonnet with an elastic band covering her head. She focused on the fudge and ignored those snapping photos of her, pretending not to hear the requests that she smile. She looked up only to toss another pound of butter into her copper cauldron.

As I returned along West Second Street, the sky threatened my big day with a dark band of gray clouds surrounding Hayward. This was clearly not a good sign. I needed bright, sunny, and hot weather to sell ice cream and to permit enough light into the shop. The sidewalk near the dairy remained more or less empty. Buck was amused at my concern, but then he didn't have a month of bills to pay or four employees behind the counter who were engaged in a detailed discussion of a classmate's hair extensions.

"This is good," Buck told me as he pointed to the sky. "It will get people off the lake and into town." There was logic to his argument. If it was bright and sunny, people would prefer to stay on the lake—fishing, water-skiing, or what have you. I was still concerned but had some errands to run. I was reminded by Bruce to get lots of change—quarters, dimes, nickels, and at least five hundred one-dollar bills to get through the weekend. I also needed ice in order to make our new line of fruit smoothies.

An hour later when I returned with ice and change, there was nowhere to park apart from a space Bruce had personally designated a loading zone by the side door. The municipal parking lot was filling up quickly. I drove around the block and was shocked by the sudden appearance of groups of attractive, casually dressed people who had descended on downtown. They moved slowly, resembling a clan of large meerkats, their heads held high and cocked in unison as they looked at the window displays on Main Street. Buck was right—they came.

I drove to the front of the dairy and gazed down West Second Street. I had never seen anything so wonderful. The benches in front of my store were filled with people, and others who could not find room were standing. Everyone held an ice cream cone or a cup of ice cream or had his or her mouth clasped around a straw, trying to inhale a West's shake.

I parked in the loading zone and grabbed my bags of money to see what it was like inside. The official greeter looked at me with a big grin and wagged his finger. "I told you not to worry."

"I will never doubt you again," I said and looked around at the bustle. Most of the tables were occupied by families with a few squirming toddlers who were carefully feeding themselves. Young girls in shorts and shorter T-shirts hovered at the dipping cabinet, struggling with their selection, while others checked out the new T-shirts on the shelf.

"Do you provide samples?" one girl asked. Behind the counter, Jennifer reluctantly reached for a taster spoon. Jen had trained the new hires and expected, if not demanded, order and calm. These personal traits sometimes came across in a seemingly hostile manner when dealing with the public, which she perceived as a threat to her clean floors, perfectly displayed ice cream, and spotless restrooms.

Liz was holding up well behind the counter. She was not as quick as Jen, but her scoops were adequate, and she was able to force a smile even while sinking her hand into the product of forced milking of many defenseless animals. A handsome college guy approached the counter and smiled. Liz moved over, pushing one of her colleagues out of the way, to help him. She slid right up the counter toward him so that the bottom of her T-shirt rode high above the mint chocolate chip.

"What can I get for YOU?" Liz asked coyly.

"Well, do you recommend any flavors?" he asked our vegan scooper.

"Oh, they're all really awesome," Liz emphasized as though she were from the beach. "But my favorite is Wild Berry Crumble." She made this up since she had never tasted any of the ice cream.

The young man was convinced and took a Wild Berry Crumble waffle cone. After Liz carefully molded the ice cream into a waffle cone and handed it to her new friend, he slowly and deliberately tucked a five-dollar bill into the tip jar on the counter in front of her. She gave him a big "thank you."

Later, I was curious and asked our ice cream Lolita why she recommended Wild Berry Crumble.

"It was easiest to scoop at the time—not too hard."

By midafternoon, a steady stream of customers had lined up for ice cream. Most had been to West's before and were surprised at the changes.

"Was that tin ceiling always here?"

"Aren't those chairs fantastic?"

I hovered on the edges to hear as much as possible.

"Are there new owners?" I heard one group ask Buck. Not realizing my vicinity, he replied, "Yep, and they came here from England—if you can believe that!"

"No, really?"

It was our busiest day so far. We served no fewer than seven hundred customers. Even as the light grew very dim, people were drawn to the glow of the dipping cabinets, which provided the only illumination in the room. In the back, empty ice cream containers filled the tables; puddles of melting ice cream colored the floor like a rainbow. My leather chairs looked as though they were furnishing a family's playroom, with crumbs between the cushions and chocolate chips stuck to the backs.

The girls behind the counter were frazzled and giddy, relieved the day was over. Their arms were sore and stained with bright blue from the cotton candy ice cream. Jen vigorously scoured the surface of the countertops while Liz emptied the tip jars and counted the change and dollar bills. They exchanged quips about their most difficult customers, ran a mop across the floor, cleaned the espresso machine, and covered the ice cream.

Buck had slipped out around dinnertime. "I think I'll go to the buffet at the casino tonight," he said.

When the girls had gone, I locked the door and drove back to the cabin. I had been gone since morning. My brother, Paul, and his wife were visiting. They had enjoyed the lake and sun all day. They had saved me a cold bratwurst and hamburger from their evening barbeque. I brought a half gallon of Almost Sinful for dessert. My brother ate ice cream from a dish. He was eight years my senior. When I was a kid, I chastised him for eating what I claimed was ice cream Mom had bought for me.

He watched as I emptied a canvas moneybag onto the table. I divided the currency by denomination.

"It's just like back when you had that paper route," Paul said. Before Minnesota adopted any child labor laws, I started delivering the *Minneapolis Star* every afternoon and the *Tribune* on Sunday morning. I was only nine years old. Every other week, I collected payment from customers in a small rubber bag provided by the bank. After counting the money and paying the newspaper bosses, I earned about eight dollars a week. Back then, Paul teased me by offering to count my collection money and suggesting he would take a cut.

He watched as I stacked piles of twenty-dollar bills. "Would you like me to help you count?" Paul grinned.

"No," I retorted. "And that's my ice cream."

Sunday was an even bigger day for business at West's Hayward Dairy. The temperature rose to the high eighties, and the sun was blinding. People were forced to remove their sunglasses so their eyes could adjust to the shadows of the dairy. By noon, a line had formed from the dipping cabinet to the front door and soon extended around the front of the building.

I jumped in to help the girls scoop ice cream. I replenished the empty tubs and grabbed a scoop. "Can I help someone, please?" I yelled.

After some intense scooping, an older woman at the side called me over. She looked very serious, and I thought this might not be good. I looked over to Liz to see whether she was appropriately dressed.

"Are you one of the new owners?" she asked. "Well, we have been coming here for forty years. We never come to town without a visit to West's. But I just want to say . . ."

Oh, no, I thought. *Here it comes. I have removed all of her fond memories. She hates it.*

". . . you did a wonderful job! We love it. It's all so beautiful," she said and went on to shower praise on the changes at the dairy. I may have blushed, and I thanked her.

By Monday, the long weekend began to wind down. The customers were either making a longer vacation of the short break or on their way out of town. It was not difficult to spot those who headed back to work on Tuesday. Fathers urged their children to make up their minds quickly so they could hit the road. I knew they were thinking of the next morning in the office—overdue project, irate boss, or reluctant subordinates.

"Do you have Wi-Fi?" a tense woman fumbling with a handheld device asked. "I need to check my e-mail." She may have had a nemesis in the office and needed to hit the ground running when she returned to work the next day; the petty grievances with her coworkers perhaps had been simmering over the weekend and would return to a boil. She sat down in one of the leather chairs while she retrieved her mail. *Never again,* I thought. She caressed the arm of the chair. I wondered what she was thinking.

Even though I worked all weekend, it had been a long time since I had felt so invigorated. The reaction to the renovations at West's could not have been better, even without the lights. I was in shorts and a T-shirt—had even caught a bit of a farmer's tan around my neck and below my shirtsleeves. I had a pile of cash to take to the bank on Tuesday morning and could begin to chip away at some of the unpaid bills. The most satisfying aspect was that, even though I did not know what the next week would bring, I knew I would not be getting on a train or going to the office the next day. Before I locked the dairy, I grabbed my bag of money and a new West's T-shirt from the shelf for my next day at work.

Beautiful Mornings

In only two months, the harsh landscape—lifeless branches, ice-covered lakes, and winter silence—was little more than a distant memory. Nature had exploded in a green abundance that hung over the active shores of Teal Lake. From the morning birdsong, the hissing of the afternoon cicadas, and the haunting evening duet of owls and loons, the dogs were in a constant state of joyous alert. In early summer, saplings, fiddlehead ferns, and wild lupine carpeted the forest floor, and in a far corner under an ancient oak, the ever-so-shy white trillium appeared for its brief annual visit, its three delicate diamond-shaped petals adding a glow to the shadows of the forest.

I took my morning coffee down to the dock. The water was perfectly still apart from a pattern created by the family of loons on their morning tour of the lake's perimeter. For the past month, their only offspring of the season rode on the back of one of the adult birds, but today he, or possibly she, swam furiously to keep up with his watchful parents.

In these two months, we completed with the speed but perhaps not the grace of Mother Nature the initial phase of our plan to dominate the Hayward ice cream and hospitality markets. While there may have been some spilled milk and projectile ice cream, the takeover of West's Hayward Dairy had gone relatively smoothly. While there had been much drama and many heated moments with my young builders, even Sparky came through and wired the lights following the Memorial Day weekend. The barn façade and cracked fiberglass canopy were as forgotten as the winter snow. In the end, the poster of Brett Favre with his milk mustache had not survived the renovations.

And people liked it. The ice cream was as good as it had always been. The espresso bar did well on its first big weekend. However, my staff suggested I might consider removing *Gelato al Caffè Affogato* from the menu as it came off as a bit pretentious and no one ordered it. Michael loved it because it was cool, Stephanie liked it because it was foreign, Jen thought it was too foreign, and vegan Liz thought it spoiled decent espresso. It was always one of my favorite ice cream treats—a small scoop of vanilla covered, or "flooded," in hot espresso, the perfect marriage of homemade ice cream and premium espresso. For the time being, I changed the name to Espresso Sundae and hoped it would catch on. Whenever a customer couldn't decide between ice cream and coffee, I insisted they try it.

I disconnected my BlackBerry and U.K. cell phones and did not bother to purchase an American cell phone. The e-mails from former colleagues grew fewer and further between. One day at the end of May, I forgot to put on my watch. Such neglect in the past would have prompted me to jump off the bus and run back to the house to pick it up. I fretted for a bit, but I wasn't about to drive twenty miles to retrieve it. After I forgot my watch again a few days later, I put it in a safe place in the dresser drawer.

I finished my coffee and set the mug on the bench. I slipped off my sandals in order to dip my feet in the lake. I felt the last of the winter chill in the water. A man in a fishing boat slowly approached the shore but shut his engine off fifty feet out. He played with some bait and a hook before casting his line toward the dock. We had been told that near our dock was a nesting area for the prized walleye, the medium-sized pike known for its mild and meaty taste.

"Beautiful morning, isn't it?" he shouted, even though shouting wasn't necessary given the short distance between us and the silence all around us.

"It sure is," I said.

"So, how do you like it here?" he asked and nodded his head toward the cabin.

"Oh, we love it. The lake is fantastic." I finished my coffee and left him to catch his dinner.

I fell slowly into a routine of sorts. I might arrive at the dairy before 8:00 or as late as 10:00 in the morning. Bruce warned me that would change once the high season kicked in. I assisted Buck with ice cream deliveries to local campgrounds and smaller ice cream shops, but I often left him to do them on his own. We might make ice cream on Tuesday, but it could also be Wednesday or Friday or whenever we needed it.

"It's going to be a hot one today," Buck said one morning. "The weatherman said it could reach ninety-five," he added and fanned himself with the newspaper for effect.

"I don't think this air conditioning works that well," Liz added from behind the counter. My attempt at a dress code had failed, and she was twisting her tiny T-shirt, exposing her navel to cool her entire body.

"Go in the freezer for a minute or two," Buck said. "That'll cool you down." Liz ignored his comment and went back to work.

"I'm off to Wilderness Walk. Wanna join me? I don't think you've met the owners, have you?" Buck thought it was important that I meet the clients. He was probably right.

"I've spoken to them on the phone," I said. Buck was not impressed. I agreed to ride along.

Tall Drink of Water, as Buck referred to Michael, loaded six containers of ice cream in the back of Buck's car. I got in the passenger side and moved the newspapers and empty fast food wrappers from around my feet. "Yeah, I need to clean this jalopy someday," Buck said.

Buck was typical of many older drivers in Hayward who believed that with age came privileges on the road, including ignoring stop signs and expecting pedestrians to wait for you to pass. Driving through yellow lights was one of his driving privileges, perhaps due to his wartime service. Nevertheless, I was more than somewhat anxious as we ran the red light across Highway 63. I watched oncoming drivers from the right slow and raise a fist to say hello—or something.

Wilderness Walk was the petting zoo on the south side of town on Highway 27 that Deanna from the humane society had once owned. The service entrance to the park was a short, steep driveway not much longer than a car's length off the highway. I watched the side-view mirror and hoped the driver behind us was paying attention since Buck had not bothered to signal his sharp turn onto an unmarked driveway. Even better, he decided at the last minute to reverse into the drive by turning left into the lane of oncoming traffic and backing down the steep grade. At the bottom, Buck asked me to get out and ring the bell so the kitchen staff would open the gate.

The gate was a high wood and chain fence sturdy enough to keep in the deer that walked freely on the other side, but it could not withstand the impact of Buck's Dodge Caravan. I wondered if he had remembered to engage the parking brake.

A large woman with bleached blond hair came through the back door of the café and walked to the gate, swishing some deer away so they did not attempt to make a run for it as the gate opened. I directed Buck inside the gate, and he reversed another hundred feet to the rear of the café. Buck lowered his car window and yelled, "I hope I'm close enough for you!"

"No problem. I'll take it in," I said. "You take it easy." I didn't mind. I'd let him sit in the air-conditioned car.

Inside, the café was filled with a busload of ten-year-olds ordering hot dogs and ice cream cones along with cups of corn to feed the animals. I made my way to the freezer with the ice cream and found the manager to sign the invoice.

"Where's Buck?" she asked.

"Oh, he's in the car," I said. "I think he's hot."

"He has the right idea in this heat," she laughed and swept the hair off her forehead before going back to serve the next group of children.

"Well, that was pretty easy," Buck said. I was not sure whether or not he was joking. I began to think the old man had an ulterior motive for asking me along on this hot day.

"Do you want to join me on the delivery to the KOA campground?" Buck asked.

My suspicions were confirmed. I suggested Tall Drink of Water could help him.

"Nah, I'll be fine," he said.

Is That Christian Rock?

After Memorial Day weekend, business initially dropped off as children returned for at least one or two more weeks of school before their summer vacations. With every passing day in early June, however, more and more tourists could be seen strolling down Main Street with a package of fudge, a new pair of moccasins, and a few souvenirs before they headed to the dairy. Local businesses, from the grocery store to the lakeside supper clubs, opened their arms to the returning visitors, whom they treated like lost relatives. The streets were lined with SUVs, foreign sedans, and other vehicles more familiar on suburban driveways than the back roads of Sawyer County.

At the dairy, Jen worked hard to keep the place in order. Stephanie was in a better mood after receiving a few text messages from her Czech boyfriend, and, while I had my doubts that Liz would be able to hold out against the temptation of frozen, sweet bovine secretions, she maintained her vegan lifestyle.

With business running smoothly at West's, Dean and I could focus on the second phase of our grand scheme to redefine the lodging business in Hayward. Over the past two months, the contractor we had hired to carry out the renovation of McCormick House had completed other projects. In that time, while I learned the day-to-day operations of the dairy, made ice cream, and managed my growing staff, Dean spent much of his days agonizing over every detail of the McCormick House renovation, including ordering furniture for the common areas and six guest bedrooms. He also helped make ice cream, and, in the evenings over dinner, we updated each other on the state of our projects.

Almost every day, though, Dean phoned the dairy. "Can you come up to look at something?" I didn't mind since the house was only a few minutes away, and I was happy to take a break. He might have been grappling with floor covering, carpet samples, or furniture measurements. Other times, he only wanted my opinion on the fabric choice for a few scatter cushions.

Working with the contractor, Dean finalized the scope of the project. He began with some handwritten notes on the back of an envelope. Over the weeks, the plan developed into a project document in the form of a spreadsheet several pages long. The list included new insulation, a new roof, removal and replacement of wood floors, converting the heating system from a smelly oil-burning one to natural gas, rewiring, a new kitchen, the installation of an air-conditioning system, and removal, sandblasting, and replacement of over thirty radiators. There was also painting the entire house both inside and out and building a breakfast terrace.

The contractor hoped to complete the project by September, just in time to accommodate tourists to the area for the autumn colors. We thought the timetable was highly ambitious, and we assumed the house would be ready by Christmas. Having been through a few renovation projects in the U.K. as well as the Teal Lake home, we had heard it all before.

As Dean said, builders were all the same. There would be delays, cost overruns were the norm, and in the end, we would feel as though we had been taken to the cleaners. We had never undertaken a project as large and requiring as much work as the McCormick House. We knew the kitchen could take six months alone, and Lord only knew what the final costs would be.

In my office, I was working on the May invoices from the wholesale milk route. For each delivery, Tom prepared a handwritten statement on a simple three-page carbon invoice that itemized the delivery and provided the cost per unit. I input each invoice into the computer, eventually generating a monthly statement. It was time consuming, but the alternative—not being paid—was less attractive.

The phone rang. I heard one of the girls answer and then ask the others, "Is Jeff here?" There was some commotion until she walked over to the office and handed me the phone. "It's Dean." Stephanie smiled.

"You've got to get up here," he said with more urgency than the usual fabric sample crisis.

"What is it?" I asked.

"You'll see." He hung up.

I found the invoicing too similar to my former life and knew that it would become something I would put off until the last minute. It was a beautiful day. The sun had lost all of its springtime hesitancy—no risk of a cool breeze. I had felt a bit of sunburn on my face and reminded myself to pick up some sunscreen.

Dean was outside the house watching two men on the roof. They were tearing off old shingles one by one and tossing them into a dumpster that had been placed on the lawn. They wore safety harnesses yet worked at a harried pace as though they were in a shingle-removing competition. I looked around, but there was no one with a stopwatch or anyone cheering or even watching.

Another workman stuck his head out of the attic window. He held a long hose that was spraying insulation in the attic. He called to someone below operating a compressor. At the front of the house, four young men groaned as they hauled the old radiators out to be sandblasted. Made of cast iron, these original units each weighed several hundred pounds.

"So, what is it?" I asked Dean.

"Look!" Dean motioned to the workmen around the house.

"Look at what? I just see people working."

"That's it! They're working!" Dean was astounded. "I've never seen anything like it. No cigarette breaks, no tea breaks. They've been working like this all day."

When I looked around, I could see what he meant. Our history of builders had been one of constant grumbling and complaints about conditions. London contractors argued they could not get good help, and their workers complained their boss was cheap. Both the English contractors and workers tolerated the situation by smoking themselves silly with hourly tea breaks. To make matters worse, if one of us was at home during the day, it was incumbent on us as the owner to brew the tea as a courtesy for the builders. As a result, building projects could take a very long time.

"You're right," I said. "Hmm. Pretty incredible."

"Wait a minute," Dean said and called to one of the workers return-ing to the house for another radiator. "Chris!" he yelled. "This is Jeff."

Chris, a young lad of about nineteen, sweat dripping from his brow, smiled as he approached me. He wiped his hand on his jeans and held it out to me. "How do you do, sir? Nice to meet you," he said.

Taken aback, I wasn't sure how to respond. "Well, thank you. Nice to meet you, too," I said. "Nice work."

"Gorgeous day, isn't it? Well, I'd better get back to work," he said and ran, not walked or dawdled, back to help the others with another radiator.

"It gets better," Dean said. "Follow me."

As we walked to the side of the house, one of the roofers lost his foot-ing and smashed his hand against the roof. "Oh, darn it!" he yelled.

"Did he say 'darn it'?" I asked as though my mother had been remov-ing shingles from the roof.

"They don't swear," Dean whispered as though it were a closely guarded secret.

In the kitchen, the walls had been stripped bare and a workstation had been set up, but no one was around. A paint-splattered radio sat on a ladder near a plug. "Do you hear that?" Dean asked, pointing to what he wanted to show me—the radio. All I could hear was the sound of an unfamiliar pop song.

"What?"

"Do you recognize the song?" Dean urged. I listened to the melody and tried to make out the lyrics: "*. . . He is the one, the only one . . .*"

"Oh my God," I said. "It's Christian rock!"

"They all go to some big church outside of town," Dean said. We knew the contractor came from the Mennonite tradition, which helped explain his skills as a craftsman. The contractor had since joined the closest thing Hayward had to an evangelical mega-church and recruited from the church's congregation.

"Do you know what this means?" Dean asked. "We aren't going to be ripped off!" He answered his own question before I could respond. The news was great and meant there would be many fewer things to worry about.

"Oh, I got these fabric samples for the living room. Do you want to tell me what you think?"

"Sure."

Banana Boats and a
Tribute to Ambrose Weeres

Although it was only the second week of June, it felt like midsummer. For a few days, temperatures had soared into the nineties. The sun was high in the sky by 10:00 AM with only a few clouds that seemed to go nowhere. Near the cabin, cicadas began to stir and whirled their cry as a warning of the heat to come in the afternoon. The dogs lay near the air-conditioning vents for much of the day to preserve their energy.

Over dinner on the terrace at the cabin, Dean and I began to lament that we might be falling into old patterns. I was spending most of my days at the dairy, checking supplies, making ice cream with Bruce, or managing the logistics of deliveries, which meant filling my car with ice cream and getting it to the restaurants, campgrounds, or ice cream shops before it melted. Dean had set up an office at McCormick House to oversee the work of the Christian builders, and he came to the dairy whenever he had a new idea for marketing the ice cream. Where was the balance? What would we do even if we made time? In London, we would go to the theater or perhaps a new exhibit, or we would spend a weekend in the country.

The answer was all around us, but that raised more questions. With over five hundred lakes in Sawyer County alone, along with several rivers and streams, forest trails, and biking paths, people came not only to enjoy the scenery but also to conquer what nature presented them. Their vehicles were topped with canoes, kayaks, and bicycles while they pulled boats—fishing boats, speedboats, cabin cruisers—and trailers with Jet Skis.

The emphasis on sports and outdoor activities begged the question Dean and I asked ourselves—*What are we doing here?* I couldn't throw a ball, I swam like a rock, and I generally ran from any activity vaguely competitive. Dean, despite his tall frame and broad shoulders, was not much more physically inclined than I was, although he had been known to hurdle a few shop assistants on his way to a Prada loafer at the Harvey Nichols summer sale.

To our credit, we did try our best to embrace the outdoor lifestyle. We began with the lake at our back door. Swimming was out of the question given my buoyancy of stone, and Dean refused to enter the water after Buck told him the large muskies that inhabited the area lakes had been known to bite humans on occasion.

Dean was convinced a pontoon boat would be the perfect way to enjoy the lake. The pontoon was an unusual sailing vessel typical on lakes in North America. With a flat bottom, the boat floated on two large aluminum cylinders. In 1950, a farmer in Minnesota, Ambrose Weeres, welded a few barrels together and attached a wooden deck on top. Not only did it float, but it gave his cows something to do on weekends. Pontoons were manufactured in many sizes, from as small as twelve feet to as long as thirty-six feet, and were often complete with full bar, stereo system, and lounge-type seating. Most were equipped with a sun canopy. Despite all these improvements, the basic design still resembled a flat deck sitting on two barrels.

On a "quiet" lake such as Teal, where speed was restricted to twenty-five miles per hour, the pontoon boat was *de rigueur* among the lake's residents, who could be seen cruising the perimeter with a pre- or post-dinner cocktail in hand. In some cases, they set a table on the boat and took dinner with them. Dean was convinced this was the key to civility on the lake. I argued that we should wait to see how well we did in controlling our other expenditures before spending on such a luxury.

So instead we bought an old twelve-foot aluminum fishing boat. The boat was designed for practicality, to get an old geezer to the middle of the lake where he could sit for the afternoon to down a six-pack of Bud Light while catching his dinner. The boat, with its three metal seats, provided few of the frills and little of the refinement of the pontoon lifestyle. The small rubber plug, not unlike the plug in the drain of a bathtub, at the back was the only thing between the puddle of water in the boat and the bottom of the lake. The vessel was propelled by a gas-powered egg beater, but due to the boat's light aluminum body, when Dean opened up the motor it raced across the lake at such speed that the bow rose out of the water at a thirty-degree angle with me at the top hanging on for my life.

It became clear that our choice of watercraft was costing us some credibility with our neighbors. On a sunny Sunday afternoon, Dean, the dogs, and I went for a slow spin around the lake. A large pontoon sailed by on an afternoon booze cruise.

"So, how are the fish biting?" the captain of the vessel asked. You could tell he was the captain by his skipper's hat and martini glass.

We explained we were not fishing but kept to ourselves that the primary purpose of our trip was to get a glimpse of the décor of some of the larger homes on the lake. The captain was confused, and there were murmurs on board. "If they aren't fishing, what are they doing in that contraption?"

"Oh, really?" the captain said. "Well, you have a nice day." He sped off. We snuck back to the dock, avoiding contact with anyone else on the lake.

My solution to our watercraft needs was a kayak, a relatively inexpensive plastic vessel that would provide an excellent source of exercise. Kayaks were also popular among the neighbors, thus eliminating any social stigma. Dean was not entirely convinced, as he thought it provided minimal protection between him and the bone-crushing muskies that resided in Teal Lake. I knew that once he saw how much fun I was having, he would change his mind.

I found the kayak's plastic seat uncomfortable and managed to get wet and stay wet for a very long time, but I persevered. I suited up in my bright yellow life vest, which, combined with the bright yellow kayak, gave the effect of a floating banana with a tumor on its side. I rarely strayed too far from the cabin and no more than a hundred feet from shore in case the vessel sprung a leak and began to take on water.

On a calm morning, with a clear blue sky and a lake flat as glass, I made the bold decision that before breakfast I would paddle to one of the islands in the middle of the lake across several hundred feet of open water. Given the perfect conditions, I had nothing to fear. The loon family appeared by my side, confident that, in my banana boat, I was not a threat. I rowed quickly with the aid of a slight breeze at my back.

In about thirty minutes, I arrived at my destination, Raspberry Island. I got out and pulled the boat onto a sandbar. There was a picnic area on the island, but I didn't stray far from my boat in case a band of pirates from neighboring Lost Land Lake appeared and seized my kayak, leaving me to fend for myself on this technically deserted island.

I walked along the shore toward the base of the largest tree on the island. The tree was home to the lake's resident bald eagles. At its base lay the carcasses of several fish and some rodents that had provided meals to the birds. I'm not sure why, but I was very surprised. I was surprised that the most majestic and revered of our feathered friends, his face on all our money, lived above a pile of trash. It was like visiting the home of a boss, a respected and well-dressed professional in the office, only to find a broken-down car in her front yard, a pile of old newspapers in the entryway, and a husband who smoked and swore at the kids. I felt like an intruder and decided to leave in case I upset the eagles.

When I returned to my banana boat, the sky to the west had darkened, and my gentle breeze now disturbed the trees on the island. Waves began to slap the sides of the logs protruding from the shoreline. I looked across the lake toward the cabin, and it seemed very far away indeed. The steep steps from the dock to the house looked no larger than single toothpicks.

I had no choice. I needed to set off before the storm came across the lake. With any luck, I would beat the rain that was not far away. I buckled up and set off. The tailwind on the way over to the island was now a blustering headwind, spraying water in my face. White-capped waves rose out of the lake. I might as well have been crossing the Northwest Territory with Lewis and Clark. I paddled quickly, as fast as I could, but progress was slow.

I hoped it wasn't a tornado. To a child growing up in the area, no storm was more fear inducing than the tornado. There was usually very little or no warning. By the time the alarm sounded, the sky could be full of mobile homes picked up in Iowa. At Catholic school, we had tornado drills. Sister Fidelis led the second grade down to the basement, where we sat against a long cinder-block hall painted a glossy gray that smelled of a mix of cleaning supplies and the Aqua Velva aftershave the janitor wore. His office was at the end of the hall. While we waited for the all-clear signal from the principal, the janitor watched us with both his good and lazy eyes. The experience did not make one feel very safe even though Sister Fidelis said in the unlikely event of a tornado we would be in the hands of God.

As I fought the currents and the wind on Teal Lake, I repeated my mantra—*Never again, never again.* I remembered looking out on the frozen lake in March and thought, *My adventure wasn't supposed to end in a shallow lake when I fell out of my banana boat.*

The loon family returned. They squawked and called as they neared me. Perhaps they were imparting advice—*Stay low in the water like us.* Or perhaps they were mocking me—*It's not so easy, is it?*

By the time I neared the shore, rain pounded against my face. I pulled my kayak onto land and briefly thought I would let it float out to sea so I would never be so stupid as to try that again. I climbed the stairs, breathless.

Dean was waiting for me by the deck.

"Are you crazy?!" he shouted. "I thought I was going to have to rescue you with the egg beater boat. You're never going to get me into those little boats after that," he said.

I tried to catch my breath to speak. I collapsed in the living room chair.

"Would you like a bacon sandwich?" Dean had calmed down. "I found this English butcher in North Carolina who prepares a Danish-style back bacon." He began to describe his find and how he wondered if Americans would take to a "bacon butty" on the McCormick House menu.

If there was anything that could bring me back to life, it was a bacon sandwich. I caught my breath just enough. "Yes," I said. I managed to add between a cough and a gasp for air, "With HP sauce, please."

When I told Matt and Dave about my harrowing experience on the water, they kindly refrained from laughing and suggested we should join them when they next kayaked down the Namekagon River. They cared too much about their hair to be considered athletic, but they had become adept at the local outdoor pursuits. They argued that river kayaking was preferable to lake kayaking—so long as you were going in the right direction, the river really did most of the work. They told Dean there were no muskies in the river, but that may have been a lie. Dean wasn't convinced.

The following Sunday, we invited our friends to the cabin for lunch. They suggested bringing their kayaks, but we said that would not be necessary.

When they arrived, Dean was making his final preparations. In order to improve our standing among the members of the lake association and to avoid any more embarrassing encounters on the water, I broke down and agreed we could purchase a pontoon. As the summer season had already begun, we got it for a good price. It was not the largest on the lake, but it had vinyl lounge seating, a stowaway table for dining, and plenty of cupholders.

Dean got behind the wheel, and the pontoon was loaded with a light lunch of cheese, bread, and fresh fruit. A couple of bottles of Chablis chilled over ice, and the motor was humming.

"All aboard!" Dean called.

We began a civilized day on the water. No one got wet, and there was plenty to eat and drink. We toasted Ambrose Weeres and his flat boat invention. We passed around binoculars to check out the eagles' nest above Raspberry Island and the loons who stayed a respectful distance from the pontoon. We waved cordially to our neighbors, who slowed to check out our new pontoon.

"Nice boat!" the captain of another vessel shouted and raised his martini glass.

He Flipped a Lot of Pancakes in His Day

At the dairy, Bruce was on the telephone.

"I see," he said into the receiver. "It's a Lions thing. Oh, I understand," he said with less than his usual enthusiasm.

"He's trying to organize the volunteers for the Sawyer County Dairy Breakfast," Buck whispered to me. "It doesn't sound too good."

"Well, if your plans change, let me know. We could sure use the help on Saturday," Bruce said and hung up.

Buck had been talking about the dairy breakfast for weeks. Held at the county fairgrounds on the outskirts of town early in the summer during Dairy Month, the breakfast was designed to promote and acknowledge the significance of Wisconsin's dairy industry. Buck usually flipped pancakes at the breakfast. "Oh, it's a big deal in these parts," he warned. "I wish I had a nickel for every pancake I flipped in my day."

Bruce had been at the dairy much of the week organizing the purchase of food and the delivery of grills and other equipment. Now he was organizing volunteers to work at the event.

Bruce scratched his head and looked at the floor. The local Lions Club was having its own event the same day, so many of Bruce's usual volunteers would not be able to help at this year's breakfast.

"Well, Dean and I could help," I said. I would need to convince Dean it would be good for business. "We could probably find a half dozen volunteers," I said, going out on a limb since that would require every one of our new friends and acquaintances to agree to help.

"Really?" Bruce asked, surprised that the two of us knew six people in Hayward. "That would be swell," he said. "Just remember, everyone needs to be at the fairgrounds by 6:00 AM. The doors open at 7:00."

"Oh, that early," I said. This could be a problem. Most of our new friends came from the bar at the Ranch Supper Club. I had never seen them before cocktail hour, and usually by the time we left them at the bar, they were "well on their way," as they liked to say. They were not exactly the types to be up at the crack of dawn to flip pancakes. Of course, I thought this was all the more reason to get them there. I'd tell them they'd started to serve Bloody Marys at the dairy breakfast.

It was understandable that the state officials recognized the industry as they did with county dairy breakfasts. There were still roughly 13,000 dairy farms with 1.25 million cows, or a cow for every fourth person in the state. Nearly ten percent of Wisconsin's workforce was either directly or indirectly involved in the dairy industry, making it more critical than, for example, the citrus industry was to Florida. Ever since the first settlers from Germany arrived in the state and saw the rolling hills and natural pasturelands of southern Wisconsin and thought, *What a great place to produce Limburger,* Wisconsin has been known as America's dairyland.

Wisconsin's dairy industry had come under threat, not from the lactose intolerant or a growing army of militant vegans but from something far more sinister—California. With its temperate climate, massive agricultural fields, the Pacific Ocean, and the razzmatazz of Hollywood glitz and glamour that could be tapped for slick marketing campaigns, California in recent years had overtaken Wisconsin in both milk and butter production. California even had the nerve to advertise its dairy industry on Wisconsin television featuring cows— clearly well-paid actors—with the backdrop of orange groves, redwoods, sunshine, and the message, "The happiest cows are from California."

In the past, the state took more direct action against threats to its number-one industry—they banned margarine. When that didn't work, the state permitted the sale of only an unappealing margarine that was not colored to resemble butter and added a hefty tax on its sale. This led to a cottage industry along the state's borders as service stations and food stores put up big billboards touting inexpensive "colored" margarine to those traveling into Wisconsin. It was only in 1967 that, under the threat of court action, Wisconsin permitted the sale of colored margarine.

The annual county dairy breakfasts, along with the giant cheese-shaped Styrofoam hats fans wore at the Green Bay Packers games, were key to Wisconsin's attempt to maintain its dairy image. I wondered how successful a cheap breakfast buffet could be, but Buck assured me, "You'll never believe it!"

On the day Wisconsinites gathered to defend the state's cheesy pride against the Goliath of California, bright sunshine soaked the hollow that was home to the Sawyer County Fairgrounds. The breakfast took place in a large pole barn. In a nearby barn, a few cows and other animals were on display, and they looked very happy. Bruce had parked the West's concession stand between the two barns and explained scooping techniques to a few Girl Scouts who would serve complimentary ice cream cones to people after breakfast.

Inside the main barn, volunteers wiped each of the long tables that could accommodate nearly eighty diners. They set out salt and pepper, jars of maple syrup, and trays of butter. At the other end, a bank of grills was set up against one wall. Buck was already at the grill flipping pancakes to put in a warming pan. He reminisced with his neighbor on the grill next to him about flipping pancakes. "I wish I had a nickel for every one of these pancakes I've flipped over the years," he said.

On the other side of Buck, an old farmer grilled breakfast sausage links in a pool of grease. He wore a straw hat and bibbed denim overalls that helped support his hefty paunch. Occasionally, he grabbed a link with his fingers and tossed it back. "I know what you mean, Buck. I've been doing this for twenty years," the farmer said.

A group of Mennonite families organized the ticket sales at the main door. The women wore light cotton ankle-length dresses, long white aprons, and crisp white or black bonnets, the type nurses wore before they switched to today's pajamalike uniforms. Some folks had already formed a line outside the door, mostly the insomniac elderly and a few farmers in their overalls coming directly from their morning chores.

Other volunteers set up the buffet line: first the pancakes, then the sausages, some optional slices of cheese, then, to my surprise and Dean's horror, vanilla ice cream scooped directly onto the pancakes followed by strawberries served from five-gallon buckets. There was milk or coffee to drink.

"Have you seen Bruce?" I asked Buck.

"Oh, he's playing the big celebrity on the radio." Buck pointed to Bruce, who was standing by the large side door talking to a woman I recognized from the local radio station. She was conducting one of the station's live remote broadcasts in which the presenter filled the airwaves with conversations and interviews between your favorite classic rock hits. She asked Bruce about his history with the Sawyer County Dairy Breakfast.

"Well, I've been organizing the breakfast for twenty-four years, but this will be my last," he announced on the radio.

"And so, Mr. West, who will take over your responsibilities at the dairy breakfast?" The announcer held the microphone to Bruce's lips.

"Well, we're looking for volunteers, if anyone is interested," Bruce added with a chuckle.

"Well, there you have it," the announcer began to sign off. "We are at the Sawyer County Dairy Breakfast and speaking exclusively with Bruce West, its chief organizer for twenty-four years, who just announced this will be his last dairy breakfast. Thank you, Mr. West. Now, back to you in the studio."

Behind Bruce, I saw Dean and Cheryl along with some regulars
from the Ranch coming through the barn door. They glanced around
their unfamiliar surroundings; perhaps they were looking for the bar.
As Bruce was busy, I instructed my friends to help flip pancakes as
Buck complained that no one had showed up.

Buck began with a lesson. "Remember, don't pat the pancakes on
the grill; otherwise, they'll go flat and hard." Cheryl, who may have
been up too late or needed a cigarette, did not take kindly to Buck's
words of pancake wisdom.

"Buck, I own a friggin' restaurant. I think I can handle a pancake or
two," she replied.

"All right, but I'm just saying," Buck retreated.

By 7:00 AM, the polka band had set up in the corner and its members were tuning up—*oompa, ooompa*. A line had formed outside the
main entrance. Bruce gave the go-ahead to open the doors. A woman
in a black and white cow suit greeted the diners as they entered the
barn. She waved her front hooves in the air and kicked her rear legs as
she walked past the polka band.

The diners gave the small ticket they had just bought from a person
at the door to another fifteen feet away in exchange for a plastic plate
and set of cutlery. Volunteers served each diner two medium-sized
pancakes and two sausage links. The diners then proceeded to Dean,
who topped their pancakes and sausage with a generous scoop of
vanilla ice cream. He chatted and joked with those holding the plates
of pancakes. He occasionally asked how they could eat ice cream with
sausage and pancakes. "I don't know—it's the dairy breakfast," was
a typical response. Next to Dean, a tiny silver-topped lady with thin
hands ladled strawberries over the ice cream.

Clara, the cow-suited lady, took a shine to Dean's English accent
and stood nearby just to hear him. She announced that he had come
all the way from England for the dairy breakfast. "Mad cow," he
mumbled.

Fathers returned for seconds, mothers cringed at the sight of their children eating ice cream for breakfast, and the kids pleaded, "Mom, why can't we have ice cream for breakfast every day?"

Bruce instructed me to keep an eye on the ice cream and make sure the volunteers I had gathered were able to keep up. "I am not so sure about them behind the grills. We can't get behind with the pancakes or we'll have a line from here to County Road B," he said as he rushed off to greet a representative from the department of agriculture who had just arrived.

Most of my volunteers were on the grills. Because there were no exhaust fans, the work was a hot and sweaty affair.

"I am sweatin' buckets," Buck announced before he turned to Cheryl. "Hey, I see you're patting those pancakes—remember what I said." Cheryl ignored him as she squirmed in desperation for a cigarette.

"Hey, Jeff?" she asked. "Do you see that big guy over there with the goofy straw hat?"

I pointed to a man talking to the radio announcer. "Him?"

"Yeah. Could you ask him to come over here? He said he would flip pancakes for me if I wanted to take a break."

"Cheryl, he's our state assembly representative."

"Well, tell him I'll vote for him. I just need a cigarette."

As I approached the representative to give him Cheryl's enticing offer, the polka band stopped playing, and a tall man in a plaid pink and blue sport coat tapped the microphone. A loud squeal slashed through the barn. The man introduced himself as the state of Wisconsin's assistant secretary of agriculture. He thanked everyone for coming out and recited some statistics about the importance of the dairy industry to the state's economy and the Wisconsin way of life. He then asked Bruce to join him on the stage.

"So Bruce, how many do you think we served today?"

"Well, I think we're over seventeen hundred," he said to audible gasps from the diners, "and they're still coming."

The assistant secretary of agriculture proceeded to thank Bruce for over twenty years of organizing the annual Sawyer County Dairy Breakfast.

"Hey, Jeff, that could be you years from now," Cheryl said. I laughed.

"And if you stopped patting your pancakes, you might be as good as Buck someday," I replied.

Buck turned and smiled. "Oh, I don't know about that. I've flipped a lot of pancakes in my day."

The assistant secretary of agriculture presented a framed certificate to Bruce. "I understand you recently sold West's Dairy. So, what will you do now?" he asked.

I listened carefully to what Bruce would say. "Well, I'll still help out when they need me."

I was glad to hear that. I relied on his help making ice cream and feared he and Jan would run off to Florida or Arizona. I had made some progress on the mechanical front—I had obtained my Wisconsin driver's license and was behind the wheel with the sudden braking and rapid starts of a sixteen-year-old. Of course, I couldn't find the hood release or adjust the clock to save my life. I took Bruce's statement to mean he would be around to help the following year.

Dean yelled that he was running out of ice cream. I ran to the concession trailer to grab another tub of vanilla.

Cheese Curds and the King of Pike

Things began to heat up. They were already suggesting it could be one of the hottest Junes on record. It was the kind of weather that would buckle roads in Britain and result in delays on the trains or the closure of London's Underground, perhaps due to excessive sweat near the tracks. Day after day, the sun appeared as a brilliant speck over a cloudless horizon. And the ice cream business was good.

With each day, more and more people congregated in the tiny town center. They bought fudge, moccasins, T-shirts—so many T-shirts. They emptied their pockets at the Packer Store and then lingered over a burger or club sandwich on the patio in front of Angler's. After lunch, they came to West's for ice cream.

I could no longer meander into the dairy at midmorning and shoot the breeze with Buck and Bob. Every day I had to check the supply of ice cream mix and other ingredients—nuts, cookies, chocolate flakes, and so on—because deliveries could take up to two weeks on any item. Already, I had run out of chocolate flakes and walnuts, resulting in delays in making two of the most popular flavors—mint chocolate chip and Almost Sinful.

There were other things as well—cups, napkins, toilet paper, and even ice. The dairy didn't have an ice maker. After I picked up several large bags from the supermarket, Buck gave me a tip: "Try Pastika's." Pastika's was a bait shop. I knew that from its nostalgic neon sign. "I didn't know they sold ice," I said.

I was as comfortable going into Pastika's as I was going into a strip club. I had no interest in fishing and no knowledge of fish, and the last thing I wanted to see was a tankful of leeches. The odor was a combination of fishy water, dirt, and formaldehyde. The walls were lined with large tanks holding every size of musky appetizer. They gurgled as air was pumped into the water to keep the fish or leeches alive. Children played with the nets, trying to catch the minnows while their fathers stood by patiently holding a container for the bait. I couldn't look.

A serious-looking man sat on a stool behind the counter. He was studying a fishing report, perhaps contemplating what to write in this week's "Outdoor Outlook," a popular section of the local paper in which each bait shop in town—a number greater than you would think—offered their assessment of the current state of play on the lakes.

"What can I do you for?" the man asked, looking up from his book.

"I'd like some ice, please—about ten bags?" I asked.

"Are you from a business?"

"Yes, I'm one of the new owners of West's," I said, pointing to the logo on my T-shirt.

"Okay. That'll be sixty-five cents per bag."

"Sixty-five cents?" I said, shocked by what seemed a very reasonable price. I knew it was only frozen water, but it seemed really inexpensive. Unfortunately, my fishing guide misunderstood me and thought I was complaining.

"Sorry, but the price of bags went up this year," he said.

I picked my bags out of a freezer outside at the back of the shop. Once they were loaded in the car, I quickly headed back to the dairy.

Earlier in the summer, Dean and I had laughed when locals began to complain about the increased traffic on the roads as the tourists came to town. Dean amused them by describing how London charges people to drive into the city. He could have been describing another planet.

"All I can say," Cheryl said as she began to relate how long it took her to get up Main Street to the post office, "is it's a real clusterfuck." Even in Hayward, traffic could bring out the most shocking language.

I was thinking much the same as I sought to turn onto Highway 27 from Pastika's parking lot. I could try the London maneuver of inching my way onto the road to force the oncoming traffic to let me in, but I knew this would likely result in an incident of road rage. My ice was basking in the sun on the backseat.

The arrival of summer was cause for celebration. From June through early autumn, towns and cities across Wisconsin held summer festivals.

Some showcased the area's ethnic roots. In nearby Haugen, there was the Kolache Festival, a tribute to a Bohemian pastry. In southern Wisconsin where there were large German settlements, beer festivals occurred throughout the year. New Glarus, or "Little Switzerland," was home to the Heidi Festival, during which the local high school drama club held a production of *Heidi,* followed by a tractor pull competition. While it was a bit tongue in cheek, Manitowoc on Lake Michigan celebrated Sputnikfest to commemorate the day in 1962 when a twenty-pound piece of space debris from the Soviet *Sputnik IV* spaceship fell to Earth and landed in the middle of Eighth Street. The festival included the crowning of Miss Space Debris.

Over the last weekend in June, Hayward held its annual tribute to the king of the pike family with the Musky Festival. When the festival began in 1949, Hayward was in the midst of a fishing frenzy. Back then, small family resorts dotted the shores of local lakes and people came primarily to fish. Across the area, records were being broken at all of the local lakes, and in that year, Louis Spray, a local tavern owner and avid angler, caught his record musky—over six feet long and nearly seventy pounds—on the Chippewa Flowage. Spray's catch created a veritable wave of interest in the fishing world, and anglers flocked to the local lakes for many years after. Only a year later, Cal Johnson caught a sixty-seven-pound fish on Lac Courte Oreilles.

To celebrate Spray's catch and Hayward's newly found dominance in the fishing world, the Hayward Chamber of Commerce held the first Musky Festival. This was just as well since nearby Cumberland had already established the Rutabaga Festival to honor the ignored member of the turnip family. Although big muskies are caught all over northern Wisconsin, Minnesota, and Canada, no one has matched Louis Spray's or even Cal Johnson's catch. Those few frenzied catches in the middle of the last century established Hayward's reputation in the annals of fishing history, and for a few days every June the chamber of commerce reminds everyone that Hayward is "Home of World Record Muskies."

As I began to feel part of life in my new town, I looked forward to the small-town festival and tribute to its history. On Monday morning, preparations for the weekend festivities were under way. Shirtless young carnival workers unloaded the equipment and set up the rides and games with the precision developed week after week as they moved throughout the state. The Tilt-a-Whirl, one of my favorite rides from the Carver County Fair, was placed on Second Street adjacent to the parking lot. Its shell-like cars swung around empty as the carnies tested the ride. A Ferris wheel, nearly three stories tall, was erected near the fire station. There was a haunted house and a few children's rides, including colorful fishing boats on a small circular track.

Buck sat on a bench watching the carnival set up.

"Pretty impressive, don't you think?" I asked.

"Well, you gotta be careful," Buck said. "These carny bastards have one thing on their mind. You know what I'm saying?" He suggested the girls working at West's did not appreciate the attention of the carnival workers. I had my doubts about this as I watched Liz fix her hair in the reflection of the espresso machine.

"I always hang around until everyone is in their car before I leave during this mess."

"Oh, it can't be that bad—it's just a little fair," I said, but then I noticed some of the young carnival workers chatting with local girls. They didn't get very far before being reprimanded by their boss, who pointed to his watch.

"Don't you like the Musky Festival?" I asked Buck, pretty certain of the reply.

"Well, it's not the same as it used to be," Buck said. "Now it's all about selling stuff, drinking, and hooligans. Between you and me"—Buck lowered his voice—"this carnival draws a pretty rough crowd. Last year, someone tried to steal our drinking fountain."

I looked to the end of the bench at the rusty old tin box that housed the drinking fountain. I had thought about removing it, but Bruce warned I would have to provide cups of tap water to customers. Perhaps someone would succeed in stealing it this year.

"It will be a good weekend for business," Buck said. "They'll be lined up out the door for an ice cream cone. Now, years ago, the Musky Festival used to be a really big deal. You know, we've had some beautiful Musky Queens in the past," Buck said. "But back then, everyone came out for the parade. You know, the City of Hayward don't even let you throw candy during the parade anymore!" Buck objected to the city's decision to forbid parade participants from throwing wrapped sweets to kids along the parade route due to the risk of injury.

"Are you going to the Musky Queen Pageant?" I asked Buck, pointing to the article in the local paper he had in his hand.

"Hell, no! Have you seen these girls? A pack of homely beasts," Buck said as he pointed to the cartoon drawings of the contestants.

"Buck, those are caricatures. Their eyes aren't really that big." The drawings exaggerated the eyes so much that the women's heads resembled those of insects rather than the doe-like innocence the artist sought.

While I had learned to accept that Buck was often right when it came to all things Hayward, I hoped he was wrong about the Musky Festival. I wanted to like it. I had even convinced Matt and Dave to come into town for the street dance.

By Thursday, the carnival was in place and open for business. A few young children from town who had been watching as the rides went up were waiting when they opened the gates. Soon, the smell of mini-donuts and cotton candy floated across the street to the dairy, and the scent of freshly fried cheese curds was tempting even the most curmudgeonly of carnival-goers.

"I think I'll get me some of those curds for lunch today," I heard Buck tell one of the girls.

By Friday morning, the Musky Festival had kicked into high gear. Peaked white tents had been erected along Main Street from Second Street to the top of the hill on Fifth Street. Like a village, the tents housed craft vendors, a semi-nomadic people who moved from craft fair to summer festival all summer and autumn. The crafts on display ran the gamut from painting and photography to handmade jewelry and woodcarving. It really was the place to go for a miniature or life-sized carving of a black bear with a fish in its mouth or—my favorite— a hanging mobile made of reconfigured beer cans.

The sweet smell of fried mini-donuts drew me to the caravans selling food at the end of the street. I had tried Buck's cheese curds the other day and was hooked. The stand, more like a U-Haul trailer painted bright green and yellow Packer colors, smelled of hot fat. Inside, a tiny woman covered in flour dipped the curds in a light beer batter before placing them in the fryer. I told her I had had my first cheese curds a day ago. Amused that there were any curd virgins left in the world, she explained that curds, an early by-product of the cheese-making process, were fresh only if they squeaked when you rubbed them against your teeth.

"They have to be fresh. After a few weeks, you might as well use them to caulk your tub," she advised. She handed me a moist, uncooked curd to rub on my teeth like a rare pearl.

"Umm, fresh," I said and held the curd in my hand, not sure what to do with it.

"You can eat it," she said.

"Yum." I swallowed the curd and realized why people dipped them in batter and fried them.

In no time the curds were ready, and she emptied the metal frying basket into a small paper container. She directed me to the condiments—either ketchup or ranch dressing. I took them straight up. The melting, stringy cheese burned the inside of my mouth.

"They're hot," she advised.

"Thanks. I see that," I cried.

Outside the dairy, the Wisconsin DNR had set up an exhibit devoted to the star of the celebration—the musky. It may not have been getting as much attention as the beer can art stand or the beer stand, but I liked it. A tall, handsome ranger in a beige uniform with a number of patches sewn on his shoulder, giving the impression of an accomplished Boy Scout, was delivering a talk to a handful of old fishermen sitting on folding chairs set up in the middle of the street. The discussion was on stocking the lakes with a type of musky that originated outside the state. This was a hotly debated issue. Many fishermen were in favor of the new and possibly larger strain of fish, while the authorities were reluctant to accept the risk of messing with the local fish population. I was impressed that I knew so much about it. Obviously I spent too much time reading the "Outdoor Outlook" in the *Sawyer County Record* and hanging around the bait shops under the guise of purchasing cheap ice.

In the afternoon, the streets resembled a Middle Eastern bazaar as crowds jostled to view the finest in beer can art and carved wooden eagles. The new central air-conditioning unit at the dairy struggled to keep the building cool. The line of Musky Festival customers extended to and out the front door, which had been propped open to allow more hot air into the building. Many held purchases from the craft show. One man escorted a three-foot carved bear standing on his rear paws and clutching a fish in one of his front paws. "Where are we going to put this again?" he asked his wife. "It's kind of heavy."

"I thought it would look nice by the front door of the cabin," she said, trying to convince him of the merits of the purchase.

"Hmm." Her husband shifted the weight of the bear carving to his other arm.

The girls behind the counter complained of the heat as their hair stuck sweatily to their necks and foreheads. I suggested they could take their break inside the hardening freezer. I realized I had begun to sound like Buck, and my suggestion was received with icy stares. I agreed to buy a fan to help circulate the air behind the counter.

By evening, I understood what Buck meant about the nature of the Musky Festival. The tourists had returned to their cabins on the lake having eaten mounds of cotton candy, mini-donuts, and cheese curds. They were either unaware or unimpressed by the evening's entertainment. Local youth gathered on the benches in front of the dairy to discuss their strategy for getting into the beer tents operated by the local Rotary Club and Lions Club. The beer tents flanked the intersection of Second Street and Main Street with a dance floor set up between them and in front of a stage. At the entrance, a volunteer with a beer in her hand checked identification and placed wristbands on those entering who were of the legal drinking age.

As the sun set on the Musky Festival, the main act for the street dance took the stage, a cover band composed of graying, potbellied rockers who may or may not have played the Minnesota State Fair at their peak. Although the sound was deafening and could be heard inside West's a block away, I walked down the street to check it out. The new Musky Queen with her crown, sash, pair of flip-flops, and a bit of attitude spoke with some of her male admirers. Miss Congeniality was watching, looking anything but congenial. Dean and our friends told me they had had enough of the dance and were going home.

I bought an Indian fry bread, a thick piece of bread not unlike Asian naan. It was a Native American treat popular at local fairs and events. I recognized the owner of the stand as a cook from the LCO school. The plastic fork could not cut through the chewy dough, so I sat on the curb to master the bread with my hands.

At the end of an almost recognizable rendition of "Smoke on the Water," I saw the bass player sneak out behind the stage, where he made himself a cocktail in a thirty-two-ounce soda cup from the convenience store. He poured a liberal amount of vodka from a family-sized plastic gallon jug and topped it with some orange juice. He caught me watching him. "It's a long night," he said and raised his glass.

"I know the feeling," I said, raising my Indian fry bread.

I had spent much of the day cleaning and sanitizing ice cream buckets in the plant room and some of the other tasks the staff did not have time or desire to do. I scooped ice cream to cover for afternoon and dinner breaks, and I stayed on to cope with the unusual crowds. "Unusual" in the number of drunk people buying ice cream.

"Do you have anything that will go with beer?" a young man asked to the delight of his friends. Jen was not amused.

The girls had worked hard. Their scoops hung by their sides like barbells holding them down. I had been keeping watch by the door. For all of his bravado, Buck had disappeared late in the afternoon. I understood why he'd want to get away. My drinking fountain was still in place but—as he predicted—it was getting ugly out there. The street was lined with empty plastic beer cups. A rather unwholesome crowd began to congregate outside the dairy.

I was cleaning behind the counter when the bass player from the street dance appeared. "Are you still open?"

I nodded.

"Could I get some espresso?"

"Oh, of course," I obliged, always cheerful when someone tried our coffee.

"Make it four shots," he requested. "I have a long drive back to Elk River tonight."

"So, you're from the band?" I asked.

He raised his eyebrows. Even if I had not seen him earlier, it would not have been hard to guess he was in the band as he was the only sixty-year-old in town with a thinning gray ponytail, silk pirate shirt, and half the Franklin Mint collection around his neck. He thought he had found a fan.

"So, do band members get free coffee?" he asked. I found the request odd, but then I was not a groupie and was unfamiliar with the protocol around street dance entertainment.

"Sure, why not?" I said. "It's been a long day."

By Sunday, I felt the celebration of the greatest pike in the lake had gone on long enough. The big stage had been removed early in the morning along with the beer tents, leaving an overpowering odor of stale beer.

A few storekeepers looked vexed as to how to deal with pools of vomit left in front of their businesses. The vendors had packed their tents and left town by early morning for their next fair. Ranger Joe was putting away his charts and photos.

"Hey, sir!" he called. "Thanks for the ice cream yesterday."

"Ice cream?" I asked.

"Yes. One of the girls brought an ice cream cone to me yesterday—compliments of the house."

"Oh, sure. You're welcome." I waved. That sounded like the work of our ice cream Lolita, but I couldn't blame her. "Good luck with the whole baby fish thing," I added.

Weary volunteers from the chamber of commerce put up barricades along the street for the last event of the weekend—the Musky Festival Parade. The parade would start at the top of Main and turn onto West Second Street to go past West's. Perhaps this old-fashioned parade would redeem the Musky Festival for me. It should at least be good for business. Buck didn't agree.

"I'm not so sure," Buck said. "People just want to see the parade." The question prompted another rant about the candy-throwing ban imposed by the Hayward authorities. "I have never heard anything so stupid," he said. "They think a root beer candy is going to knock some kid's eye out. It's crazy!"

"So, you're not going to watch the parade?" I asked.

"Oh, no. I'll be here. It's a really big deal."

By "big deal" I learned Buck meant it was the longest parade on the planet. It spanned much of the afternoon. At times I looked around to see if Leonid Brezhnev or Fidel Castro were in the viewing stands and whether Hayward had its own stockpile of cruise missiles to haul down Main Street on the back of a logging truck. Instead of missiles, the parade featured nearly every fire truck from Sawyer, Bayfield, and Washburn counties. God help those whose home caught on fire during the Musky Festival parade.

I laughed at folks who brought lawn chairs out early in the morning to stake their spot on the parade route. These were not just chairs they had thrown in the car but comfortable seats with cupholders. Others brought picnic baskets with sandwiches and cookies. I thought I saw someone order a pizza. No wonder Buck was annoyed they couldn't throw candy—people were getting hungry! During the second hour of the parade, a steady stream of customers came into the dairy for a burst of calories to take them through to the end.

In addition to the display of firefighting might, there were marching bands from area schools, some baton twirlers, veterans groups, and, so it seemed, anyone with a classic car or at least an older vehicle. A group of Shriners came through on tiny scooters, weaving in and out in a synchronized manner and careful not to lose the fezzes on their heads. One of the many highlights of the parade was the float carrying the newly crowned Musky Queen in her evening gown. She mastered the parade wave, but so did Miss Congeniality, who appeared to be slowly moving to the front of the float in a grab for attention.

After a few more groups, including anyone with a scooter or four-wheeler, as the popular open-topped all-terrain vehicle was called, the parade fizzled out. Parade watchers began to pack up their equipment to head home. Children took advantage of the blocked-off streets to play a quick game of tag. A few parade stalwarts remained glued to their folding chairs as if they had melted to them and the chairs in turn had adhered themselves to the pavement.

Just when I thought the longest summer festival was over, I heard marching music. Some continued packing their things, but the others knew what it was and came out of their comatose state. Some even rose from their chairs to get a view around the corner. A huge group of uniformed men turned onto Second Street. Their knees lifted high in the air. Trombones swayed. They were loud, clear, and very good.

It was Marty's Goldenaires. They were a serious marching band, with a conductor, nice uniforms, and a magnificent sound that was out of place in this parade. Perhaps they were lost and had gone to the wrong parade.

"They always make up the caboose of the parade," Buck said. Because the band stopped at every corner to extend the performance for the crowd, there was a gap at the end of the parade. Nevertheless, the crowd, or the segment that had not expired from heat exhaustion, loved Marty's band. Those who had been sitting comfortably in their lawn chairs rose to their feet and clapped to the music. Even the children were mesmerized by the color guard waving oversized flags and the instruments reflecting the bright sunlight. The horns filled the air, and people tapped to the "1812 Overture" and "The Ballad of the Green Berets," and then the band mixed in Lionel Richie's "Dancing in the Streets" as they passed in front of West's.

As the Goldenaires turned the corner, the parade was over. The crowd dispersed, and many who were still hungry came in for ice cream.

"It's the same every year," I heard a middle-aged woman tell another. "Too long."

"Perhaps I should get myself on the parade committee," her friend suggested.

"Thank God for Marty and the Goldenaires," her friend replied as though Marty, now deceased for forty years, were still marching in the parade.

I turned to Buck, who was standing with me outside the dairy.

"Guess that's it for the Musky Festival," I said. He could tell I was dejected and agreed with his take on the festivities.

"Afraid so," he said.

Everyone Has Ice Cream
on the Fourth of July

While the Musky Festival may not have proved the quintessential small-town event I hoped it would be, in Hayward, provided you looked for it, there was always a Norman Rockwell moment just around the corner.

We had had our strongest weekend at the dairy over the Musky Festival, serving over one thousand customers on Saturday alone. By the end of the month, ice cream sales had grown considerably over the previous June. I would have liked to attribute the growth to improvements in the store's appearance and comfortable seating area. The leather chairs were a hit with the children and their sticky hands. I wanted to think it was my new coffee bar, but coffee sales were insignificant when compared to the ice cream sales. More likely, it was the hot, sunny weather and what many businesses described as an uptick in tourist traffic.

Whatever the reason, as I saw lines reaching the corner, I could not help but think that in only a few months, we had joined the ranks of the world's ice cream mavens. If only my instructors from the University of Reading Ice Cream Course or my classmates from Unilever could see me now. It was time: *Ben and Jerry, take your Chubby Hubby off the shelf. Almost Sinful has arrived!*

My staff had a different view. "We need more help, Jeff," they whined in unison.

"I have a friend who would be great," Jen said. "Her name is Suzi."

My first thought was that it was a bad idea to hire a friend of the other employees, but the alternative would have required advertising the position and interviewing a number of people for the job. I agreed to meet Suzi the next morning.

When I arrived at the dairy, she was waiting for me in one of the leather chairs. I caught her laughing with the girls behind the counter. Once she realized who I was, she blushed and tried to cover her smile.

Suzi had bright blue eyes and blond pigtails, and she looked as if she had grown out of a bottle of suntan lotion. She wore athletic shorts and big sneakers. She said she was on the soccer team and was going to play that afternoon with some friends. We discussed her surname, which had an abundance of vowels and very few consonants. "It's a Finnish name," she told me.

Suzi had worked at the Super 8 Motel cleaning rooms. I caught her glancing at Jen, who must have coached her in what to say. "So I really like to clean." She looked up again at Jen, who nodded her head slightly to acknowledge the good answer. Suzi went on to describe how she always wanted to scoop ice cream and liked people. "And I'd work really hard and do a good job."

In a way, Suzi was not unlike the young lawyers I interviewed for positions at the bank in London. They might have been more subtle and clever than her in conveying their work ethic, their interest in the job, and those qualities they would bring to the position. For the most part, though, it was all crap. Within weeks of their start date, they became difficult and demanding, and they only cared about their bonus, their vacation time, and the size of their office or cubicle. But perhaps Suzi was different. Perhaps all she wanted to do was scoop ice cream, and I had the power to make her dreams come true. How could I deny her such an opportunity?

"And because I'm on the soccer team, I'm a good team player," she added and looked over to the girls, who were eavesdropping on the interview.

"Well, that's nice," I said. Notwithstanding the coaching and canned responses, I liked Suzi. She was earnest and would meet any criteria for Finns in the workplace.

"One final question," I said. Suzi sat up in her chair as though she was ready for the ultimate test.

"Who is Gerald Ford?" I asked. Of course it was a trick question, but I wondered about the state of history education in the schools. Would she know the name of the thirty-eighth president of the United States and the only president not to have been elected either president or vice president?

I could see her mind working. She glanced over to her friends, who were no help, and then she looked down at the table.

"Oh, I know," she declared. "Is it the old guy who sits here all day?"

"No," I laughed. "That's Buck." She looked deflated, thinking the answer could cost her the job. "But don't worry. You got the job."

I felt bad about the Gerald Ford question. Suzi raised her arms as though she had just scored a goal.

"Oh, thank you!" She bounced up and ran to her friends and coaches behind the counter.

"On one condition," I added.

"Oh, sure, what is it?" Suzi asked.

"You start tomorrow," I said.

Suzi took to her position with gusto, and, armed with the proper scooping technique, she mastered malts and sundaes and how to sanitize equipment and buckets. Jen watched over her as a mother might her daughter. Buck thought she talked too much and was a bit sassy with him.

With less than a week until the July Fourth holiday, preparations were in high gear. Bruce had warned we would need a healthy stockpile of ice cream. I ordered additional cones, syrups, and other supplies and made a few trips to my favorite bait shop for ice.

I wasn't sure what to expect from the Fourth of July, having spent the holiday in London or Hong Kong for the previous twelve years. These places had not been hotbeds for celebrating American independence. The last few July Fourths I had spent in the United States were at my law firm's office in New York as a junior associate, where I filled most of my evenings and weekends faxing prospectuses around the world from the firm's telecommunications room. If I craned my neck, I might have been able to see fireworks over the East River from my office window. Apart from burned hamburgers, warm beer, mosquitoes, and charred and missing fingers, I was not sure what my first July Fourth in Hayward would be like. After the Musky Festival, my expectations were low.

Unlike the Musky Festival, there were no big events scheduled, no street vendors selling crafts, no street festival or carnival. However, the holiday meant a long weekend at the height of a hot summer, so anyone with a car and a few extra dollars wanted to be in Hayward or a town just like it. Like any other town in America, Hayward hosted a fireworks show. I was told it all took place near the baseball field between the intermediate school and primary school about four blocks from the ice cream shop.

As in previous years, the dairy would take the concession trailer to the site of the fireworks display in order to provide fireworks-goers well-deserved ice cream treats. Bruce said he would take the trailer up there with his pickup. In the past, Bruce closed the ice cream shop and focused on the captive audience a few blocks away. In a departure from tradition, I decided to keep the shop open during the evening and asked Suzi to stay behind in the store while the others worked out of the concession trailer at the fireworks.

The holiday fell on Monday. The long weekend and continued dry heat meant record days at the dairy even before the fourth. In fact, the morning of the fourth seemed relatively quiet.

"They're all on the lake this morning but will come in for the fireworks," Buck assured me. "I'm not so sure it's a good idea to stay open. You know, everyone will be uptown for the show." Buck reminded me that he had disagreed with my decision to keep the shop open during the fireworks, but then again he disagreed with any change in the established way of doing things. He was often right about these things, but I had a hunch it could be good for business, as people would be driving by the dairy on the way to the fireworks display.

"Well, we'll see," I said.

By 5:00 PM, Jen, Steph, and Vegan Liz had organized their scoop stations in the concession trailer. Dean and I arrived with the first load of ice cream. We hoped to meet Matt and Dave and some other friends to watch the fireworks. The trailer sat on the edge of a parking lot facing an open field. Ropes closed off a section at the other end of the field where the fireworks had been set up for the evening show. People began to arrive four hours before the fireworks, carrying chairs and blankets and scoping out their preferred viewing position. I recognized some of them with their chairs, picnic baskets, and coolers from the Musky Festival parade.

To the left of the field behind a row of large trees was the baseball diamond. I recognized the deep voice of the announcer-turned-restaurateur who called the game between the Hayward Hawks and their rivals, the Spooner Rails. I recognized Buck by his back as he sat at the top of the home team's stands. He seemed to be talking the ear off the man sitting next to him. No doubt Buck was reminiscing about his own days on the team.

"Hey, Buck," Dean shouted. "Why aren't you playing out there?"

"Well, look who's here," Buck replied, laughing. "I didn't think you English folks celebrated this one."

"What do you mean? We celebrate the fact we got rid of you lot," Dean shouted back. Buck fended the joke with a wave. The people around him laughed.

At the bottom of the stands, the Lions Club sold burgers and hot dogs out of a cinder-block concession stand. The Rotary Club had set up a tent to sell beer. Another group sold popcorn. Country and western music played on the radio from the concession stand.

There was no fancy beer can art for sale or expensive cheese snacks. The Hayward Civic Club sponsored the fireworks display and relied on donations from vendors such as the dairy and others. Bruce had always subsidized the price of cones, charging only a dollar for a small one. It was a community event, and despite it being the height of the Hayward tourist season, the crowd was primarily made up of Hayward residents, along with some people with second homes on the lakes who liked to think of Hayward as home.

Men and women walked from the game to the food stand and the beer tent. Many had traded in their Packer wear for a red, white, and blue shirt. Others, however, sported at least a small Packer emblem to show that their true and foremost allegiance was to football. Some had clearly spent the afternoon at the beer tent and were slurring their words.

As the sun was setting on a perfect summer day, the vision could not have been more American if Betsy Ross herself were sewing a flag in one corner and an evangelical preacher were shouting in another. I felt I was on the set of a film and would not have been surprised if some young ruffians from Spooner came into town to challenge the local kids to a line-dancing showdown.

Jen was in charge of the concession trailer. She wiped the counter as Stephanie served the few customers who had already lined up. Both had worked the concession trailer at previous July Fourth celebrations and were ready.

"Was Suzi okay at the dairy on her own?" Jen asked.

"Oh, I think she'll be fine," I said. "It wasn't too busy."

With the concession trailer up and running and hopefully well stocked for the evening, Dean went to find our friends and I returned to the shop to check on Suzi. I entered through the back. She had her head in the dipping cabinet, struggling with some reluctant ice cream at the bottom of a container. On the other side, a mob had formed and extended to the door. Suzi surfaced from the cabinet with a giant cake cone.

"Hi, Jeff!" She smiled when she saw me.

"Busy?" I asked.

"Well, I could use some help," she suggested as she handed the cone to the customer. "Everyone decided to stop here on their way to the fireworks."

"Okay, let me think," I said. Everyone else either was working at the concession trailer or was out of town. The crowd did not seem as patient as usual. They were sunburned and tired from their day on the lake, and they were anxious to get to the fireworks. The people at the back peeked around to see what was taking so long. I picked up the phone. It was a desperate move, but this was serious—the crowd could turn ugly. I dialed and waited.

"Hello?"

"Hi, Dean," I said. "What are you doing?"

"I just found the guys. You coming back soon?"

"We have a problem," I said. I explained the predicament at the dairy and that we needed someone to help scoop. While Dean had scooped many ice cream cones for himself and once even tried serving a few customers, he soon decided it was not for him.

"Who's working?" he asked.

"Just Suzi. I'll be here, but I may have to go back to the concession trailer."

"Okay," he said grudgingly. "I like Suzi."

"Thanks. Be quick, please." I hung up the phone and picked up a scoop to help the next customers.

"Is Dean coming to help?" Suzi asked as though a favorite uncle she did not see very often was coming to dinner. The kids were not sure what to make of Dean. They had little experience with non-Americans. His accent reminded them of someone on television. When he stopped by the shop to use the phone, pick up a package, or make himself a smoothie, he joked with the girls and encouraged them to have fun. When Suzi had first met Dean, she was nervous until she realized not all Brits were as direct and mean as the judge on a singing competition.

Dean was at the dairy in no time—just as the concession trailer phoned to say they were low on mint chocolate chip and Almost Sinful.

"Hi, Dean. We're going to work together!" Suzi shouted when he came through the back door.

"I think I need a new West's T-shirt," Dean said, ignoring the line of customers waiting for ice cream. "What color do you think would suit me, Suzi?"

Suzi stopped halfway through making an ice cream cone to consider the question. She looked at Dean and scanned the selection of T-shirts. "Hmm," she thought out loud. "I think the light blue. It would look nice with your eyes."

I loaded the car with more ice cream and set off. The sun was beginning to set, and there was a steady stream of cars heading to the school grounds. The parking area must have been filled because people were parking on the streets just a block from the dairy and walking. As I got closer, the traffic was stopped. I would never get through. I turned the corner in the opposite direction and found a spot to park. I pulled out the dolly that I carried in the backseat, stacked the ice cream on it, and began to walk—quickly. I had to carry the ice cream at least three blocks. The stack of plastic tubs began to sweat in the humid night air. I wove between slower-moving groups.

"Hey, we'll help you with that ice cream," they joked.

As the sun dipped below the horizon, the trailer glowed against a red sky. The baseball game had just ended—the Hayward Hawks had handily defeated Spooner. When I reached the concession trailer, a line of at least fifty people stretched into the field. It was a rush between the end of the game and the beginning of the fireworks. Some classic Madonna played from the radio station. Buck stood by the door at the side of the trailer, licking a small ice cream cone. All was good in America.

"Hey, girls! The boss is here!" Buck yelled when he saw me. Jen, Liz, and Steph ignored him. They focused on getting through the line so they might be able to watch the fireworks themselves.

The field between the concession stand and where the fireworks were set up was nearly full of families and groups sitting around blankets eating, drinking, and waiting for the big show. A few men and some women sloshed their way through the crowd in search of loved ones. As it got darker, parents rounded up their children to sit by them. Some parents lit sparklers for the kids. Some young children looked fearful and held the sparklers as far away as possible.

I unloaded the ice cream into the freezers in the trailer.

By counting the empty ice cream cone boxes, I figured we had served over six hundred customers out of the concession stand. "Pretty good night, huh?" Buck said. "Everyone has ice cream on the Fourth of July. It's America!"

From across the field, the first fireworks were launched. It was more of a teaser to get the crowd's attention. After a minute, there was another, and then like popcorn, they came in quick succession. Heads tipped back and mouths opened to make the audible "aww" or "ohhh." The girls leaned out of the trailer to get a better view of the sky. Customers still waiting for ice cream turned around to watch the show.

I stood next to Buck, who had probably seen as many fireworks displays in Hayward on the Fourth of July as there had been. He was as enthralled with the show as a child watching for the first time. "They're good this year," he said.

The fireworks rained down on the crowd, the hot sparks disintegrating above them. The line for ice cream disappeared, and the girls came out of the trailer to watch the show. Although exhausted from the heat of the trailer, swarms of mosquitoes, and long lines of customers, they were smiling and upbeat. Jen and Steph had made themselves ice cream cones. The ice cream had become very soft, and they laughed as it dripped over their hands.

Vegan Liz stood by them watching the show with her arms around her stomach. She was going to be a high school senior in the fall and told me she wanted to go to the University of Chicago. She was surprised to hear it was my alma mater. The inner-city school wasn't the typical choice for small-town kids such as Liz—or me.

"I bet it has changed a lot," she said. At times I forgot how young my staff were. While it seemed like only yesterday, I had graduated from college before Liz was born. I joked that in twenty years she would return to Hayward and buy the ice cream shop from us.

"No way. I can't wait to get out of this town," Liz said. I was happy for her. I knew exactly what Liz wanted, although her decision to pursue studies in Chinese seemed further than she needed to go.

As she watched the fireworks explode above, her head tilted back, she seemed pretty content in her small town. I hoped she would re-member that.

For the finale, there was the largest aerial bouquet of every color, with brocades of bright light shooting off at all angles. It lit the ground below, revealing billowing plumes of tinted smoke rising from the end of the field. An acrid smell filled the area. At the very end, and a sur-prise to even the most experienced in attendance, five towers of fire shot up from the launch site.

"Whoa, look at those suckers!" Buck shouted like a forty-year-old at a Nickelback concert. The girls laughed. The field erupted with applause and screams.

When I returned to the dairy, Suzi was covering the ice cream. Dean wiped tables.

"Dean said we could leave most of the cleaning for the morning," Suzi said.

"I'm sorry you didn't get to see the fireworks," I said.

"Oh, we did—we could see the fireworks from the corner." Suzi pointed outside. "It got quiet just before they started," she added, in case I thought they had left customers waiting while they checked out the display.

I asked Dean how he had enjoyed his night at the dairy.

"It was fun. Suzi works very hard and gave me some tips on how to make malts," he said.

"I like working with Dean—can he work with me again?" Suzi asked as she counted dollar bills from the tip jar.

"Of course. He can work here as much as he wants," I said.

"Hey, Dean. We did pretty good—twenty-two dollars each." She exchanged the one-dollar bills for tens and fives from the cash register.

"Great," Dean said. "But you can keep mine, too."

"Really?" Suzi shouted, surprised that someone would give up his tips. "You worked hard too—you deserve it."

"No, I insist." Dean smiled as he held up his hand to resist the money. Suzi looked up, surprised, her face framed by the rectangular menu board as the light of the pendant lamp bounced off her blond hair.

"Sweet deal. This is the best Fourth of July ever."

And, there it was—my Norman Rockwell moment.

I Did a Bad Thing

I did a bad thing. I came up with several excuses: the continuing and unbearable heat in July had much to do with it; long hours from opening West's at 9:00 AM, making ice cream, doing deliveries, and running around all day until closing at 10:00 PM; and the crowds of people both at the dairy and all over town that made travel, as Cheryl called it, a clusterfuck. The sweltering conditions and busy days took their toll on everyone as our cooling system failed to provide relief. Customers quickly ate their dripping ice cream and left in search of a breeze. I even saw Buck break into a sweat while reading the newspaper. The girls stood in front of the small fan I had bought for them. Liz cooled herself by rubbing an ice cube around the back of her neck.

In the plant room, there was no air conditioning. Condensation dripped from the exterior walls of the walk-in freezers. Periodically, ice built up on the compressor coils, and we had to shut down the system and spray hot water on the units to remove the frost.

We had not established a proper schedule for ice cream production other than making it when needed. There were no doubt better ways to track inventory, but for the moment I relied on one of the staff to say something along the lines of "Jeff, I think, like, you know, we may be out of strawberry ice cream." This prompted me to scour the freezers for one last bucket of strawberry that had been misplaced in the stack of maple walnut. More often than not, I found one or two buckets that would get us through another day. Nevertheless, I called Bruce. He found Kenny. Buck was always around, and we set things up to make more ice cream.

Bruce liked to start extremely early in the morning. "It's not so dang hot," he said.

I arrived just as he assembled and sanitized the equipment. I hauled out cases of ice cream mix, filled the vat, and organized the other ingredients. We always began with vanilla because it was the most neutral in terms of both flavor and color and would permit us to make other flavors without cleaning the vat and machine. We always followed vanilla with chocolate chip and cookie crumble because vanilla was the base for those. We finished with any flavor involving color such as mint chocolate chip or Wild Berry Crumble or, due to allergy concerns, any nut flavor such as butter pecan or maple walnut.

As the summer progressed, we improved on our assembly-line production. I continued to run the finished product to the hardening freezer. Buck often got behind with the lids as his fingers tried to maneuver the plastic in place. "It's these damn latex gloves!" he complained, hoping we would let him work without them. "The damn heat doesn't help, either," he rationalized.

It was hot. Bruce had Kenny wipe his brow a number of times as a surgeon might ask a nurse in the operating room. When Dean helped, Bruce allowed him to fill the three-gallon containers.

After four hours, we were beat. The heat and constant standing had taken its toll. Buck strolled off to his car without saying anything. After cleaning the floor and the machine of all spilt ice cream, Bruce said he would return to disassemble and clean the freezer later when it cooled off.

I was heading to my office, which, small in size, was the coolest spot in the building apart from the refrigerators or freezers. Behind the counter, Jen, Suzi, and Michael ran between customers. Their hair was dripping with sweat. Liz steamed milk for a cappuccino with a sour look on her face. As I walked by, she warned me under her breath, "We seem to have an unhappy customer at the table over there with the kids."

I looked over the counter and saw a woman with long, brown, curly hair that stuck to her cheek due to the heat. She had a table full of children licking the bottoms of their ice cream cups or crunching the ends of their cones. Dirty napkins, broken cones, and puddles of melted ice cream covered the table. One young child may have been licking the dripped ice cream off the table.

Oh, great, I thought and attempted to sneak into my office without her seeing me. This presented a challenge because she was perched in her chair ignoring her litter as she sought out a person of authority. There was always the chance she would assume I only worked here.

As I turned the corner to the restroom hallway, her voice came at me like a semi-truck.

"Excuse me," she called. "Are you the manager?"

Although she sported a massive and pregnant belly under her print skirt, the woman moved deftly through the crowd. I wondered if I should move aside; it was not clear whether she was going to stop when she reached me or plow right through me. I stood my ground.

In my defense—and so long as we disregard the whole customer is always right doctrine—I tried to do the right thing. I listened to her. I gave her the sense that I was interested in what she had to say. But I was hot. I was tired and smelled of vanilla ice cream. Her arms flailed, fingers pointing, and her voice was harsh and direct. There were accusations that Michael looked at her as though she were from another planet. I attempted to humor her by claiming *he* was from another planet, as evidenced by his haircut, and that he looked at all customers with a vacant expression. We were concerned it might be drugs, but I did not tell her that.

In any case, she was not amused. Her primary grievance had nothing to do with Michael's extra-planetary origins but was that he had not offered her child-sized portions of ice cream, or "kid's cones." After several requests, I had agreed that the staff could serve a very small cone to those who asked for a kid's cone at a reduced price. My new friend had not asked for kid's cones and had received the regular-sized cones for her children, but she heard someone after her receive one at a savings of fifty cents per cone. That's it.

I should have known this pricing policy was going to be a problem. But I was reluctant to put the item on the menu because the "under fives"—as we referred to those youngsters—made up a large segment of our customer base.

My limited customer service skills suggested that I should just give her the difference in price or give her a coupon for some free cones. She continued to scream and dictate in my ear, doing neither of us any favors. I decided, *No.* She had insulted my staff and questioned my management, and I was having a bad day. I was hot and did not care.

I stood my ground. I explained the policy. Now, at this point—well, actually, it should never have gotten to this point—I am sure Ben or Jerry would have rolled over, offered her money back and free ice cream for life, and named their next flavor in her honor—Berry Bitch. I knew it was going badly, very badly.

"I would offer you the difference, but it looks as though your children had no problem eating the larger cones," I said, pointing to her messy brood and my filthy table. The youngest was gnawing on the

table leg. "All I can suggest is that next time you request a kid's cone."
I turned my back to her to go into my office. I closed the door, took a
deep breath, and hoped she would leave.

Of course, this was not what happened.

"What an asshole," I heard her say through the closed door.

Steam began to billow out of my ears, and the top of my balding head
turned beet red. I had seen the "red mist."

I opened the door quickly to startle anyone on the other side.

"Excuse me," I said. I looked at the woman. "Did you just call me an
asshole?"

She was surprised by my angry tone but stood her ground. She did
not respond. I looked at the busybody standing next to her, waiting for
the restroom. I turned to her.

"Did *you* call me an asshole?" I repeated the word to maximum
effect, but I may have resembled something close to it in the process.

"No, no, oh no, I wouldn't say that," the other woman said and
looked to the mother to implicate her.

"Well, I didn't think you'd hear me," she said.

"Well, I did hear it, and I think it is time for you and your children
to leave!"

"I am waiting for the restroom," she replied.

"Sorry, there is a public restroom up the street for you," I said.

"Are you kicking me out?" she asked as she fondled her pregnant belly.

"Yes, and the next time you feel like ice cream, try Dairy Queen."

I waited for her to collect her gaggle and leave. I scanned the room
Clint Eastwood style to see if anyone else had something to say. A
woman sitting near the restroom looked at me.

"May I help you?" I challenged her. She melted into her stool.

Regret flooded over me even as my friend and her little ones were trickling out the door. I wished Dean had been here. He would have either
given her the free ice cream or somehow charmed her into believing

she got a very good deal. And this wasn't me. I was meant to avoid confrontation.

Then again, the heat may have been a factor. In the *Sawyer County Record,* there had been a definite spike in reported cases of disorderly conduct. A man was charged and fined for the crime while being attended to in the hospital's emergency room. It was alleged that he yelled and swore at staff, shouted profanity, and threatened to come back and kill them. A sixty-year-old woman was fined for disorderly conduct even though the charge of endangering the safety of a family member by threatening him with a kitchen knife was dismissed. In the same week, on a street with the innocent name Day Care Drive, a man was sentenced for pushing a young child and was ordered to attend anger management counseling.

And then there was the case of a young, sweet woman known as Bambi. Dear Bambi was placed on nine months' probation for battery to a man with a blunt instrument and one year's probation for disorderly conduct. She was also ordered to attend anger management counseling. I vowed never to have another exchange with a customer like I had had with the pregnant lady. The thought of attending an anger management session with a very angry Bambi was too frightening.

When I told Dean the story, he was shocked. "She called you what?" He was sorry he hadn't been there to help with the situation, but I could tell he also feared what impression I may have left with the other people in the room. "So, how many customers heard any of this?" he asked.

Dean, who had a much better disposition for dealing with such situations, was right: I cannot and will not please everyone. I thought I would use the experience as a lesson in customer service. My outburst was a poor example for my young employees, even those on temporary work permits from outer space, and I might have scared away a few customers who may have witnessed the exchange.

The next morning, I gathered my "scoop troops" around for a discussion. I asked if they thought any of the other customers had heard anything. They looked at each other.

"No, I don't think so," Michael said, but no one to any degree took seriously what he might have observed.

I announced it was time to change the official "kid's cone" policy to include the item on the menu. We would implement the policy change as soon as we updated the programmable cash register and menu board. There was general agreement among the staff that this was the right time for the change.

"Most other ice cream stores offer kid's cones, like Culver's," Michael said.

"That's soft serve," Liz said, as though the distinction might matter.

The other lesson was for me alone. I had come to Hayward in search of a less-stressful existence. There had been many times at the bank when the pressure, anxiety, and lack of control built up in me like a volcano waiting to explode. When the explosion came, it was usually in a quiet room away from others who might be singed by molten lava spewing from my split skull. Then I blamed it on the job—on the corporate world. But I couldn't do that anymore.

I reminded myself I sold ice cream—not blood transfusions—and it should be all sweetness and light, not life or death. Later, there were many times when I wanted to tell an unhappy customer just that—*it's only ice cream.* Instead, I repeated the mantra to myself and kept in my pocket a stash of cards entitling the holder to a complimentary ice cream cone.

It was another very hot day. Business boomed. Bruce was finishing the cleanup from the day before. The stainless steel vat shone, and the opaque rubber tubes were all hung in their places. Bruce scratched his head while examining a small object in his left hand.

"Howdy," I greeted Bruce. I was happy to see him. After my incident with the unhappy customer the day before, I was looking forward to a better day. Bruce continued to examine whatever was in his hand.

"I think we may have a problem," he said. He held up a steel nut that had broken in two. It came from the contraption that held the cylinder in the freezing chamber of the freezer. I took the nut and examined it closely.

"It looks broken. Can we get a new one?" I asked.

"Oh, sure, that's no problem. The problem is here." Bruce pointed to the hollow chamber inside the nut. "You see"—he paused—"these ball bearings are held in the nut. When it broke, they fell out. I found eight of them while I was cleaning the machine, but I'm still missing eight ball bearings."

I immediately sensed where this was going yet could not bring myself to such a conclusion. "Could they have been washed down the drain?"

Bruce indicated that he had rinsed all the parts in a bucket where he found the broken nut.

"Was it broken before we started?"

"No, I screwed the nut on the cylinder myself when I put the machine together." He recalled his steps. "I think they're in the ice cream," he said.

As the information traveled to the nerve endings of my brain, I imagined a small child cracking his teeth on tiny ball bearings and then a class action suit. The court would be filled with young children sporting broken smiles. The plaintiff's lawyer would look at the jury and point to me. "If it wasn't for this man and his quest for ice cream profit, these children would have beautiful smiles. They could have been models or child actors." The jury would be in tears.

I thought of my outburst the day before. *Oh, Karma, is that you?*

I wondered if there was a way to detect the ball bearings. I knew it was only an attempt to stave off the inevitable, and I could not imagine taking a load of ice cream down to the hospital and asking if I could borrow their radiology department while I took X rays of a couple hundred containers of ice cream.

We had a recall procedure in place for just such a disaster. All containers were marked with a number identifying the day on which the ice cream was made. We also maintained a logbook of the number of containers made of each flavor. I reviewed the log and made a rough calculation—the ice cream that could contain the ball bearings had a street value of nearly two thousand dollars. The value of the ice cream used in the shop was much greater. The cost of this was the equivalent of a day's takings in the shop. *Ouch!* On top of it, this meant the day I had spent with Buck and Bruce making ice cream was all for naught. *Ouch.*

We identified the ice cream made the day before and moved it to a separate area of the freezer so no one would use it. So far, nothing had been used apart from some deliveries to the local convenience stores earlier in the morning. I asked Tom to return to the shops and retrieve the ice cream so it would not fall into the hands of any customers.

Bruce thought that, more than likely, the nut had cracked at the end of the session; otherwise, the machine would have broken down earlier.

"That would have been the butter pecan," I said as though we were detectives solving a crime and had come to an important breakthrough. We removed a third of the butter pecan batch from the freezer. Sitting in the hot plant room, the ice cream would melt in no time. Because we were confident we had lost only eight ball bearings, if we found them, we could stop and rest assured that the remainder of the batch was not contaminated.

By the afternoon, the ice cream was soft enough to pour. Using a sieve, I took my time since it was still quite thick and the pecans had to be removed by hand. Finally, after draining twelve three-gallon containers of ice cream, I saw in the bottom of my sieve four small silver balls. At the bottom of the next container, I found two more ball bearings. They might as well have been gold. We were missing two ball bearings. It was possible I had missed them. I resigned myself to taking more ice cream out of the freezer to melt.

Tom returned from the route. I told him the good news.

"Well, I picked up the ice cream. The only problem is they had already sold two five-quart containers of butter pecan," he said.

"Do they know who bought them?" I asked.

"They know one of them."

"Really?" I said.

Tom smiled and then held out his hand to reveal two ball bearings. I was relieved yet alarmed at the thought of the required tooth replacements and veneers.

"Were they okay?"

"Oh, for sure. They were fine. I gave them a couple of tubs of free ice cream. I hope that was okay?" Tom asked.

"That's perfect," I said.

A few days after my encounter with the pregnant woman and product recall, Dean and I had dinner at the Ranch. Happy to see us and now completely recovered from the early-morning pancake marathon at the Sawyer County Dairy Breakfast, Cheryl took our drink order. She placed the margarita I ordered in front of me and put her hand on my arm. "This one's on me. From what I hear, you may need it," she said with a mischievous smile.

"Oh, no! Why is that?"

Cheryl related how she had run into a friend who owned another restaurant in town. Her friend was a sweet lady but not exactly discreet. She described for Cheryl how a family with a number of children had been in her restaurant and had told her about the crazed new owner of West's Dairy.

I put my head on the bar. Cheryl continued, "Apparently, you started screaming and kicked this poor woman and her kids out for no reason." The restaurant owner told them that she could not believe "mild-mannered" Jeff would do such a thing.

"I have one question." Cheryl interrupted her own story. "Was she really pregnant?"

I nodded, my head still on the bar.

"And you wouldn't even let her use the toilet?"

I nodded again.

I looked up at Cheryl. "Do you think many people have heard this story?"

"Hmm." Cheryl folded her arms and grinned. "I think it is safe to say that story is now legend in Hayward."

Where's Buck?

It was one of the hottest Julys on record for northern Wisconsin. West's Hayward Dairy produced nearly 4,500 gallons of ice cream. Events such as the Honor the Earth Powwow on the LCO Reservation and the Lumberjack World Championships attracted thousands of visitors to town. Sales in July were twice that of June. Our bank account was flush with cash. Over the course of the month, we served over 20,000 customers and sold 9,654 cake cones, 6,138 waffle cones, 3,999 sugar cones, 1,219 malts and shakes, and 752 sundaes, as well as smoothies, espresso drinks, and iced coffees. We introduced three new flavors for the season—a traditional black raspberry, pralines and caramel, which was one of my favorites, and a banana ice cream we called Chunky Musky. The West's Latte, a shake made of espresso and ice cream, was a hit, but the public remained unconvinced of the Espresso Sundae's deliciousness.

I was proud of my young staff. They remained in good form and smiled through the blistering heat, steady stream of customers, and sticky mess. However, some of them began to complain of a strange phenomenon: after a long day or night of work and after they had gone to sleep, they reenacted their day in an "ice cream dream."

Jen in particular, and not surprisingly, was susceptible to the ice cream dream. In her dream, she was working alone on a busy afternoon

and ran out of mint chocolate chip. She ran through the freezer but
could not find any. She searched through each stack until her hands
were freezing. Customers yelled at her to help them. She then looked
in other places one would not expect to find ice cream—the cooler, the
dry storage area—but the mint chocolate chip eluded her. Once she
even searched for the ice cream on the scorching-hot roof.

"I had a dream like that!" Suzi shouted as Jen reported her dream
ended when she woke in a cold sweat. "In mine, I couldn't find my
scoop," Suzi said. "It was a really busy day. Customers were around the
block." Suzi pointed to the street corner. "Everyone was working really
hard, but I couldn't find a scoop. Everyone started yelling at me. It was
so horrible."

The heat even got to Bruce, who could otherwise make ice cream
anytime of the day on any day of the week, and he announced he was
taking a few days off to go to his cabin in the woods outside of town.
"It's just too dang hot," he said. "Things will begin to slow down now
that it's August."

Only Buck seemed to maintain his cool through the dairy's busiest
month. He managed this by avoiding being anyplace near the shop in
midafternoon when the sun was highest and we were busiest. He said
he played cards at the senior center, but the girls suspected he went
home to his air-conditioned trailer for a nap. He might stop by later in
the afternoon or evening but usually just to check in before dinner.

Despite his disappearing act in the afternoon, Buck's mornings were
very predictable. He arrived at the dairy by 7:00 AM every day, including Sunday. He removed the lids from the tubs in the dipping cabinet.
He made coffee for the occasional customer who came in to use the free
Internet access. He made some ice cream deliveries, but I tried to make
sure I took any large and heavy orders.

I suspect in the past he had helped the kids scoop ice cream but now
recognized he would have a hard time keeping pace on a busy day. I
didn't mind. I liked the way he held court at his favorite seat, with a

newspaper in front of him. Just as I enjoyed hearing his animated stories of old Hayward, customers would listen for the mere price of an ice cream cone. People often asked about the changes at the dairy, and Buck happily told them all about Dean and me and what we were doing at the "mansion."

Many customers who came back year after year recognized him and liked to catch up. Once a couple was so engaged in their conversation with Buck I assumed they must be related. After they left, I asked Buck who they were. "I have no idea," he said. "But they sure knew a lot about me." He laughed. I was not convinced he realized it was because of the stories he may have told them in the past.

At times his language was a bit too salty, and I did point out that even if he said it with affection most parents did not appreciate their children being referred to as "little bastards." And I was tempted to intervene when he was giving advice on local restaurants, knowing that not everyone would appreciate the charms of the co-op.

On the second Saturday in August, I arrived at the dairy just before 9:00 AM. The door was locked. Buck was not there. I thought perhaps a customer had called and requested a delivery, but there was no note or evidence that Buck had been in yet. The coffee was unmade, and the dipping cabinets were still closed as they had been at the end of the last shift. Liz had been waiting on the bench outside for me to unlock the door.

"You don't know where Buck is, do you?" I asked. She did not.

I gave him an hour in case he had gone out for a late breakfast. At 10:00 AM, he still had not turned up. I called his house. There was no answer. I did not remember him saying he was going anywhere. Where would he go, anyway?

"Did Buck say he was going anywhere today?" I asked Liz.

"Buck? He never goes anywhere," Liz said, showing little concern for the man who tormented her for her vegan lifestyle, which he once associated with communism.

I thought about driving over to Buck's house but realized I had never been there. I knew where the mobile home park was but was not sure how large it was or how I would find his home apart from following the old man smell or looking for the mount of a deer's head fastened to the front like a hood ornament on a car. I knew it was a traditional long, narrow trailer that had been long ago driven to its location and parked on a platform, but Buck rarely talked about his home.

In fact, my only knowledge of his home came from a grisly scene he once described. Buck had come home one afternoon, and the screen door was open. When he walked in, a large black bear was eating a box of cookies he had left on the kitchen table. Rather than turn and run far away, Buck sneaked into the living room and grabbed his rifle off the wall. As he chased the bear to the door—to avoid a mess in the kitchen—he shot the animal. The bear fell on the cement slab outside his door.

"What did you do with it?" I asked.

"It was so dang big, I couldn't move it," he said. "I called a buddy who likes bear meat, but he couldn't come around for a few days. It began to stink by the time he got there. Oh, but you know what I did? My daughter liked the teeth and wanted to make a necklace out of them, so I yanked the buggers out of his mouth."

I was not worried about Buck taking care of himself even if he was lost in the woods and surrounded by a pack of wolves. I had noticed he was wobbling more when he rose from his stool, as though he might be lightheaded due to blood pressure or sugar levels. Then I thought about his driving habits and became very concerned. Bruce and Jan tended to look after Buck, but I had probably seen more of him over the summer than Bruce had, and, after all, he did work for me. Where could he be?

I wasn't sure I was prepared for such responsibility. Taking care of Buck was like operating the ice cream machine. I wasn't ready. I didn't know what to do. When my mother became sick I was thousands of miles away. It was up to my brother and sister in Minnesota to take on the role of caring for her. I could only provide support by phone. I left London as soon as I got the call, but she died just hours before my plane landed in Minneapolis. I was too late.

I called Bruce at home in case he knew where Buck might be. Bruce was not home, but Jan said she would call Buck's former wife to see if she knew anything. I was sure there was most likely a logical explanation, but the man was nearly eighty and a driving hazard on the road, and he lived off a diet of burgers and fried chicken. Anything could have happened.

Jan called back. She could not get hold of Bruce or Carol, so she had driven over to Buck's house. "His car was gone. I looked in the windows, but no one was there," she said. "He must have gone somewhere."

I again thought of my few times in the car with Buck and assumed that he must be in jail or a ditch somewhere waiting for help. I was now worried. I was in the middle of my own ice cream dream, and I could not find the old man who came with the dairy. I checked the freezer and cooler to make sure he had not fallen and knocked himself unconscious. I almost checked the roof. Notwithstanding the climb on two narrow ladders to get there, Buck once followed me up to the roof like an agile and aging orangutan.

I had to make a delivery to the campground. I asked the girls to make a note if they heard anything of Buck's whereabouts or if he returned while I was away from the shop.

When I returned to the dairy, Buck was sitting at the table.

"Where were you, Buck?" I yelled, happy to see the old guy. "Suzi was very worried," I added.

"I was not!" Suzi shouted from behind the counter. "He says mean things to me. *You* were worried, Jeff."

"He thought we should call the police," Liz said.

"Oh, I just went down to the big auction at Springbrook," Buck said. "I thought I told you I was going there today." I vaguely recalled him telling me about an auction notice in the paper.

"Did you buy something?" I asked, pointing to a cardboard box of miscellaneous stuff in front of him.

"Oh, no, it was all junk, not worth anything. I had this box in the car. I bought it at your auction at the mansion in the spring. Paid two bucks for the whole box," he said. "I found something in here you might like." Buck picked up a couple of eggcups made of clear glass in the shape of chickens. He carefully lined them up on the counter. "I thought you could use them for breakfast when you're done with the house."

I picked up an eggcup to examine it. It was quite sweet, something I would have saved if I had seen it before the sale.

"Great," I said. "Thanks. Now, don't be running off like that again, Buck," I scolded.

Buck smiled. "Oh, don't worry about me. I never go far. But I'll let you know."

〜

The Demo and the End of Summer

By the third week of August, the throngs of summer tourists had vanished. With the beginning of most schools or at least school-related activities such as football, soccer, golf, or girls' volleyball, families with school-aged children disappeared from the streets. There was still a steady stream of customers at West's, but sales dropped by half of what they were at the beginning of the month.

There was only one thing left to do before the end of the summer— go to the fair. The Sawyer County Fair had taken place at the end of August for nearly one hundred years. It had been ages since I was at a county fair. Dean heard they served deep-fried Twinkies and imagined how delicious they must be.

Saturday was the big day at the fair. We went early in the evening. We started in the hall in which the dairy breakfast had been held. The tables displayed the winners of the garden competition. Heads of lettuce and cabbage and bunches of carrots with bright green manes were placed on plates ready to serve with the blue, red, or green ribbons beside them. Baked goods, pies, cakes, and cookies were lined up but could not be touched.

"Where do they sell those Twinkies?" Dean asked.

We moved to the barn with the livestock. Cattle, pigs, sheep, and goats stood politely in their pens after three days at the fair. They had been scrubbed, combed, and judged, and now they were being sold. Sold!

We arrived for the annual livestock auction. Children who had raised the animals on the farm had agreed to give them up and auction them off, with the proceeds going to fund kids programs about farming and tending to animals.

"Why would anyone buy a pig or a cow? Are they farmers?" Dean asked. The people who heard him looked around to see who was going to reveal the truth about the fair's livestock auction to Dean.

"They're going to eat them!" one of our friends exclaimed. Dean grimaced in despair as though he had stumbled on some unusual ritual or had never considered where a bacon sandwich came from.

It was somewhat hard to watch as a young lad held onto the small pig he had cared for much like a pet all spring and summer, only to sell it to the salivating bald man in overalls with bacon and pork chops on his mind. We quickly left for the food stalls in search of deep-fried Twinkies.

Fortunately, no animals suffered in the production of the Twinkie, nor were many plants or really any other material of nutritional value wasted in the making of one of America's favorite snacks. As a child, I loved Twinkies—delicious and ever-so-moist yellow sponge cake surrounding an unusual white cream. Even back then, when *nutrition* seemed like a word from the future, people sensed Twinkies were bad for you. My mother bought them only on rare occasions.

There was not a long line for the deep-fried Twinkies. Dean rushed to the caravan selling the golden gems and ordered. He told the woman he had never had one. She was vaguely amused and assured him he would not be disappointed. Her fried Twinkie stand shook and leaned as she moved around inside. We watched as she impaled the Twinkie with a wooden spear, dipped the cake in a light batter, and submerged the stick into a pot of boiling fat. After a minute, which seemed like an eternity for Dean, she pulled it out. At this stage, it resembled a corn dog. She placed the stick on a plate and squirted chocolate sauce from a Hershey's bottle over the Twinkie. "Enjoy," she said.

We looked on in anticipation as Dean bit into his first Twinkie. "Ah, shit!" he blurted. He jumped up from the bench and tried to open his mouth to relieve the pain of the scalding white cream that oozed from inside the Twinkie.

"So, do you like it?" I asked.

"No, it's bloody disgusting! I cannot believe you eat that," he said, referring to all Americans, including anyone at the fair who heard him. He placed the Twinkie on the plate and was going to leave it. I couldn't resist. I picked up the stick and blew on the molten white center before taking a small bite. It was greasy and had lost much of its spongy texture from the frying. *Not that bad*, I thought.

The crowds began to stream toward the entrance to the main attraction of the evening—a true spectacle of man versus man. Like ancient Romans heading toward the Colosseum to witness the gladiators do battle, the people of Hayward knew that when this battle was finished, the field would be littered with bodies and there would be only one victor. Of course, the bodies would be that of beaten and immobile cars, as this was the annual demolition derby!

"The demo," as most people knew it, was possibly the most-attended event of the season and the highlight of the Sawyer County Fair. The arena was designed for the demo with a dirt-covered ring about the size of half a football field. At one end was a path by which the cars entered the ring. Cement blocks surrounded the field to prevent cars from jumping into the crowd. On a hillside, several hundred people sat in metal bleachers, but three times as many sat on the hard weed- and thistle-infested ground around the ring. Families brought blankets, folding chairs, and picnics. I saw Bruce by the beer stand. Buck was already at the front of the bleachers. "You gotta get there early," he had warned me. Our contractor from the B&B was there with his family. Most of the other workers at the house were in the crowd.

After standing in line at the beer stand, alcoholic refreshment a req- uisite for watching the demo, we found a relatively painless spot on the grass behind the bleachers but high enough to see the action. The announcer, dressed all in white, introduced himself and described the sequence of events.

The participants in this challenge were all from Hayward or within a sixty-mile radius of town. Local mechanics spent the year searching for the largest and hardiest American car. The cars were from twenty to thirty years old. They were stripped of all glass, including headlights. The bodies were reinforced and painted with numbers, and often the mechanics sought local sponsors and painted their names on the side of the vehicle.

The announcer, from Kentucky, stood in the center of the field on the back of a flatbed truck and attempted to warm up the crowd with some jokes. He started to tell an Ole and Lena joke, typically silly and mildly amusing humor about an old Norwegian couple. It was a risky move for someone who was not Scandinavian or even from the Upper Midwest.

"Ole is on his deathbed," the announcer began, to cringes from the audience. "The doctor told him he has only a few hours to live. He catches the scent of his favorite bars wafting through the air. With all the strength he can muster, he drags himself into the kitchen." The announcer mimicked a dying man walking across the flatbed truck. "Ole sees a pan of fresh bars cooling on the rack. He cuts into one and bites into the delicious cake." The announcer licked his lips before continuing. "Lena comes, smacks Ole's hand, and says, 'Shame on you, Ole! Dese are for after de funeral!'"

The crowd laughed and applauded the announcer's efforts at regional humor. Buttressed perhaps by the response, he tried another, more off-color Ole and Lena joke that did not fare as well with the crowd, which only laughed nervously.

The announcer moved on quickly and asked the audience to stand for a moment of silence in honor of fellow citizens serving in the armed forces to protect the American way of life, including our constitutional right to demolish things.

With the formalities finished, the truck stage maneuvered to the edge. The local fire department drove a large truck to the center of the field. Three uniformed firemen unfurled the fire hose and sprayed water on the field to prevent sparks. The participants revved their engines and began their procession into the stadium. They drove a lap in formation as the announcer named the drivers and the sponsors, including most of the local restaurants and bars in town. Even Marge from Turk's Inn was a sponsor. In the case of one driver, the announcer indicated the sponsor was his mother-in-law.

"We expect to see a McCormick House car here next year," our friend suggested.

"Only if I can drive it," Dean replied.

Finally, the participants took their positions, with three cars at one end of the field and three at the other. What happened next was a surprise for those of us who had never seen a demolition derby. There was no racing around the track; all the action took place in the center of the field. Upon the countdown, the cars sped toward the center, directly at those coming from the opposite direction. Some made a last-minute 180-degree turn and put the vehicle in reverse so the back end rather than the engine received the impact from the oncoming driver. The crowd roared with the initial and near-crippling blow of a large Chevrolet station wagon to a Buick sedan. At the edge, one of the faster cars swerved at the last minute to miss the lumbering oversized Oldsmobile headed for it and promptly turned around to catch the sedan with a direct hit on its side.

The action was quick. After a few blows, two participants stalled and were out of the competition. Smoke streamed from the engine of a large black Pontiac that took a direct hit from the station wagon. Crewmembers examined under the hood, and the fire department prepared to take action if necessary. On the smallest car, the rear of the vehicle was dragging on the ground. Like a wounded warrior, the car's driver won the approval of the crowd, who cheered as he drove furiously around the edge, swinging at cars like a launched harpoon while still protecting its rear. The large wagon, however, was invincible and gave a solid blow to the wounded car's side. At the end of the round, there was only one car moving. The second-place finisher could proceed to the final round provided the crew could get it in motion.

The second round started cautiously as drivers adopted a strategy of evasion in order to remain in the running. Facing jeers from the crowd and warnings from the announcer, they mixed it up. With three piled on each other in the center of the field, the fourth made a series of blows to the sides and rears of the others. As the cars disentangled, one was caught on a piece of torn metal from another car, and the two drove around in circles until they separated.

While the drivers moving on to the final round made adjustments or necessary repairs, the announcer introduced a special treat, one that answered the question—*how far will Americans go to amuse themselves?* He said it was an exciting new event and, subject to the approval of the crowd, could be a feature at next year's fair.

From the far end of the parking lot, what sounded like a series of chain saws began to roar. Gasoline fumes filled the air as tiny vehicles with a single man on top rushed to the field. It was a riding lawn mower race. But these were not your ubiquitous riding lawn mowers that men drove on their suburban estates each Saturday; they were modified push mowers with amplified engines and makeshift seats to give the impression the driver was riding something the size of a Cuisinart. The lawn mowers briefly rested at the starting line as though stopping was not an option. When the whistle blew, they streamed around the ring. The sound was deafening, and the crowd laughed and cheered. The oversized drivers struggled to balance their mowers around the corner. Two on the inside track leaned too far and toppled to the ground, but they quickly picked up their blender on wheels and completed the race.

Most people had never seen the mower race and could not believe it. I saw Buck laughing uncontrollably. The contractor's wife held her hand to her mouth in disbelief. Dean and I—the newest citizens of Rome—could not believe we were watching grown men racing on mini-lawnmowers as though they had jumped off a Benny Hill skit.

"Do you think this is closer to the Ascot or the Henley Regatta?" Dean yelled to be heard over the grinding of the mowers, suggesting the event could become a feature on the season's calendar in Hayward following the dairy breakfast and the Musky Festival.

The announcer named the first- and second-place finishers and, based on the crowd's reaction, said the mini-lawnmower races would be featured at next year's Sawyer County Fair. This was met with great applause and approval of the citizens, including Dean and me.

There was a further delay of the demo final as two of the four finalists struggled to repair their beaten vehicles to compete. The crowd grew restless. The beer tent at the back of the field was swamped. Those of us on the ground removed thistles and dried, prickly grasses from our behinds.

With the finalists to the demo in the field, nervous crewmembers looked on. It was doubtful that two of the vehicles, clearly injured beyond repair, would withstand many blows. The sun began to set behind a wall of towering pines on the other side of the Chippewa Trail, casting a long shadow on the field of action. The victorious station wagon from the first round, with barely a dent on its body, stood as a symbol of past summers when many in the crowd piled their families in for a summer vacation to the Wisconsin Dells or even the Black Hills of South Dakota to see the figures of the presidents on the side of Mount Rushmore.

Soon after the action began, one of the damaged vehicles stalled in the center of the field after a quick but mortal blow by the station wagon. The car sat there, unable to move except by the pressure of the cars around it. The driver had no choice but to stay in the vehicle until the round was finished. Before long, there was just the station wagon and a 1980 Volvo that was no match for the wagon but still running. The wagon skillfully pursued the sedan until it made a solid blow to the passenger side and pushed the old Swede the length of the field to claim victory.

The driver jumped out and raised his hands into the air. The announcer shook his hand, patted his back, and named him the winner of the nine-hundred-dollar first prize. The citizens of Rome rose to their feet to applaud their new gladiator and then headed to the gates of the Colosseum for deep-fried Twinkies.

AUTUMN

A Plan

Summer moved on like a good friend leaving town after a short visit. By the middle of August, the days remained dry and sunny, but in the evening there was a chilly reminder that autumn was approaching. On the drive from Teal Lake to Hayward, a group of overly sensitive maples in a low-lying valley turned crimson overnight, seemingly ashamed by the premature closure of their chlorophyll-producing glands. Hawks began night flights to warmer havens, and some Canada geese flying in V-formation chose to head south early this year.

On August 24, the temperature fell below the freezing point. Petunias withered in their baskets with shock and betrayal. In front of a small home near Main Street, a woman in a pink blouse and white straw hat plucked her wilting flowers. Written on her face you could see the guilt for not taking the precautionary measure of covering the basket with a sheet or plastic overnight. "It really snuck up on us this year," she said. "It's been so hot."

At the dairy, Jen and Liz were preoccupied with returning to school. They would be seniors at Hayward High School and were thinking about college. I joked that a college education was overrated and they could make their career at West's Dairy.

"Oh, that would be so gross!" Liz screeched, reminding us how she couldn't wait to leave town. Jen hoped to be a teacher, and I felt sympathy for her students, already knowing what a taskmaster she would be.

Although business remained steady, the dairy takings fell by fifty percent from the beginning of August. I walked the empty streets of Hayward that only a few weeks before had teemed with happy ice-cream-eating tourists. It was sad. An older couple from Iowa rummaged through the two-dollar rack in front of the T-shirt shop. *This cannot be happening,* I thought. *Come back, everyone. Have another ice cream cone. Please!*

"It's the same every year," Buck said. "You know, it's the kids. They're gettin' ready for school—football practice, cheerleading, and so on."

This not only affected my bottom line but my staff as well. Jen, Liz, and Suzi had decided to sign up for the cross-country running team. The coach was a popular teacher, and the girls hoped to shed a few ice cream pounds they might have gained over the summer. I attempted to convince them not only that was there scant evidence that ice cream consumption led to weight gain but also that team sports created an unhealthy competition among peers. They easily saw through my pleas and questioned my argument.

"Jeff, I think you don't want to work. You don't like scooping ice cream," Suzi said.

"How could you say that, Suzi?" I said.

"It'll be okay," Jen said. "I'm sure Buck will help," she added in an unusual display of sarcasm.

Cross-country practice began at 3:00 in the afternoon. The girls changed into their running gear and jogged out the door. I looked at Buck, who was sitting in a leather chair, watching the traffic.

"I guess it's just the two of us, Buck," I said. He mumbled something inaudible and removed his hat to scratch his head.

Labor Day weekend in early September was the official end of the season. Once again, people flocked to Hayward for the three-day weekend. The weather was good and business was good, but there was a general sense of "this is the end" for everyone. In contrast to the long weekend at the beginning of the summer when people were excited and looked with joy toward the coming weeks, these customers knew the season was changing. For many, it was the last weekend to enjoy a warm day on the lake. Others got a head start on winterizing their home by replacing the screen windows and doors with thick-paned storm windows and doors, removing the dock so the ice would not destroy it, and covering the boat.

I decided that the Tuesday following the Labor Day weekend was the opening of a new chapter. After such a hectic summer, I looked forward to the quiet months ahead. Back in London, I had often dreamed of owning my own little coffee bar where I could exchange pleasantries with customers, take care of paperwork between serving people, and keep a dog-eared paperback classic behind the espresso machine to fill the quiet times. I would play cool jazz music, some swing classics, or perhaps trendy new music to give the impression that I was young and hip. This was my chance. Anyway, Buck would be here to help me when I needed to run errands or when a lost tour bus came through town and stopped for ice cream.

I drove up Main Street to the post office. The street resembled a scene from an end-of-days movie. The buildings remained intact, but those who had survived were driven underground, where they kept supplies of canned beans and fruit cocktail. A few cars were parked in front of the bakery, but they may have been left there overnight. Many shops were closed as the owners took the morning off to have an end-of-the-season breakfast at the Norske Nook.

At the dairy, Buck sat at the bar, fixated on my surprise gift for him— a new flat-screen television. He had been a good sport all summer and hadn't complained once about not having a TV to watch.

"So, what do you think?" I asked. "I said I would make it up to you."

"It sure is a fancy one. I bet you bought it at Wal-Mart." Buck thumbed the remote control like a kid with a video game.

"Wait till I tell Little Bob," Buck said. Bob had made himself scarce for much of the summer. He disliked crowds, and without a TV there seemed little point in stopping at the dairy.

The television sat on the wall opposite the ice cream counter. "This way, Buck, you can watch TV while serving customers," I said as a reminder that he had promised he would help me.

"Ah, sure, Jeff. I'll help you out when you get stuck," Buck said. "I made the coffee already." He held up his mug as his attention was drawn back to the final round of *Family Feud*.

I waited to put on my cool jazz background music until Buck turned off the TV, whenever that might be. I installed a small counter for a work space next to the espresso machine. I unpacked my laptop and a stack of unpaid bills as well as customer invoices to be input into the accounting system. I had put off most of the data entry for a few months—actually, since April, when we started. My goal was to input all the data for April on this, my first day at work.

By late morning, the first customers of the day sauntered into the dairy, a family from Rockford, Illinois. They ordered two ice cream cones and three milk shakes. I looked over at Buck, but he was multi-tasking—watching the late-morning news out of Duluth and reading the *Minneapolis Star Tribune* at the same time.

The pattern repeated itself every ten minutes. By 1:00 PM, a line had formed at the counter. I had to say something. I needed help, but when I turned to Buck, he was gone. A man with a bushy beard who had been chatting with Buck looked up from the newspaper. "He said he was going to lunch," the customer said.

"Great," I mumbled.

"He said he might stay and play some cards after lunch."

"Fantastic," I said under my breath.

It wasn't until after three in the afternoon when the last of my after-lunch crowd left the shop. Buck was nowhere to be seen. My lunch consisted of a caramel shake with a dollop of hot fudge. I made a cappuccino and sat in a leather chair. I watched the school buses stream down Dakota Avenue.

Buck shuffled through the door. "What's this? Sittin' on the job!" he said.

"Where have you been? I thought you were going to help me," I said.

"Oh, sorry," Buck said, with a touch of sincerity. "I got talked into playing a few hands of gin rummy."

I wasn't going to begrudge the old guy a card game, so I let it drop. "Did you win?" I asked.

"Sure did."

Buck pulled up a leather chair and looked out the window. "Look at those buses—half empty, each of them. What a waste," he said.

At 5:00 PM, we closed for the day. I punched a few keys, and the cash register chugged and whirled out a small report of the day's business. In the summer, the report could take a minute to print, but now it took only ten or twelve seconds. We took in little more than $250—most in the form of ice cream cones, about a dozen malts and shakes, a few sundaes, eight cups of coffee, three lattes, and one mocha.

Between serving customers, I had managed to input invoices for only the first week of April. My arm was coated in a sticky ice cream film, and my shirt was splattered with milk shake. Though my hands shook after five espresso drinks, I was exhausted.

As I locked the door and headed to my car, Buck turned to me.

"It was a pretty good day," he said.

The next day, I had a plan. First, I got to the dairy early before Buck arrived. I turned on the music I had preselected, a combination of modern jazz and some swing classics from the 1930s. I set the *New York Times* on the bar and made a cappuccino.

"What the hell is this?" Buck said, pointing to the speaker above the door when he entered the shop.

"Tommy Dorsey," I replied.

"Hmm. I see. Well, it takes me back," he said quietly and sat down at the counter.

The music distracted him, or so I thought. He glanced at the *New York Times* skeptically as though it were something foreign and fingered the corner to measure the weight of the paper or to determine if the newspaper ink smeared his hand.

"Sure you don't want to watch the *Today* show?" he asked.

"Nah, let's listen to music today."

"All right, I guess I could read this fancy paper." Buck picked up the *New York Times*. "What's this? Two dollars! You paid two dollars for this?"

"It has a crossword and a sudoku puzzle," I said.

Buck unfolded the newspaper and spread it across the counter, using his hand to remove any creases.

It was early in the day—too early for ice cream. I set up my laptop and began to reconcile my checkbook.

Ahh, I thought to myself. *This is what I was looking for.* Before long, I felt I was making progress. There were few customers in the post-apocalyptic Hayward of early September to distract me. Buck was engrossed in his new newspaper and seemed to be enjoying it. "I have to say, you sure get your money's worth in this one," he said. "The articles go on a bit—not like the *Sawyer County Record*."

Little Bob, handling a walking stick, came through the front door. He was wearing the same khaki trousers and red shirt I had last seen him wearing in June.

"Well, look who it is, Jeff," Buck said.

"Hey, Bob," I said. "Would you like a coffee?"

"Oh, sure . . . Yeah, that would be swell," he accepted as he maneuvered himself onto the tall stool by the bar across from Buck.

"Were you at the co-op?" Buck asked

"Oh, yeah, had a donut."

"Who was your waitress?" Buck inquired.

"Oh, the little redhead. She's real nice to me," Bob said, perhaps a bit smitten. "So that's a new TV," he added, pointing at the blackened flat screen. "I guess *The Price Is Right* would be starting about now."

"Well, Jeff thinks we should listen to music today," Buck said, nodding in my direction.

"Oh," Bob said, deflated.

I suddenly felt like the evil babysitter forcing the kids to bed before their usual bedtime.

"You can turn on the TV. I don't mind," I said. Before I finished my sentence, I heard the announcer yell for some very excited man to "come on down!"

My quiet morning disturbed, I took the time to run some errands. Over the course of the summer I had looked forward to my errands, unlike in London, where I encountered an ever-changing uniformed staff at my bank or the surly attendant at the dry cleaners who always gave me the impression I should expect to see stained or ripped trousers. After a few months in Hayward, everyone seemed to know who we were and vice-versa. At the bank, Mary Alice and Joan kidded me for my ice cream–coated twenty-dollar bills but bristled when I suggested I launder them. There was Lois at the bakery, Ann at the bookstore. It was as though people in Hayward had no last names—a bit like a night at the Grammy Awards with Cher and Madonna.

These folks had taken the place of my friendlier coworkers in London, who gathered around the water cooler for some light gossip or predictions on the next *Big Brother* evictions. Apart from the errand banter, there was the promise of free food. Provided you arrived by late morning, the bank had freshly baked cookies and the bakery offered samples of their European breads slathered in Wisconsin butter. At Angler's, Mary Beth had unlimited chips and salsa on Mexican night—Thursday.

There was no free food at the bookstore. In fact, there was a sign on the door banning all foods and, based on helpful drawings, singling out ice cream cones as particularly unwelcome. I questioned Ann about the fairness of the policy—I allowed people to bring books and magazines into the ice cream shop. After all, I joked, they had already wrapped their large selection of pornographic magazines in cellophane to protect them from dripping ice cream cones. Before I left Buck, Little Bob, and Bob Barker, I made an iced latte to smuggle into the bookstore for Ann. She had been investigating a juvenile prank where someone had flipped the Beanie Babies on display so their butts faced the customers.

I was afraid she had checked the store's security cameras and was on to me.

Back at the dairy, Bob was gone, and Buck had turned the TV to another episode of *Classic Bowling*. *Oh, this is a classy place,* I thought. Buck was behind the counter. In front of him was a seemingly lost young woman in a business suit with a stylish handbag. She held the delicate strap with her hand rather than over the shoulder like the golf-bag handbag most women in town carried. Her blond hair was pulled back tightly, and she was keying something into her BlackBerry. Buck looked frustrated.

"Jeff, this lady here wants one of those bullshit mocha drinks you make," he said.

"That's okay, Buck. I'll get it," I said. "You go back to your bowling show."

"Oh, I know how it ends," he said. "A perfect score." Buck shook his head as he shuffled behind our fancy customer.

I turned to the woman. "So, what kind of milk would you like in your 'bullshit' mocha?"

She looked over the tops of her tortoise-shell spectacles. "I'll have a nonfat mocha, no foam, half the chocolate," she said before returning to her BlackBerry. "Oh, and you can hold the bullshit," she added.

"Certainly."

The rest of the day, there was no cool jazz, only the drone of whatever Buck was watching on TV. My checking account remained unbalanced, my paperback sat gathering dust and coffee grounds behind the espresso machine, and my thought was, *So much for my dream.*

Although I sold only a half dozen espresso drinks, I could not call the dairy a coffee bar if I did not offer a machiatto or caramel cream latte. My options were limited. I could strap myself to the counter all day, but this would be a short-term solution only; in a matter of weeks I would run out of the building and throw myself in front of a passing school bus. I could give up on my dream and close the coffee bar so I could leave Buck to sell ice cream cones. Or I could hire someone to work either full time or at least a few days each week so I could retain a portion of my sanity.

Perhaps there was another option. I recalled going to coffee bars in Italy. Most of the baristas behind the counter were older men—true professionals in crisp white shirts and black aprons who took pride in their work. They were not known for their award-winning smiles or pleasant conversation, but they produced a great cappuccino.

"Buck," I said, "could you come here, please?" I thought, *This is never going to work.* "I would like to show you something." By making the request intentionally vague, I might at least get him off his stool.

As he approached the espresso machine, I said, "Buck, I'm going to train you to be my new barista."

"Bartender! What the hell you talking about?" Buck said.

"No, a master of this coffee machine." I grabbed the handle of the steam wand.

"Nah, I can't do that," Buck said and stepped back. "I'll stick to my regular American coffee. That's good enough for most people."

"Come on, Buck. Let's at least try," I pleaded.

Buck approached the machine with trepidation, as though he were embarking on an alien spacecraft. It was all too foreign for him. "There sure are a lot of bells and whistles on this contraption." He shook his hands in the air.

"It's really pretty easy once you get the hang of it," I said.

The machine was a true Italian espresso maker with three "heads," just like an Italian coffee bar. I had bought it from a Starbucks in Minneapolis and had it refurbished. The machine was not as old as my ice cream maker, but it made a nice shot of espresso.

"We'll start with a simple shot," I said, beginning my lesson. I explained how first we ground the beans and filled the head with the ground espresso. "We tap it down to remove excess air and place it in the head of the machine." I thought Buck might struggle with this part because he suffered from arthritis and was shorter than me, and the machine sat quite high on the counter. I pushed a button for a double shot, and Buck watched as the rich, dark nectar poured slowly from the head into a small cup.

"It sure smells nice, I'll say that much," Buck said.

I pointed out the golden *crema* but realized this was perhaps too much detail for Buck. "It's very strong. That's why many people prefer it with milk." I filled the metal pitcher with cold milk for steaming.

"Now, we'll make a latte." I thought this was going well so far, so I expanded my lesson. "*Latte* is the Italian word for milk," I said. When I trained the kids, I tried to give them the cultural, historical, and linguistic lesson to show not only that I was a coffee connoisseur but that I had traveled. "It is more or less the same as *café au lait,* as the French would call it."

"Café olé—sounds Mexican to me."

"No, *au lait,*" I distinguished.

"Oh, like an Ole and Lena joke. Did you hear the one . . . ?"

I thought the old man was messing with my head. "Never mind," I said. "It's not important." I realized this was not going the way I had hoped. Just for that, I thought, Buck was not going to hear my story of the connection between the Capuchin monks and the cappuccino.

When the milk reached a temperature of 140 degrees, I pulled the steaming wand slowly from the liquid to create the froth on the surface. I took a spoon and poured the milk slowly over the coffee, holding back the froth until the very end. I held up the coffee to Buck.

"You see, the milk, or the fat in the milk, enhances the flavor of the coffee—mellow, pure, and ever so slightly sweet. Truly marvelous." Buck now looked at me as though I had become possessed by a drug. I couldn't help it. I loved coffee. It was my greatest vice—simple and pleasurable.

I handed my perfect latte to Buck to try. He approached it as though I were handing him a crack pipe. He took a gulp, leaving a milky mustache on his top lip. "It's nice, but"—Buck hesitated and handed the cup back to me—"I'll stick with American coffee. You can make your fancy coffee drinks. I'll make malts because I know you don't like that machine," he said, making a not-so-subtle point.

So much for the greatest generation! They had saved us from fascism and launched the nuclear bomb, but they were afraid of an Italian coffeemaker. I wondered how things might have turned out differently if the Italians had strapped a giant espresso machine to the front of their flimsy tanks. The Americans might have run into the sea.

"All right, Buck," I said. "We'll have it your way."

I poured the latte in the sink, the froth sticking to the drain stopper. I returned to my other options and remembered a piece of paper in my pocket. It was a telephone number Lois had given me.

A New Plan

I discovered that the bakery was a key communication point in Hayward. A few weeks earlier, while mulling over my own important decision— sticky bun with plenty of caramel and pecans or fried cinnamon roll with thick white icing—I let it be known that I might be looking for additional help at the dairy during the autumn and winter months. The next time I was sampling a *rustica* loaf, Lois slipped me a note with a name and telephone number. "I highly recommend her," she said.

After Buck left that evening, I dialed the number. Vivian sounded cheery and grateful for the call. I could hear *Wheel of Fortune* in the background and thought it might work. We arranged to meet at the dairy the next day before it opened.

It was a beautiful morning again, somewhere between summer and autumn. The sun had already burned through the dawn chill. Vivian sat outside at the end of the bench in front of the office window. She cupped her hand over her eyes to block out the sun so she could see me walking over to her. She sat on her other hand like a nervous schoolgirl. She wore light white trousers and on her feet simple white sneakers, which she kept close together under the bench.

Although we had not met, she seemed to know who I was. She smiled as she rose from the bench and wiped her palm discreetly before shaking my hand. "You must be Mr. Miller," she blurted with enthusiasm.

I chuckled and said she should call me Jeff.

She returned to the bench as though we would conduct the interview outside.

"Would you like to go inside and have some coffee?" I asked.

"No, I'm fine out here. It's such a beautiful day," she said as though she really meant it. This was fine with me as I saw Buck was already in the dairy. Vivian fiddled with a folded piece of paper, a reference from a previous employer, which I decided I did not need. She told me she was seventy years old. I said I couldn't believe her, and it was true. Her skin was smooth apart from a few lines around the eyes, and she seemed to burst with youthful energy.

Vivian had heard that I was from the city and told me she was born in "Manhattan, New York." When she was thirteen, she worked in a soda fountain in New Jersey. "I scooped a lot of ice cream," she said. When she was sixteen, she came to Hayward. She was vague on the circumstances of her leaving home at such a young age. Her aunt—also Vivian—owned and operated the Ranch Supper Club.

"So, you were named after your aunt?"

"No," she said, as though I had asked the most ridiculous question possible.

"That must have been a wild place back then," I said. I recalled the photograph of her aunt atop a swaybacked horse.

"Oh, it sure was, but my aunt Vivian ran a tight ship."

"I met my Cecil at the Ranch," she said. Cecil had been her second husband. Again, the story as to what had happened with her first husband was somewhat mysterious. I knew I would find out sooner or later, so I didn't pry. Cecil had a carpet-fitting business, and Vivian helped run it for years. "All it left me was a pair of bad knees," she said. Although Cecil had been dead for ten years, Vivian spoke of him as though he had just gone to the store for some milk.

Vivian reminded me of some of my mom's friends—women who had lost their husbands years ago and who formed strong ties with other widows. It may have been their generation or their loss, but they were independent and made the most of what they had—like a bunch of sassy Bea Arthurs. Vivian mentioned she had gone to Rice Lake with Lois for some shopping and lunch, and I thought of how mom and her friends made an adventure out of a trip to Target and some endless shrimp at Red Lobster.

I had to hire Vivian, but I let her continue. She had a pleasant voice and a warm smile and was so happy. She spoke of her cleaning prowess with gusto. She said she had her favorite products, and even some homemade cleaning solutions, but understood if I wanted her to use store-bought products. This seemed a bit risky to me, but I said it would be okay so long as I was not around while she used them.

"Oh, you are wicked, Mr. Miller—I mean, Jeff!" she slapped my arm.

She said she knew everyone in town and liked most of them. "My aunt Vivian taught me that you should be friendly with everyone because you never know . . ."

"She was very wise," I said.

"So Vivian, . . ." I paused for effect, and it worked because she opened her eyes wide and leaned into me. "Can you start tomorrow?"

"Oh, yes!" She jumped to her feet and leaned over to give me a big kiss. "Thank you! You won't be sorry."

"There may be one little problem." I held out my thumb and index finger to demonstrate the size of the issue, but it was only an estimate. I feared it could be a much larger problem.

"What's that?" Vivian continued to smile.

"Do you know Buck?" I asked. The smile on her face vanished, and her hands moved to her hips.

"Yes, I know Buck," she said.

"Well, he's often here. He helps out when we need it, but he can also be a bit ornery." What I did not tell her was that Buck thought he could manage the store with only me to help him.

"Don't you mean he is a stubborn old fool?" she said.

"You could say that, I suppose."

"Look, I can handle Buck," she said. "My aunt Vivian taught me that, too." With that, Vivian said good-bye. She smiled as she walked, if not skipped, down the street toward the bakery.

I stood up from the bench and peeked in the window. There was Buck reading the paper. I took a deep breath and opened the door. Buck looked up and gave me a look, the dead eye, as though I had betrayed him. I attempted a friendly "good morning," but it was to no avail.

"What were you doing with her?" Buck did not beat around the bush.

"Well, . . ." I paused in search of an explanation or at least a plausible story to bide some time. "Well, you remember I said we could use some help when I am not around—especially making that 'bullshit' coffee." I paused, but Buck still looked at me, shooting daggers. "So," I said, "Vivian said she could help out when we needed her." Of course, I meant five days each week.

"Bruce and I never needed any help," Buck said.

I told him I would need to spend more time at McCormick House since the renovations were nearly complete and we would be opening the bed and breakfast in a month or so. It sounded plausible. "Anyway, she seems like a very nice lady. Do you know her?" I asked.

Buck tutted. "Do I know her? Of course I know her. Everyone knows that old lady!" Buck said before he muttered something else under his breath.

"It will be fine," I said, more to reassure myself.

Buck was sore the rest of the day and barely spoke to me.

That Is a Lovely Blouse

By August, Dean and I understood West's potential. We couldn't have been happier with the summer's business. We tried to keep our expectations low for the first year. Nevertheless, the dairy's takings for June, July, and August exceeded our predictions. It was at times a *Rocky Road*, but we had to pinch ourselves: it was *Almost Sinful*. We felt we were well on our way to joining the ranks of America's ice cream greats.

At the same time, we knew the heady days of summer with booming ice cream sales were coming to an end, or more likely a screeching halt. We had to rely on the wholesale milk and ice cream route to carry us through the winter. Bruce assured us this was possible. Over the course of the summer, we had managed to retain existing wholesale customers, who without a written contract could have taken their business to another vendor or food purveyor. It was clear that action was required to shore up support among existing customers and to solicit new ones.

After our brief exposure to the milk route back in April, Dean and I agreed the best thing we could do for the wholesale business was to

ensure we never had to deliver milk again. So far, this plan was working well. The customers loved our driver, Tom, and we paid him hand-
somely and hoped he would never want to take another vacation.

We also agreed we needed a strategy to grow the milk business.
Unfortunately, I was not much of a salesperson. Back in my paper route
days, we boys were offered fabulous prizes, such as portable black-
and-white televisions or brightly colored Panasonic cassette players, for
securing new customers. Pine Street was a tough market. It was an old
neighborhood where death seemed to provide the only turnover. I never
got that cassette player.

When I was a young lawyer in private practice, at cocktail parties I
was expected to entertain and impress clients with my charm and brilliant legal mind. It soon became apparent that I was not convincing at
either entertaining or impressing. I put it down to a fundamental problem I had with the firm billing me at over two hundred dollars an hour.
I thought at such a rate, there should at least be a massage or free lunch.

Dean, however, made a name for himself in the technology boom
selling software to large corporations and had proven to be an accomplished salesman. Every year, as a top performer in the company, he
won incentive trips for us—to the south of France, the Caribbean,
Hawaii, and Bali. I was never exposed to Dean's high-pressure selling
techniques—I was convinced after only a pint of lager at the Queen's
Head.

While we were the only local provider of milk and ice cream, large
food purveyors who delivered truckloads of frozen food to local restaurants sold milk as a loss leader, making it impractical for many
local businesses to buy from small West's Hayward Dairy. There was
one exception, and we knew the key to any growth in West's milk business was to win back the Hayward schools milk contract. The school
milk contract was bread-and-butter business for any milk distributor.
The federal government required schools to provide milk packaged in
eight-ounce containers as part of the school lunch program. It was a

captive market with nearly a thousand students in the Hayward schools with change in their pockets and only one thing to buy—our milk.

West's had supplied the Hayward schools with milk for decades; however, in the summer prior to our purchase, the contract was lost to an upstart business that acquired its milk in, of all places, Iowa. It was unclear how this had happened. Bruce claimed the new outfit sold below its cost in order to get the business; others suggested there were some personality clashes that contributed to the decision. Previously, the school milk contract accounted for nearly forty percent of the dairy's wholesale milk revenues. Bruce always said, "Don't worry; you'll win it back." It was unfathomable that Iowa milk would be sold in Wisconsin. Surely we could secure the contract.

In early August, the Hayward schools sent a request for tender for a new three-year contract. Given the potential to increase our winter business by forty percent over the next three years, the pressure to win the contract was great. I notified the sales representative from our supplier. He was based in Duluth. He had met with us briefly at the time we had acquired the dairy just to make sure we were not thinking of signing up with his competitor. He said it was great news about the Hayward schools, and he would be right down to talk about it.

"You need to get the bid right the first time," he said, suggesting this may have been the problem in the past. "How about lunch?" he asked. It had been a long time since Dean and I were on a business lunch, so we jumped at the opportunity.

We met the representative at the dairy.

"Oh, we got trouble here," Buck joked when he arrived, assuming we were scheming something.

The sales representative drove us to a restaurant on a lake ten miles out of town—a rib shack popular with tourists and one of our supplier's favorite places. He suggested the BBQ feast for the table. The feast was served somewhat oddly on the inside of an aluminum garbage can lid: ribs, chicken, pulled pork, and brisket, as well as fries, beans, and corn on the cob. It was not the lobster sandwich at the Four Seasons or the sushi sampler at Nobu, and we felt as though we were eating from a trough, but it was very tasty and hit the spot.

"Would you guys be up for a game of golf at a local course?" the sales representative asked. Neither of us golfed, so we declined. Most of the meal was reserved for chatter about life in Hayward and what it was like living in Duluth on the shores of Lake Superior. He enjoyed his ribs possibly more than we did. After he polished off the last of them, he soaked up the remaining baked beans with the last French fry, leaving nothing but business.

He pointed his bean-soaked French fry across the table to emphasize this point. "What you got to do in these situations is go in aggressively so they can't turn you down. Once you've got your foot in the door, you have it made," he said.

"But it's a three-year contract," I said. "If we lock in a price now, we could go three years without making anything or very little." In my head, I tried to calculate the profit using the price he was suggesting. The proceeds might be enough to pay the driver but not enough to pay the gas. I looked at Dean. We decided to let it drop for the moment and enjoy the lunch because it might be all we'd get out of the deal.

Our sales representative drove us back to the dairy. He left us with two baseball caps with the company logo. "Now, remember what I told you," he said. He then rushed off, we assumed to play nine holes some-where between Hayward and Duluth.

Dean and I contemplated our next steps. We agreed that we could not be too aggressive but needed to bring something to the table. We heard rumors that the school and the kitchen were not completely happy with the current provider. There had been some delays, and some of the milk had been past its sell-by date.

"We need to meet with the school," Dean declared. I wondered if that was such a good idea. After all, we did not come across as locals or even as people who knew anything about delivering milk.

"It will be fine. I've been in these situations many times," Dean said.

The deadline was approaching. We put together a bid and arranged to meet with the head of the school kitchens and the school business administrator. Their offices were in the intermediate school that housed the third through sixth grades. The school was typical American cinder-block design and about twenty years old. Like the rest of the building, the offices were designed to withstand the destructive knocks and spills of eight-to-eleven-year-old children. In the windowless conference room, the furniture had been borrowed from the classrooms—a worktable more appropriate for art projects and hard chairs that sat low to the ground. The seats were made of the composite material that could withstand earthquakes and radiation. I tried to sit in the most convincing businesslike manner even though my knees rose to my chest. Dean, several inches taller than me, resembled a contortionist.

The business administrator for the schools was a short, bald, Italian man with a big belly and an air of more fascist authority than respect. He lived up to the historical nickname Bruce had given him. The coordinator for the kitchen was young and attractive with a professional manner. It was unlikely she spent much time with her hands in a vat of macaroni and cheese. Although classes had not begun, she had been in the kitchen getting things set up for the first day of school. They both took to the Lilliputian chairs as second nature.

As soon as they entered, Dean began. "I love the office," he said, looking around as though searching for a window or anything that might be remotely lovable.

"Well, thanks," the administrator said. "We do what we can."

I now understood what Dean meant when he described his work as "rolling shit up a hill." He began with an unsolicited description of our move to Hayward, how we loved the town and its friendly people. He then turned to our passion for milk and ice cream and for doing the most with the shop to expand its business, and how we hoped to give back to the community as much as possible. This was all true, but Dean delivered the message with such passion I feared they would suspect we were selling snake oil, not milk.

Apparently, according to Dean, we would be on call at all hours to meet the needs of the school. I looked at him and bit my tongue. He was good, though.

"You know, I have been looking at your blouse," Dean interrupted himself, turning to the head cook. "It is really lovely," he said.

"Oh, thank you." The cook beamed. "You know, you have the best accent. I could listen to you all day," she said.

Oh my God, I thought.

At this point, he could have stopped, but Dean was the type who needed to seal the deal and was looking for insurance, so he turned the conversation to McCormick House.

"Oh, yes, what is going on up there? It looks fantastic since you painted it," the administrator said.

"Well, we wanted to a create a . . ." Dean began to relate his vision for McCormick House. "The best thing about completing the project is that we'll have a big party, and we would like you to come if you can make it." I looked at Dean as though he were speaking in tongues.

"That would be fantastic!" the business administrator said. "My wife would love to see the house."

We spoke some more about the milk deliveries and presented our bid, which would be considered by the whole school board.

"Don't hesitate to call us if you have any questions about the bid and how we put it together," Dean offered, just in case they would have liked to rig the bidding for us.

Outside the school building, I turned to Dean. "Big party? Since when are we having a big party?" Although Dean had mentioned a shindig, we were getting concerned about some of the expenses.

"Well, they surely can't turn us down now if they would like an invitation to the most anticipated opening in Hayward in many years," Dean said. "Anyway, it would be nice to show off the house when it's done."

"You seemed to enjoy that—the hard sell," I said. I knew people in sales got a rush or high when they were in their element. Perhaps Dean missed it.

"It felt good, I must admit. I still got it," he said, quickly adding that he did not miss it for the world.

"It will come in use next year when we try to get West's into the supermarkets," Dean said. He had been working on a design for packaging the ice cream in half-gallon containers so we could expand the wholesale business over the next season. "That will be a great addition to the business."

The following week, a school board member came into the dairy to give us the good news. The school board had accepted our bid and had awarded the new three-year milk contract to West's Hayward Dairy.

"That's fantastic," I said as he shook my hand. "Can you tell me, was our bid much lower than the other guy's?"

The school board member smiled and said, "They didn't bid. West's submitted the only bid."

"Really," I said in the very ambiguous manner I picked up living in Britain, somewhere between a question and a statement and meant to hide my shock and disappointment while conveying only mild surprise to the listener. *You've got to be kidding me,* I thought. After toiling through numbers to come up with a minimal margin to cover costs and overheads, we could have charged much more and still won the bid since we were the only game in town. In my head, I calculated the money we could have made if we had known there would be no competition.

"So, I hear you're having a party at McCormick House when it's done," the school board member said.

"Yes," I said. I hesitated but knew what I had to do. "I'll make sure you get an invitation."

"Oh, my wife would love that."

Musky Capital of the World?

A high-pressure system stalled over Wisconsin, bringing continued sun through the middle of September. Everyone seemed to enjoy the warmth. Tourists who put off their vacations to save money or avoid the crowds were especially pleased with their good fortune. Vivian was engaged in conversation with a couple from Indiana. She regaled them with stories of old Hayward, and because her Cecil himself hailed from Indiana, she inquired, indirectly, if they knew him.

Buck listened to Vivian's story and felt the need to correct her when she misrepresented an important fact or detail. They quarreled over the specific dates and historical bits like a married couple, prompting the customers to ask, "So, how long have you two owned the dairy?" This unthinkable suggestion drew a quick rebuttal from both of them.

"No, this is the owner." Vivian pointed to me. She changed the subject by telling them all about how we had come to own the dairy less than a year ago and how we were refurbishing the old mansion on the hill. They looked at me as though I were some sort of circus freak. "Oh, my, that's nice," the wife said.

"Say, I think the new *Record* may be out," Buck said.

"Why don't I see if it is?" I agreed as a way to get out of the shop.

Second Street was quiet. I chatted with Deanna outside the gallery. An old cocker spaniel looked on—to the extent his sight permitted. I couldn't remember if this was her blind or deaf dog. I told her Dean's birthday was coming up. She advised me she had a new inventory of sock monkey greeting cards. I promised to return after I got the paper.

On Main Street, locals ate lunch on the patio of Angler's. It was Thursday, and they had come for the bar's Mexican specialties. Mary

Beth served drinks to some tourists seated on the patio in front of the bar. While they waited for their food, they closed their eyes and tilted their heads to the sky to bask in the warm sun. Others went about their routine as well. The owner of the pet boutique and bakery washed her store windows. Next door, the manager of the Celtic store played his Irish whistle, which competed with the marching music emitting from the outdoor speakers that lined Main Street. A few aging tourists found themselves passing the day downtown. They moved at a far slower pace than the hordes of summer. They pointed and chuckled at some of the T-shirts on display—a potbellied man with orange suspenders and a green John Deere hat was tempted by a *What happens in the deer shack stays in the deer shack* shirt. "I should get that for Uncle Mitch," he told his wife.

"Oh, for sure, dear. That would be perfect."

Looking back at this moment, I thought, *The poor bastards—they have no idea what is coming their way.* They sipped their margaritas and dipped tortilla chips in chunky salsa. It was the calm before the storm, the quiet before the attack.

Inside the bookstore next to the front door was a bundle of the latest issue of the *Sawyer County Record.* Ann was organizing the porn magazines on the top shelf. She stood on the bottom shelf but still struggled to reach the glossy cellophane treasures at the top.

"They just arrived. Let me open them for you," she said. She grabbed a pair of scissors to cut the twine that bound the papers. I picked up a copy and glanced at the headline. I took a second look. I could not believe it. I left a dollar on the counter. She was too busy eyeing the man checking out one of the unwrapped porn magazines to say anything.

Group Says Spray's World Record Musky Is a Fraud: Asks Hall of Fame to Disqualify 1949 Catch.

The headline's implication was too great to get my head around. For nearly sixty years, Louis Spray's musky catch was the standard by which the king of the freshwater fish was measured. More importantly, due to

the Spray fish, Hayward had staked its claim as the Musky Capital of
the World. The good townspeople had built the world's largest plastic
fish to commemorate this world-record catch, and now the entire basis
for what we know as modern Hayward was being challenged. This was
big news!

As I walked down the street, I scanned the article that covered nearly
three pages of the paper—and it was a broadsheet. I walked past the art
shop without giving a thought to the new sock monkey greeting cards.

To understand the gravity of the story, one must begin with the fact
that it was about the musky. The musky, or muskellunge, is the largest
of the freshwater pike, and the largest fish found in the area's lakes. It
was hard to imagine the lakes were home to a fish that measured over
five feet long and weighed nearly seventy pounds. That's the size of an
awkward adolescent child swimming around the bottom of the lake.

The great musky was also the most elusive of fish. Those who fished
musky preferred to call themselves musky "hunters." They did not
grab a six-pack of beer, rod, and reel and jump in the boat for the day.
They planned their attack to the last detail, taking into account weather
conditions, water temperatures, and the time of day. These men and
women might go days casting their lines without even a bite or sight of
a fish, only for the satisfaction and possible glory of catching the Big
One someday.

So what organization would have the audacity to challenge Hayward's
record musky, and what could be the basis of their claims? According to the article, the Illinois-based World Record Musky Alliance, or
WRMA, had commissioned the ninety-three-page report to authenti-
cate the veracity of the Spray catch, relying on independent experts who
carried out critical photographic and taxidermic analyses of Spray's
fish. The report concluded that the catch was not nearly as heavy as the
claimed sixty-nine pounds eleven ounces and was at least ten inches
shorter than the sixty-three-and-a-half inches Spray claimed.

The WRMA study made these conclusions without a fish to measure or weigh. The Spray musky, which had been mounted and displayed proudly in Louis Spray's tavern in Rice Lake, fifty miles south of Hayward, was destroyed when fire consumed the bar in 1959.

The WRMA relied on Canadian experts in photogeometry—part geometry, part physics. The Canadian experts reviewed photographs of Louis Spray holding the fish when it was caught. Knowing Spray's height, they reconstructed a 3-D model of the fish. In the report, the WRMA said it was the equivalent of using DNA testing to solve criminal cases that had gone cold. However, the photogeometric reconstruction had little to do with DNA testing and more to do with photographs of a young man representing Louis Spray in white sports socks holding a cardboard cutout of a fish. Based on Spray's height and likely angle at which he held the fish, the experts claimed they could accurately measure his catch.

In addition to such cutting-edge science, the WRMA's report relied on circumstantial evidence to conclude that Spray was, basically, a crook and a liar. According to the report, after reeling in the fish, Spray and his fishing buddy stuffed it with ice to increase its weight before taking it to the Stone Lake post office to be weighed. They were accused of either colluding with or duping the local postmaster, who might not have seen cans of beer chilling on a bed of ice inside the belly of the fish. Spray's fishing buddy at the time had previously been caught using such tactics to win a fishing contest.

The report raised a question—and admittedly a reasonable one: how could one man achieve such success in the boat? You see, when Louis Spray caught his "record-breaking" musky in 1949, he was already the world-record holder with a 1939 catch. In fact, this was Louis Spray's third world-record musky! He was either the luckiest fisherman to have lived or, as the WRMA's report suggested, something was very "fishy" indeed.

The report was submitted to the Fresh Water Fishing Hall of Fame and Museum, the Hayward-based self-proclaimed official keeper of freshwater fishing records. The WRMA requested that the Spray record be disqualified or at least moved to the category of "myth." In its place, Cal Johnson's fish, caught in Lac Courte Oreilles, also near Hayward, the same year and which still hung in the Moccasin Bar in Hayward would assume the title of the record catch.

Back at the dairy, I could not wait to ask our expert. I am not sure I had seen him so disarmed. He was, albeit ever so briefly, speechless.

"Buck, what do you think?"

"Well, between you and me"—Buck looked around to see if anyone could hear—"Spray was a bit of a scoundrel."

"He was nasty," Vivian added from behind the counter she was wiping.

"Do you think he stuffed the fish with ice?" I asked.

"No, I don't think he even caught the fish!" Buck said. Buck's theory was that Spray had bought the fish from a Native American who had caught the musky by spearing it. "You see, Spray claimed he shot the fish in order to land it in the boat." Buck was referring to the old and rather brutal tactic of dealing with a reluctant catch. He believed this was just a story to explain the fact there was a hole in the fish caused by the harpoon used to kill it in the first place. Spray collected prize money, if any, and endorsements and hung the mounted catch on the wall of his bar as a magnet to attract customers.

The *Sawyer County Record* interviewed the director of the Fresh Water Fishing Hall of Fame. The director was relatively new to the job and perhaps unhappy about the uncomfortable position in which he found himself. He stated the hall of fame had a process for reviewing such submissions as the WRMA's request to disqualify the Spray record and would not rush to any judgment one way or the other.

The director, however, made a curious statement to the newspaper: "Let me state that the National Fishing Hall of Fame does not view this as us against the WRMA, or Wisconsin against Illinois. We are a national organization." This unsolicited comment told me there was more to this story, that there was some entrenched interstate dispute between the Illinois-based WRMA and Hayward's Fresh Water Fishing Hall of Fame. The *Record*, in its usual attempt to avoid anything controversial, shied away from this story.

I later looked into the WRMA. The group had been around for only a year, and its mission, among other things, was "to library [*sic*] and disseminate scientific muskellunge record data, and continue the search for a legitimate world record muskellunge." I only needed to look at the WRMA's website to understand what drove the director's comments. Notwithstanding the WRMA report's science-based tone—complete with cardboard cutouts—and professional veneer, the WRMA was otherwise very dismissive of Hayward's hall of fame and described it as merely a group of local fisherman trying to preserve the records in Hayward.

Now, they might have a point. The Fresh Water Fishing Hall of Fame was established by a group of local semiprofessional fishermen, and it was more than a gateway to the largest fiberglass musky. The hall of fame also became the self-proclaimed keeper of world-record fishing catches. The government had not tasked them with this role; they had appointed themselves.

What I did not know—I must have missed the coverage in London's *Financial Times*—was that until fifteen years ago, Louis Spray's catch was not even considered the record holder. Until then, the record had been held by a 1959 catch from New York State. However, research carried out by the Fresh Water Fishing Hall of Fame itself had determined the New York catch was a fraud. The hall of fame disqualified the catch, returning the record-holding title to Louis Spray and to Hayward.

So what would this august record-keeping body do in this case when a plausible argument for fraud had been raised regarding the Louis Spray catch and, if Buck's opinion was worth anything, the argument could be true?

"It's all about money!" Bruce shouted from the back of the room. "These Illinois people," he said. "They hope to disqualify the records one at a time. Eventually, one of them will catch a fish that will become the new record and get all the money, endorsements, and whatnot that comes with it."

All this talk of greed and money got Buck worked up. "They should keep the record here! It's always been Spray's record, and it should stay that way," he said.

"But I thought you said he didn't even catch the fish," I said.

"Oh, it doesn't matter. It's still Hayward."

Special Visitors

By the end of September, the combined forces of autumn were building. The oaks, maples, and other hardwoods peaked at brilliant reds and auburns, and the birch forests that covered the hills and valleys were set for an explosion of ochre. Near the cabin a golden leafy carpet lay over the forest floor, and the morning dew released the earthy scent of decay. Spike and Freddie jumped like children through the leaf piles I left at the edge of the lawn.

Buck was in good spirits. He had taken his ex-wife to dinner. Before dinner, they took a drive around some of the lakes to measure the changing colors. "I think the colors are going to be good this year," he said. "The peak color won't be for days yet," he confirmed. He told me a few stretches of highway I must see but also gave me a schedule as to when the best days to go would be.

One afternoon after an ice cream delivery to a resort on Lac Courte Oreilles, I stopped at the edge of a cranberry bog to watch the harvest.

The bog was small compared to a corn or soybean field. The farmer flooded the bog after freeing the ripened berries from their vines with a cultivator. The berries floated to the surface, turning the bog into a vast crimson-to-purple lake. The farmhands used a boom-type material known as the "cranbarrier," similar to that used to contain oil spills in the sea. These men in rubber overalls pulled the cranbarrier across the bog to an area where others guided the berries onto a conveyer belt that was lowered into the bogs to load the berries into waiting trucks for transport to Ocean Spray for juicing.

There was also a healthy crop of local fall-time festivals. These were clever ways to extend the tourist season after the waters cooled and the vast majority of summer visitors returned to the city. The festivals brought out the locals and the leaf spotters in the area for one last bite of cheese curds or fry bread for the season.

Stone Lake, a dot on the map twelve miles south of Hayward, transformed its two village streets into an outdoor mall and amusement arcade for the annual Cranberry Festival. The event typically attracted some thirty thousand visitors. Buses took some people to the nearby bogs to witness the harvest firsthand, but most stayed in Stone Lake, content with a slice of cranberry walnut bread or a bag of berries with the intention of making fresh cranberry sauce for Thanksgiving. Dean and I planned on going to the Apple Festival in Bayfield, a village on the shore of Lake Superior surrounded by apple orchards.

Hayward's Fall Festival wasn't nearly as large as the Cranberry Festival or Apple Festival or even the Musky Festival. It lasted only a day with a few vendors, including a local greenhouse that sold the world's largest potted and colorful mums, large pumpkins, and knobby gourds. It had more of the small-town charm of Hayward's Independence Day celebration.

Of course, we had been to the Fall Festival in Hayward. And just as it will thirty years from now, my mind turned to a year ago where it all started. I had sat on a bench with a Blue Moon ice cream cone. Dean had laughed at my selection. Blue Moon remained a popular choice for West's youthful clientele, and I occasionally snuck a spoonful when no one was looking. Matt and Dave had obligations in the city and couldn't make it for the anniversary.

As new chamber of commerce members, we were asked to supply ice cream for the Fall Festival ice cream social. The ice cream would be served with the entries to the apple-baking contest. In addition, and as a special honor, the chamber advised me they would like Dean or me to sit on the panel of judges at the baking contest. I told Dean they were looking for an international judge. He agreed, but reluctantly.

It was midmorning. The sky was gray. There was a light drizzle. Dean handed me a latte and sat down next to me in a leather chair.

"I was telling Suzi about the B&B. She says she would like to work there someday," Dean said. "Did you know she worked at the Super 8 Motel?"

I laughed. "Here she told me she only dreamed of scooping ice cream."

"Cheers," Dean said and raised his coffee. I followed suit. "Can you believe it has only been a year since we were first here?" I shook my head—it *was* hard to believe.

A chamber of commerce representative was setting up a few folding tables for the ice cream social and collecting entries for the apple-baking contest.

"Why would they need an international judge?" Dean asked. I shrugged.

"That's a nice sweater. Where did you find that?" I asked. Dean wore a light blue shirt with a fine navy V-neck sweater.

"Oh, I found it in a box. I guess I packed all my sweaters when we moved. I thought it would be springlike when we got here. It's nice— feel it." Dean brought my hand over to touch his sleeve—very soft.

"What are you wearing?" Dean pointed to my new red-checked shirt.

"It's flannel," I said. Over the summer I kept to a strict wardrobe of West's T-shirts, but as it got cooler I needed something to put over the T-shirt. "I found it at Wal-Mart. It was only eight dollars—everyone in town wears these." Dean rolled his eyes.

"Jeff, you have a closet full of nice shirts—just roll up the sleeves," Dean scolded. "You don't have to wear an eight-dollar shirt." Although Dean didn't walk around town in a suit, tie or ascot around his neck, he liked to keep to certain standards, and it was often noted at the Ranch that he was a snappy dresser.

"Everyone here wears flannel. Kinda butch, don't you think?"

"It's a gingham blouse," Dean shot back, and we laughed. Dean looked around to see what was expected of him as a judge. "I suppose I should get out there." He caressed the arm of the leather chair as he got up.

Fortunately for Dean, there were no more than a dozen entries in the contest. He moved to a folding chair behind the card table with the other judges. His arms were folded like a petulant child who wanted to go home. Chef Jeff was the organizer of the contest and a judge. The other judge was his buddy, a local fishing guide. A young woman from the chamber of commerce explained to Dean the judging criteria: "Each entry can receive a maximum of six points for taste, three points for originality, and three points for presentation." She pointed to the plastic-wrapped disposable plates on which most entries were submitted, and a lovely frosted apple cake that sat on a raised glass cake stand—clearly an early frontrunner.

"You need to try Sally's entry," the organizer told the fishing guide. "She works for me."

As the noon deadline loomed, a large woman in a yellow and black Hayward Hurricanes sweatshirt trotted to the table with what looked like a basketball covered in pastry or the world's largest apple pie.

"Whoa, that's a big one," Chef Jeff said as he took hold of it.

"I used five pounds of apples in the single pie," she said. She reluctantly handed the pie to the judge as though it were her firstborn wrapped in pastry, and it could have been by the size of it.

"Well, the contest was not to use the most apples, but it does look like a nice pie," the organizer said. The woman shrank and retreated.

People began to gather in front as the judging was about to begin.

"When does the ice cream come out?" I heard a man about Buck's age ask.

"As soon as the judging is completed," the chamber representative dismissively told him.

A large dinner plate with a healthy portion of each entry was placed in front of the judges. Dean looked a bit green at the sight of his plate. While the other judges dove into the entries, Dean focused on the judging cards and nibbled a piece of apple-cinnamon bread.

While the judging took place, I returned to the dairy to organize the ice cream for the social. People sat in the leather chairs and tables, waiting for the free ice cream. Jen had been clear in advising them there would be no free ice cream inside the dairy.

"Will you be serving all of the flavors at the ice cream social?" a woman yelled to me.

"No, just a few," I said.

"How about free coffee?"

"No," I said.

Jen was serving a few people who were unaware that we would be giving it away in a few minutes.

By the time I returned outside with the portable dipping cabinet, four tubs of ice cream, and two scoops, the judging of the apple-baking contest was finishing. The organizer stood by his worker, Sally, and announced, "The winner of this year's Fall Festival apple-baking contest is Sally for her oatmeal and apple bar." The gathering of twenty or so persons showed little interest in the winner. They had come for the free food.

By the look on Dean's face, I sensed he had been overruled. The organizer was still congratulating Sally, his employee, on her victory. "Can you believe this?" Dean said. "The whole thing was rigged from the very beginning!"

The woman who made the five-pound apple pie was headed toward Dean. I moved out of her way to demonstrate scooping technique to some novices from the chamber of commerce. Dean tried to explain that there wasn't anything wrong with her pie, but that all the other entries were very good as well.

A few customers still walked into the dairy, oblivious to the line for free ice cream outside the front door. I could have said something but decided I could use the additional sales.

Suddenly, I looked up from the dipping cabinet and was startled at what I saw. Other customers looked, and some children pointed impolitely. Our attention was drawn to a single family—the man was tall, blond, and about my age. He was with his wife and several children ranging from five years to early teens. By the man's beard and denim trousers with large buttons and black suspenders, and by his wife's dark blue dress falling well below the knee and her white apron, one could tell they were Amish. The boys dressed like their father and the girls with blond curls and simple dresses came from central casting. The older boys anxiously peered past their father to see the ice cream. The father stood in the center of the shop, hesitant in a new place. His wife and daughters stood shyly behind him.

I announced to the shop but was speaking for the benefit of the Amish family that if anyone would like free ice cream, it was being served outside along with the apple desserts. The father smiled and tipped his hat and ushered the family outside.

Most Amish live in Pennsylvania, Ohio, and Indiana, although Wisconsin had the fourth-largest Amish population in the country. They preferred the rich farming country of southern and central Wisconsin. In the 1960s, there had been an Amish settlement in Sawyer County, but it had disappeared as members moved or left the community to join less restrictive Mennonite churches in the area. The Mennonites shared many of the same beliefs as their Anabaptist cousins, the Amish, but they also enjoyed the conveniences of running water, electricity, and vehicular travel.

Most likely, this Amish family lived near Chetek or one of the other communities near Eau Claire, sixty to a hundred miles south of Hayward. I did not see, hear, or smell any horses, so I assumed they had gotten a car ride to Hayward. Like most people, the Amish were not averse to catching a ride.

The other customers watched the family. Some gawked, and a tourist tried to take a photograph, but the children quickly turned their faces to avoid a graven image. Most people, however, kept a respectful distance. Part of it was, while Americans generally knew little of their Amish neighbors, they knew the Amish preferred to be left alone. And part of it was, people didn't question why anyone would be here. It was free ice cream, after all.

Dean showed none of this reserve. He was so thrilled with his new customers, he quickly forgot about the drama of his apple-baking judging debut. He escorted his new friends from the farm to the front of the ice cream line and scooped large portions for each of the children. He chatted with the older boys, who described a game they played on their farm. It sounded as if they were describing baseball, but Dean did not know the difference. The young Amish girls held onto their brothers and giggled as Dean spoke.

"Jeff, they have never met a British person," Dean yelled to me. "Yet they call you lot 'English.'" At home, the Amish often spoke a German dialect and referred to English-speaking Americans as "English."

Dean turned to the mother, who was sampling the five-pound apple pie. "What did you think of that?" he asked and wrinkled his nose.

The woman, who could bake a better pie blindfolded, smiled and said it was very nice.

"I thought it was a bit dry," Dean said. The woman smiled and nodded slightly to agree. As they finished their desserts and thanked us for the ice cream, the family's escort pulled up in a van. They got in and pulled away. The children waved from the back window.

Dean smiled and waved. "I wonder why they came here? I told them to come back next year," Dean said.

"That would be nice," I said. I doubted, however, we would ever see them again.

I looked down at my shirt and its bright red checks. Perhaps it was a mistake—I didn't have to dress to blend in.

So He Was Some Sort of Terrorist?

By early October, the autumn colors were at their peak brilliance. The winds picked up. The forest was showered in yellow and gold and smelled of ancient oaks or a large glass of dry Chablis. The path to the cabin glowed as the sun penetrated the bright yellow canopy of leaves that clung to the branches. At any moment, a single leaf might lose its grip, float to and fro, and brush the leaves and branches with a rustle and slight whistle, until it softly landed on a leafy pillow. This sound, multiplied by millions, created a dull rumble all around the cabin.

It was a busy season for the Chequamegon National Forest. The red and gray squirrels and chipmunks worked all day gathering nuts and pinecones for the winter pantry they created somewhere on the property. The terrace at the back of the house became a collection and transfer point and rattled the dogs to distraction as they ran back and forth with each passing rodent. The sky resembled the approach to Heathrow, with flocks of birds lined up one after another on their route south for winter. The bears became more active as they bulked up for their winter slumber. Deer carried on as usual, but one wondered if they knew what was coming their way.

I knew what I had to do. I looked out the door over the lawn covered in leaves ten inches deep. If I did not rake and collect the mounds now, rain would turn the delicate piles into heavy masses of pulp. This would create more work to move later in the autumn or a muddy mess if left until spring. Raking and gathering leaves was one of my least favorite chores. When I was young, I convinced my mother to allow me to wait until the last of the leaves had fallen so I would not have to repeat the task in a week's time. "Oh, that will be fine, dear. But you don't want to be raking in the cold," she would say. In the end, I raked the frosty leaves in early November in gloves and under a stocking hat.

Of course, this was not like the backyard in town, where you gathered the leaves from a few trees to provide mulch for your borders. Here, surrounded by hundreds of trees, the leaves kept falling. I waited until the sun shone through the branches with only a few oak leaves clinging to otherwise bare limbs. The lawn was swollen with mounds of leaves spun by an autumn breeze. I started to rake and bag them, first in one direction and then another. I formed a few piles of leaves that would be easier to bag. Before long, a callus had formed between my thumb and index finger even though I had barely made a dent in the leaves. I realized there would be hundreds of bags.

This can't be right, I thought. *There must be an easier way.* I threw down my rake and went inside to look for a bandage to protect the tender break in my skin. The dogs greeted me with abandon as though they were updating me on the squirrel and chipmunk activities. I covered my other hand and palms with bandages as a preventive measure.

I returned to my chores but noticed our old neighbor from down the shore marching through his lawn with what appeared to be a jet pack on his back. Attached to the jet pack was a long tube that blew the leaves neatly in the desired direction. He blew the leaves into a wooded grove at the edge of his property where it didn't matter if they rotted. I threw down the rake—again. I needed to get myself a jet pack.

By mid-October, God's builders were putting the final touches on the new B&B. With its new light gray exterior with white trim, McCormick House shone in the bright autumn sun above Shue's Pond and once again took its position as Hayward's first home. Inside, the painters— between donut, cigarette, lunch, and soda breaks—removed the last of the dark, Victorian color scheme from the bedrooms and began varnishing the new mahogany doors. Dean would have preferred to have the doors French polished, but he could not find anyone in the north woods familiar with the technique of waxing the stained wood. In the end, he was happy the varnish was not too glossy and gave the appearance he desired.

The morning frost disappeared except where it was protected by the shadow of the house. The local sandblaster was back and stretched the power cord for his air compressor from the house and across the lawn. We had first met him in June when he came to sandblast the cast-iron radiators that were removed from the house. Then the radiators sat outside in the summer sun and rain and turned a brilliant rusty orange that required his attention once again. The workers, still feeling the groin pain from moving the cast-iron radiators out of the house in the spring, looked at the beasts sitting in weeds and tall grass and wondered if there might be an easier way to haul them into the house and upstairs.

An old-timer was called in from the co-op's heating supply store. He was the only man in town familiar with the radiator system found at McCormick House and was recruited to refit the home's iron horses. Carrying a sizable paunch, he stood in the shade on the front porch with his hands tucked into the bib of his overalls. He shook his head at the disarray of rusting radiators in the bushes and went inside. We assumed he would relish the task of working on the old system, but if he did, he did not show it. I heard him ask the foreman if there was any coffee around—the sign of a craftsman.

Before noon, the men had hauled most of the radiators into the ground floor and were working on the second floor. After the radiators were placed in position, our expert got to work reconnecting them to the water pipes that extended through holes in the new wood floor. He made some connections and began to tinker with the valves. Once they were all in place, he fired up the system—two new natural gas boilers that replaced a dirty oil-burning furnace. As the water started to pump through the system, bangs and knocks emanated from the floors and walls, and the radiators rang throughout the house. Our expert moved from room to room, bleeding air from each radiator by adjusting the valves until the banging ceased.

In some cases, the radiators leaked and dripped on the new and still untreated wood floor, much to the consternation of Don, our master floor finisher, who showed up on a tip that the radiators were being installed. The new oak floors were protected by cardboard and plastic, but Don admonished the workmen to set the radiators down gently to avoid marking the wood. Don then followed our furnace man around with a rag to wipe up any water that dripped as he tightened the radiator valves.

Don was known throughout the area for his polished wood floors. He was short and thin with tiny spectacles. A liberal, he enjoyed discussions of war and politics and upsetting the Republican majority in the area. He was also an unofficial restaurant critic. Knowing that we ate most of our meals in restaurants, he shared his thoughts on some of the new and established places.

For the most part, Don's conversation returned to floors—how to appreciate them and how to care for them. His work was in demand by the second-home owners who required oak, walnut, and birch flooring in their large, newly built log cabins. "They spend thousands of dollars on a beautiful floor and then clean it with harsh chemicals. Do they not appreciate my work?" he asked. It sounded like a warning.

Don did not lay the floor—that was for the hired laborers employed by the general contractor—but he oversaw the selection of the floor type, advised on the best source of wood, and supervised the methods used. When he came around to the house to check on progress, he picked through the unused flooring pieces in order to match the grain of the piece that was fitted next to it. Don returned at nearly the last stage of the project to apply the appropriate finish and to buff and polish the floor. This was a three-day process during which no one apart from Don was allowed in the house. For him, this was the final act of the renovation, and it was a solo one.

As the day progressed, Don was engaged in a heated discussion with our furnace man about the governor of Wisconsin. In response, it seemed the furnace expert allowed more and more water to leak from the system. Don ran for more rags. The furnace man smirked.

With completion of the project imminent, we turned to planning the party to celebrate the opening of McCormick House. We chose the fifth of November for the occasion.

"Great. We'll do a Guy Fawkes theme," Dean said. "How about fireworks?"

I liked the idea of fireworks but was not sure about the Guy Fawkes theme. While Americans were aware of many British traditions, such as the Royal Family, they were confused by others, such as Boxing Day and spotted dick. But I was pretty certain that no one in Hayward had heard of Guy Fawkes or his foiled attempt in 1605 to blow up the Houses of Parliament by placing thirty-six kegs of old gunpowder in the cellar of the Parliament building. I doubted many would understand why this treacherous event was acknowledged each year with bonfires and fireworks. Dean said he would include a little history lesson in the invitation.

We invited everyone who worked on the house and their spouses or significant others, including the contractor, his crew, the electricians, the plumbers, and even the painters. We knew the painters would be there because they had been asking about a party since they started work. We invited the radiator guy and Don as well as the few friends we had made in town and, of course, the school cook, business administrator, and certain members of the school board.

Dean arranged to meet with the local pyrotechnic, who ran a fireworks store on the LCO Reservation. Her name was Chantal, and we were warned. Dean asked Chantal around to the house to get her ideas as to where it would be safe to set off the fireworks and generally what kind of show we could have in Hayward. Chantal was excited by the job.

It was a mild afternoon in late October. Guys were still working on the new terrace at the back of the house and a new external staircase leading up to the second floor. Don had sealed off his domain on the ground floor for his final act. Painters and electricians used a ladder to climb into a window on the second floor. Another group of carpenters had begun to erect the cedar fence around the back of the property.

Chantal arrived, very blond and tanned. Her bright blue eye shadow matched her sweater with a plunging neckline. She was local and knew most of the crew. "How you all doin', boys?" she asked.

"Hey, Chantal," many replied in unison.

"Scotty, I haven't seen you around in a while." She winked at one of the younger members of the crew.

"You know—wife and kids keep me busy," he said. Chantal rubbed his shoulder as if to make it better. At that point, Dean appeared and pulled her away.

I was busy with the landscapers when I saw Dean lead Chantal to the front of the house. He pointed toward Shue's Pond as the direction toward which he wanted to see the fireworks. Chantal followed Dean and stood behind him as he pointed to the tree line across the pond.

She pointed with her right hand in the same direction but placed her left hand on Dean's behind. Dean must have thought it was a bee or dragonfly because he jumped forward, let out a big screech, and then laughed when he realized what had happened. Chantal, showing no signs of embarrassment, laughed as well.

As Chantal finished and was saying her good-byes to the crew, Dean tried to pin down the issue of insurance and liability in these types of cases.

"Oh, honey, don't worry," she said with a flourish of her hand. "I have two million in coverage for the both of us. If a kid gets his eye blown out, we'll get him a new one!"

"Great," Dean said. "I guess we're covered."

"Listen, I'll get over here at about 7:00. We'll have a couple beers, and then I'll start the show," Chantal said before she left through a hole in the fence.

"It's going to be quite a show," Dean said, turning to me.

It was less than a week before the party by the time Don finished the floor and was satisfied that the finish had cured to withstand the furniture and foot traffic. The carpet fitter, a silent young man in a large black cowboy hat, came to lay a new neutral carpet in the guest rooms and upstairs hallway. In order to save some money and because guests would not be allowed in the kitchen, we purchased prefabricated cabinets that arrived in large boxes. A group of builders unfamiliar with the prefab side of the business argued over the directions and placement. The electrician hung new chandeliers in the living room and tested the low-voltage spotlights in the hallway and in the ceiling of the veranda at the front of the house.

As the painters completed a final coat of varnish on the mahogany doors and the carpenter fitted the chrome handles and locks, McCormick House was nearly complete. The rooms looked larger than before, the trim painted white to frame the polished dark wood of the doors. The walls were a cool "Shaded White" and the floors golden like spilled honey. There was the strong scent of varnish, paint, and carpet.

It was the moment Dean had been waiting for. He had measured every piece of furniture, light fixture, and picture frame. He called the movers to arrange delivery of the beds and new furniture we had purchased for McCormick House. I phoned Kenny and bribed him with an invitation to the grand opening if he helped move our furniture that was stored in the basement. Most of the carpets and furnishings had been measured and bought for the house. I looked at them for the first time. I could be sitting in a room at the National Gallery, except Dean hadn't put anything on the walls.

I hadn't been looking forward to the move into town. As the time neared, I wasn't sure I liked the idea of taking care of strangers. I suggested we should try to spend as much time at the cabin as we could—at least when we didn't have guests—making that our primary home. The morning of the party I had to pick up some things for the gathering. Dean was still unpacking items for the house. He said he didn't need my help. In fact, he asked me to stay away while he hung paintings and set out further accessories for the rooms.

When I returned through the kitchen at the back of the house, Dean yelled, "Just wait a second." He moved from room to room, perhaps plumping cushions. "Okay," he called, and I walked through. Dean stood in front of a large mirror in the dining room next to the long antique mahogany table. He beamed with pride as he presented the dining room. Above the buffet hung an oil painting of an unknown nineteenth-century gentleman bought in the Cotswolds. I liked it for the shimmering effect of the gold shirt studs. "People will think it's Robert McCormick," I said.

"I suppose it could be," Dean said, always looking for an angle. "I might have to tell guests that until we can find a picture of him."

As I looked around, though, I saw this wasn't just a business venture or the home of a long-gone lumber baron. There were things I hadn't seen since January, when we packed our home in London for moving, and others that for lack of space had been in a storage facility for years.

In each room, Dean had placed one, two, or even more pieces that reminded us of the dozen years we had spent together. They were lovely objects, paintings, sculptures, and vases. For us, however, they were like a collection of snow globes—souvenirs, each had story. These were the good times, when we weren't in the office or on a business trip—days spent rummaging in antique warehouses, Sunday afternoons biting our nails at auctions. They brought back small adventures—weekends in Paris—or larger ones—a two-year stint in Hong Kong. Each painting, sculpture, or antique cabinet called to mind a story, even if only how we managed to fit a large piece of furniture in the back of a London taxi—*'fraid that's not gonna make it, guv'nor.*

In the living room, Dean hung the eighteenth-century prints of garden schemes—searched for up and down Portobello Market one Christmas. On the upstairs landing were two large blue and white ginger jars—the largest overhead bags Singapore Airlines had ever seen. There was a lacquer cabinet we bought in Macao in September 2001—a very long night spent glued to the television in a Hong Kong hotel. In the library, a sad Victorian desk from a stone cottage in Longborough sat nicely in the window overlooking Shue's Pond. The desk was of no significant value, but with a new leather top and brass hardware, it would be fitting for Robert McCormick himself.

The caterer arrived with her husband to put up a tent at the side of the house where the food would be served. Even though it was November and we expected a cool night, we hoped guests would eat in the tent before returning to the house, thereby avoiding any spills or stains on the new carpets and furniture.

By 6:00 PM, McCormick House was filled with most everyone we had invited. People began to mill about the house. Everyone looked as though they were going to a wedding. Men in pressed shirts with ties and jackets, women in dresses. Even Buck put on a clean dress shirt, took off his dairy cap, and ran some spit over the few hairs on his head. I got a whiff of Aqua Velva aftershave as he walked by me upon hearing the food was in the garden.

An advantage of inviting the people who helped restore the house was that there was no need to provide a tour. Each worker proudly showed his wife or girlfriend around, pointing out details of the restoration he had carried out. The electrician gestured to the lights and described for his wife the work required to install the dimmers. He played with the switch, providing an impromptu light show. One of the painters noted the fine differences in the shades of beige that could be found in the house. "I know. I couldn't really tell the difference, either," she added.

Don nervously looked on as people walked on his floors with damp shoes. At one point, I saw him in what appeared to be lecturing mode, talking to Dean about caring for the new floors.

I found my sister, sister-in-law, and four of my nieces huddled in the library. They had previewed the house while the work was being done, but my sister was describing some of the furnishings she had seen when she visited us in London with my mother.

"Looks like you already know everyone in town," my sister-in-law said.

"I've never seen these people before," I joked. I kidded them about their husbands, who had turned down this invitation to go on a hunting trip.

"Jeff, do you know what today is?" my niece Angela asked.

"Of course," I said. It would have been her grandmother's, my mother's, seventy-eighth birthday.

"If she ever asks, tell her this party was for her," I said.

The evening was cool with a mild drizzle. Dean began to fear rain might spoil the fireworks. Chantal, on her second beer, was not bothered.

"Don't worry—those suckers fly even in the rain," she said.

"Hi, Buck!" I greeted our old friend as he bounced against the hallway wall after walking inside from the yard. "What do you think of the house?"

In one hand he held a flimsy paper plate piled high with Swedish meatballs covered with an extra helping of barbeque sauce and in the other a glass of soda. He put the cup on the polished buffet in order to pick up another toothpick of meatball.

"Well, I must say," he said, holding up a hand covered in barbeque sauce, "it's quite the place you got here, Jeff. Real good job—and nice grub, too." He wiped his hand on his trousers.

"Well, there's plenty more food outside," I said, with the emphasis on *outside*.

Chantal took her position on the sidewalk at the front of the house. We encouraged people to move to the front lawn or the front porch. Due to the drizzle, most remained on the porch since it was not as muddy as the scattered lawn. About ten women managed to squeeze themselves onto a new teak daybed. Others crowded around them. I saw the contractor looking at the crowds gathering on the porch. I could tell he was thinking the same thing I was.

"Do you think the porch will hold everyone?" I asked.

"Oh, for sure. I don't think there'll be a problem," he said. "We can always fix it if it does come crashing down," he joked.

With no introduction, Chantal set off the first batch of fireworks. She wore black to hide herself as she ran between the fireworks she had arranged behind a wooden barrier on the street below. However, she left uncovered her long blond hair, perhaps intentionally since it took on the hue of the ever-changing fireworks—bright yellow, then blue, then pink.

The display was loud and impressive as mortars shot well above the trees of Shue's Pond. People watched from their cars that lined the streets. The smell of gunpowder drifted up to the house, and smoke filled the street below.

"It's better than Hayward's Fourth of July fireworks," one woman said as she smoked a cigarette on the daybed.

Dean was speaking to another woman on the front lawn.

"Now, tell me again. This Guy Fawkes was some sort of terrorist in England who blew up Congress?" she asked.

Wishing to avoid the ins and outs of the persecution of the Catholic Church in old England, Dean said, "Yeah, it was something like that."

As the finale neared, Chantal ran frantically between the remaining blasts. With beer bottle in one hand and lighter in another, she lit the fireworks and darted behind the protective barrier, her hair the color of a malfunctioning traffic light.

The police arrived after some complaints of noise, but the show was nearly over, so they stood by to watch. With the final starburst, the crowd on the porch broke into applause. Chantal grabbed a bottle of beer and looked up to her audience.

"Way to go, Chantal!" someone yelled. Others hooted and hollered. There was applause all around. Chantal took a deep bow and waved her beer bottle and lighter above her head.

The Hangover

The party was a huge success. We thought people would leave after the fireworks, but they stayed until the last Swedish meatball was eaten, the last bottle of wine drunk. We figured that if each of the hundred people who attended the party told five people about the place, and each one of those persons told just two more about the changes at the house on the hill, even those in town who had not heard of Dean or Jeff would know us now. And we did it in less than nine months!

While the fireworks were a crowd pleaser and the food was plentiful, McCormick House was the biggest hit of the evening. Her old bones stood proud and showcased well the talents of the local craftsmen and our old furniture. The inexpensive paintings from auction houses on Lots Road looked as though they had been there for years.

But with every party, there are a few hangovers. Although neither Dean nor I drank very much, our hangover knocked at the door the following morning.

"Hi, guys," our contractor said. He carried a large envelope. "Gee, thanks for the party," he said. "The guys all appreciated it."

"It was our pleasure," Dean said.

"Well, I got some bad news, as they say." The contractor chuckled nervously. He moved quickly into a justification that was clearly designed to set us up for the final blow.

"We really did a lot of work last month getting the house ready. Also, the invoices from the subcontractors started to come in. So, what I am trying to say"—he stumbled, but we knew what was coming—"is that this month's bill is a bit of a doozy."

Dean took the envelope and pulled out the summary. Since work on the house had started in June, the contractor presented a bill at the beginning of each month setting out the work done the previous month; materials purchased; hours for the contractor, foreman, and crew; and any other expenses. Over time, the statements grew, but we had hoped we had seen the worst the previous month. That was not the case. The bill for October was thirty percent greater than September's.

Without saying anything, Dean passed me the page. When I looked at the figure, a lump the size of a tennis ball formed in the back of my throat and dropped to my stomach with a thump. *How? How was it so expensive?* We had now spent more than twice the original estimate, and the renovations amounted to much more than what we paid for the property. In addition, the fence was not yet finished, and we had already postponed landscaping the grounds until spring in order to stave off the expense.

Of course, I knew how it had happened. No expense was spared. We used the finest materials, and the quality of work was superb. I understood why the contractor had waited until after the party to present the bill.

As we sat in shock, the contractor left. My next thought, naturally, was to wonder how we were going to pay for this. We had burned through most of our reserve fund set aside for the renovations. In addition, the revenues from the dairy's summer, which, as Bruce had warned, would be needed to get through the winter, had been spent on draperies, flat-screen televisions, DVD players, and oak finials. The dairy was now bringing in less than a hundred dollars a day. We had one booking at the B&B, and that was not until Christmas!

We had only ourselves to blame. We wanted the best, and McCormick House looked fantastic. The local supplier did not sell twenty-five-watt low-voltage lights, so we ordered them from California. The replica of the original front door—"You want it in mahogany, we can get one made in Canada." The chrome door furniture and skeleton keys came from Fulham Road in Chelsea, and most of the lighting was imported from Chelsea Harbour in London. In the past, we did the same—went over budget on projects—but it wasn't a problem as another bonus was just around the corner. Now there were no more cash bonuses.

Behind the contractor came the others to thank us for a great party and then dump their final invoices. As we laid them on the table and began to calculate the numbers, even the relatively small bills added up. The total sent a chill down my spine. "Perhaps it's time to see the bank manager," Dean suggested.

"It's a good thing we invited him to the party," I said.

"Sure. We'll ask him if he enjoyed the champagne and then hit him with our request."

Ha

By mid-November, autumn was like the pleasant colleague who had been transferred to another office after only a short period. You really wanted to get to know him, but he was already gone. Temperatures plummeted overnight to below twenty degrees, and we woke to a fresh coating of snow. Ice formed along the shoreline of Teal Lake. Within a month, the lake would return to its annual glacial state. The loons looked frantic as they squawked and called. They were some of the last of the migratory birds to leave for the winter, perhaps looking for a cheap flight.

On their morning walk, the dogs gingerly stepped on the ice-coated puddles in the driveway. The doe that had fed in our lawn all summer returned for the last bites of clover. Dean bought an ax with a view to splitting some wood that lay on the ground in the forest around the cabin. After twenty minutes of heaving at the rotting logs, he cracked open the telephone book and ordered a few yards of precut logs from a local expert.

We looked forward to returning to the cabin on quiet days during the winter to rest and sit by the fire. Although we had no guests at McCormick House, we began to move our personal belongings into town and to sleep at the house. The dogs seemed excited with the move. The large bay windows were the perfect height for terriers to ward off the dangerous Toyota that might be driving past on Fourth Street.

At the dairy, Buck watched the traffic heading toward the school on Dakota Avenue. Vivian filled a coffee mug from the air pot.

"Morning, sweetheart," she said. "I was just pouring us some coffee. Would you like me to make you a latte?"

"That's okay. I'll get it," I said and opened a small under-counter refrigerator for the milk. Vivian took a mug to Buck, who was sitting in a leather chair looking down the street. Vivian sat at the counter and picked up the *Sawyer County Record*.

The place was spotless. Vivian had spent much of her first two months scraping every bit of dried ice cream off the floors, walls, doors, and possibly the ceiling. She ran a tight ship—just like her aunt Vivian. And, most impressive of all, she seemed to have tamed Buck, either through homemade baked goods or gentle persuasion. From all appearances he had gone from feral tomcat to lovable tabby. Possibly it was all for show, and when I wasn't around they fought like crazy, but they appeared to be the image of the happy dairy family.

Business had been slow since the weather turned cooler in October. At times, the daily takings just covered what I paid Vivian and Buck. Dean and I had talked about closing the shop a few days each week or for a month or two in the winter. I really didn't want to do that. I knew Vivian could use the paycheck, and where would Buck go?

I joined Buck in the leather chairs. I looked down the street. Past Pastika's Bait Shop and the Norske Nook, I could see one of Hayward's three water towers. One was near the school and covered in high school graffiti referring to rival Spooner's collective manhood. Another was seen from the back of McCormick House and read, *Hayward: Home of World Record Muskies.* The water tower in back of the Norske Nook was an early model resembling a coffee pot with a lid on it. HAYWARD was spelled out in large capital letters stretching around the entire tower so that you could see only a few letters from any given direction. From where I sat at my ice cream shop, I saw only HA. *How appropriate,* I thought, as though the landmark were laughing at me.

A year ago, I had been sitting comfortably in my seventeenth-floor office with a pension and savings that ensured a comfortable retirement and a nice collection of shoes. As time elapsed, it was easy to forget about the stress associated with my corporate life. It was easy to forget about the simmering office politics that threatened to boil at anytime. *But was this the answer?*

Since the McCormick House grand opening and our realization of the dire financial straits we found ourselves in, I had been preoccupied with money concerns. We put together some figures showing the dairy revenues from the summer as well as projected earnings from the B&B. We scheduled a meeting with the bank the following week. The bank would likely lend us the money we required to pay the remaining debts. We had no mortgage on the property, but what would be our interest rate and term? How was this going to hamper our ongoing cash flow? I thought about what my friend in Dubai told me, "Whatever you do . . ." I thought about Dean, and my role in bringing us to Hayward. *Oh, what have I done?*

Perhaps there was another explanation. As I looked at the joking water tower, I thought of my father. I didn't know the man, but I knew he wasn't the type to stay in one place. Before I was born, he had moved his family no fewer than three times—from one farm to another. There was a period when my parents owned a tavern in Mankato. *What was he looking for?* My mother was very different—cautious. After my father died, she stayed put in the same town for over thirty-five years. Perhaps I was genetically predetermined to take risks. My other brother had, moving his young family to southern California thirty years ago. He started his own company, did well.

"What's wrong?" Buck asked. "You seem bothered about something."

"I don't know Buck." I sighed. "Business seems very slow these days."

"Aww, you can't worry about that. It's always quiet right now. In a week, the deer hunters will be in town. That will help business."

"But it's a long winter," I pleaded.

"Look, between you and me," Buck said, "Walter West supported a wife and five kids on this business for years. I'm sure you and Dean can support a few little dogs. You'll do fine."

Even though he was not aware of the financial straits brought on by the renovations at the house, I appreciated the old guy's support.

We sat for a while. There was little traffic on the street, and a sleety mix of rain and snow began to blow.

"Well, actually, I don't think *this* will be good for business, Jeff," Buck said.

"Thanks for reminding me." I laughed.

Little Bob arrived. Buck and Bob got themselves in position for *The Price Is Right*. Vivian got up to make room for Bob at the counter.

"Don't mind me. I got work to do," she said. "Would you like a coffee, Bob?"

"Oh, yes. That'd be swell," Bob said as he climbed onto the stool.

"What are you going to do if something happens to Bob Barker?" I asked. The host of *The Price Is Right* had been on since this version of the show's beginning in the 1970s. He had been preserved in some sort of Hollywood game show brine and looked fantastic. Buck and Bob both looked at me as though I were crazy.

"Well, I think he's only about eighty," Bob said with a straight face.

I realized my *faux pas* and let it drop.

"So Bob, you going hunting this year?" Buck asked.

"Oh, sure. I'll probably go out around the house," Bob said.

Everyone in town was gearing up for the opening of deer-hunting season. Most men and many women kept a calendar, counting down the days until the season opener, like children before Christmas. For the past week, hunters in pickups arrived in town sporting their fluorescent outfits—the fashion conscious wore the entire blaze-orange catsuit. They came from all over the region to take advantage of the larger deer population in the north woods. Local bars and businesses put up signs welcoming them. At Wal-Mart, the cashier's aisles, usually laced with sweets and chocolates, Hollywood gossip, and other impulse buys, were now lined with hunting magazines and beef jerky.

"Jeff, he's going to go hunting with his walker," Buck said, making fun of his friend.

"Well, I don't want to fall down," Bob said.

"So, if you shoot a deer, how will you get it out of the woods?" I asked. I was now very curious as to the sight of the old man in the woods with a gun and a walker.

I shouldn't have laughed at Little Bob. Surely he was a much better shot than I ever was. My older brothers were avid sportsmen and attempted in vain to convince their younger brother of the same. When I was about ten years old I was signed up for a gun safety course required for all underage hunters.

Mr. Frogman taught gun safety in addition to driver's education. He was also my junior high gym instructor. For years, I was convinced the man was sent to this earth to destroy any budding self-esteem I may have had. I aced the firearm safety written exam, as I would the written driver's test, but when we got to the shooting range, it was a different story. We all took turns—boys and girls—with our .410 shotguns, appropriate for shooting rabbits and other small game. Whenever it was my turn, Mr. Frogman called out: "Everyone stand back, Miller's up again." I never heard what happened to Frogman, but imagined the headline—*Bizarre Gun Range Accident Claims Instructor's Life.*

"Well, I got it all planned," Bob began. "I bought some rope, and I'll tie it to the walker. I should be able to pull it out that way."

"Well, good luck with that." I said. I tried not to laugh. I looked over at Vivian, who was giggling. I decided I had to find some way to keep the shop open all winter. I would miss this too much.

Without Garnish . . .

I lived overseas for twelve years, yet one of my favorite holidays was Thanksgiving. Most British are vaguely familiar with Thanksgiving—

certainly more so than Americans with Guy Fawkes. They know it as a quaint American custom at which a Christmas-like dinner is served in November. Fewer know of the connection between Thanksgiving and a group of English religious fanatics who were chased out of Britain nearly four hundred years ago.

Because of the large American population in London, it was generally considered tacky to engage in mutual recognition of your fellow countrymen. Even at the bank, one never entered into sentimental conversations about the old country with colleagues. Since Europeans had adopted softer toilet tissue, power showers, and dry cleaners that washed and pressed shirts in days rather than weeks, there was little reason for Americans to seek each other out to commiserate about the squalid conditions of Chelsea and Kensington. Many Americans who had lived in London for years began to blend in. The women shopped at Harvey Nichols instead of Harrods; the men wore brightly colored corduroy trousers, spoke in odd mid-Atlantic accents, and drank at lunchtime. They skied at Courchevel and named their daughters India and their sons Luc.

Americans who had not been in London long might shell out the punitive airfare to fly home for Thanksgiving, but the rest of us knew London as a great place for Thanksgiving. Not only did many hotels and nicer restaurants offer a Thanksgiving special, but the supermarkets also stocked up on turkeys, cranberries, and yams. Around Thanksgiving time, whether you were picking up your turkey from the butcher at Sainsbury's, marveling at the selection of sweet potatoes, or placing your order for pumpkin and pecan pies from the Pie Man on Chelsea Green, there was a quiet acknowledgment of a fellow member of your tribe, and it was acceptable to make a friendly inquiry about his or her Thanksgiving plans.

During my first year in London, Dean, whom I had just met, made Thanksgiving dinner for me. It became a tradition, and by our last year, it had become a hot ticket. There was a lavish buffet with roast turkey, sweet potatoes, cornbread, and endless champagne. We invited between thirty and fifty people—mostly English.

It would be difficult to replicate those dinners in America, even with a lovely and large home. Most people with any social graces would have an invitation with family or friends. And who in their right mind would put their Thanksgiving at risk with an English cook who might be tempted to put "bubble and squeak" on the menu?

There were uncanny parallels between the plight of the Pilgrims and our own story. Of course, it may be a stretch to compare our corporate ennui with religious persecution, even if, at times, life at the bank felt like persecution. And the Boeing 777 that brought us to America, while cramped, was far quicker than and lacked the pestilence of the *May-flower*. But we did come from England, Buck thought we at least looked like men of God, and I had always been partial to a buckled shoe.

Like the first Pilgrims, we were poorly equipped and perhaps not as self-reliant as we thought. We found a group of locals who did not chase us away with pitchforks but welcomed us to their community and helped us stave off starvation. Bruce taught us how to grow ice cream. Buck taught us how to place the ice cream in cornucopia-shaped waffles and creamy blended drinks, and Vivian, with a cheerful and motherly manner, sold the ice cream cornucopias to those passing through town. Christian brothers and sisters rebuilt a humble dwelling—or a seven-bedroom mansion with heated marble floors in the bathrooms—to protect us from the pending winter. We were thankful for Cheryl and her cocktail bar and for our bank manager, who had approved our new loan, allowing us to survive another year.

A traditional feast with our new neighbors would have been appropriate, but they had plans, and we wanted to get out of town. With the opening of deer hunting, Hayward was under siege. Shots could be heard from all sides, as though the deer themselves had taken up arms to attack. Hunters raced from one end of town to another in search of more jerky snacks or the mysterious lap-dancing bar in the woods.

Dean, for whom hunting meant men and women in fancy dress on horseback, was especially appalled by how hunters exposed their slain trophies on the back of their open pickups or tied to the roof, rear, or front of their vehicles. The story of Thanksgiving would have been very different if the Pilgrims had to dodge the bullets of Wisconsin deer hunters.

We accepted an invitation from a friend in Minneapolis for a traditional gay Thanksgiving. We knew it would be delicious and fashionable, and there would be plenty to drink. There would be a tasteful, gilt-framed mirror surrounded by large bouquets of seasonal flowers and tiki torches on the front walk. As we left town, we took a route avoiding any area where Little Bob with his walker and loaded weapon might be found.

Our friend Larry was a consummate entertainer with a large coterie of friends who looked forward to his parties. Larry's guests were primarily middle-aged men. Together, we wore Banana Republic's entire fall line of cashmere sweaters. We drank a fine California wine in oversized goblets. Many of the guests were couples who had been together for up to twenty years in various stages of bliss. A forty-five-year-old man brought a young man he had met a few weeks ago. The younger guest was buff and wore a tight T-shirt, and everyone wanted to sit by him. Another brought his daughter, the product of a youthful indiscretion, and her attractive fiancé, who stood nervously like a deer in the Wisconsin woods. One man brought his mother, who adored her son nearly as much as they both adored their Merlot.

In stark contrast to many other American Thanksgivings, there was no football on the television and no discussion of Minnesota Vikings or Green Bay Packers. Everyone stood in or near the kitchen. A younger professional couple—a happy family in search of a womb—described their attempts to adopt. They were thinking of meeting a pregnant woman in Tennessee who had three children already and a boyfriend who had just been sentenced to eighteen years in federal prison. Those

of us with a basic understanding of the federal sentencing guidelines—
he was a bad man—stayed clear of the discussion.

At Larry's Thanksgiving, the focus was not on the size of the bird—
there was a turkey on a grill and another in the oven—but the size of
the centerpiece. He had made by hand a large chocolate cornucopia—
including dark, milk, and white chocolate fruits and nuts—covered in
gold leaf and sprigs of orchids.

Larry and others began to fill the table with bowls of Brussels
sprouts, sweet potatoes, mounds of mashed potatoes, homemade cranberry chutney, and a large turkey—golden brown. Gareth brought his
famous twist on the green bean casserole. There was a lime Jell-O mold
with carrots, an ironic tribute to the midwestern roots of most of the
guests. Larry invited the father among the group to carve the turkey.

We raised our glasses, for we were all thankful for something, even
if only a fine meal and a fine wine. Larry welcomed Dean and me to his
annual celebration. For us, the year had progressed at such a pace that
we rarely had had time to sit and think about the enormity of the
changes we had made. But as we raised our glasses, we were thankful
for our new home on the edge of the wilderness.

Dean turned to me and whispered, "And here's to our bank manager."

"Cheers," I replied.

"Wait! Wait!" Larry screamed as he ran back to the kitchen. He reappeared with a large bouquet of parsley that he placed with skill and
grace on the platter next to the turkey. "Without garnish," Larry said,
"we might as well be lesbians!"

The table raised their glasses again and cheered.

WINTER

A Long Winter

By early December, winter had placed a steely grip over Hayward. A blast of Arctic air from the Yukon Territories slashed its way across the border through North Dakota, Minnesota, and northern Wisconsin, as it would do all winter. After growing accustomed to the Saharan heat of the past summer and mild autumn, even many locals were shocked by the initial blast of cold weather and avoided going out until their bodies acquired some natural resistance.

It had been over twenty-five years since I had spent a winter in the Upper Midwest. Any hardiness in my natural disposition had been tempered by years of mild—albeit damp, dark, dreary, and utterly dismal—English winters. Even as a child, I dreaded the cold. I looked to my weatherman for some explanation or hope but was left envying those kids in Florida and California. I questioned the sanity of my ancestors and wondered to what extent it was hereditary.

"How bad can it be?" Dean asked before the move when I advised him to buy a down jacket.

It was minus five degrees and snowing. I prepared myself for a walk to the dairy. Dean drank his coffee by the window while the dogs looked out, puzzled by the snow. They barked at the bundled mounds of unrecognizable figures moving down the street.

"It's beautiful, isn't it?" Dean said. "I think I'm going to love winter."

I ignored him. *You innocent fool,* I thought.

I doubled my cashmere scarf and threaded it around my neck. I pulled a wool cap over my ears before donning the thick, down-filled parka I had found in the basement. It was no longer the height of fashion, but it would do the trick. I pulled the parka hood over my head and zipped the fur-lined snorkel. The snorkel was better than a simple hood as it zipped up from the bottom around your chin. I had to admit I looked a bit like an aardvark, but I would be protected from almost all wind.

"What do you think?" I said, my voice muffled by the fur lining.

"You look ridiculous."

"Someday, you'll want my snorkel."

Thick snowflakes fell slowly to the ground in clumps. A layer of snow already covered our walkway. Across the street, a neighbor lady got in her car. She worked two blocks away at the bakery but drove to work every morning. I thought of asking for a ride to avoid the cold, but then I would miss the snow.

Main Street was quiet apart from a crew from the public works department hanging balsam garlands around the street lamps. Two men stayed in the warm truck, another two wound the natural balsam around the lamps. Another worker stuck evergreen treetops in the dirt that filled the concrete planters along Main Street, and yet another followed with white lights.

The buildings I had derided by the end of the summer seemed prettier in this winter scene. The log exteriors, gingerbread, and wooden balconies looked more natural iced with fresh snow. I could have been walking inside a snow globe. When I turned onto Second Street, however, a blast of cold air knocked my breath away. I pulled my furry snorkel closer for the rest of the walk.

Near the dairy entrance, I met my neighbor, who had parked her car and was walking to the bakery. "Hey, I could have given you a ride," she said.

"That's okay. It's nice and brisk." I shivered.

Buck and Bruce chatted over coffee. My protective winter outfit amused them.

"Say, ya think you'll be warm enough there, Jeff?" Bruce asked.

"Yeah, you don't want to catch a cold," Buck added.

Vivian came to my defense. "Ahh, you look very warm, sweetheart." But she then said, "Don't you have snow pants?" referring to the quilted trousers mothers put over their children's pants in the winter.

"Very funny. You're all fired!" I replied.

"We're only kidding. Would you like a latte?" Vivian asked.

"Yes, please."

"It's only five below this morning," Bruce commented.

"Yep, it's going to get a lot colder than that," Buck chimed in to add to my dread.

"So, how much snow are we getting, Buck?" I asked, knowing full well he had been studying the jet stream's movements all morning.

"Well, the guys in Duluth said four to six inches, but that's probably lake effect snow up there," he said, referring to the news meteorologists as if they had been having breakfast at the co-op. "Eau Claire says three to five inches, and the Hayward radio said four inches—but they don't know what the hell they're talking about."

"I think we'll get four inches," Bruce said. "It's coming down pretty hard now." And he was right. The snow had filled the sky since I left the house.

"Perhaps it's time to bring the benches inside." I pointed to the painted benches left next to the store from the summer.

"We used to put those away in October!" Bruce said.

"Let's wait till the snow stops," I said, wondering if it would ever stop.

Traffic moved slowly as wipers fought to keep up with the snow. Across the street at the fly fishing shop, the owner, in a fishing cap and vest, sat in the window tying flies at a type of sewing machine; he was oblivious to the deteriorating conditions outside. He recognized that fishing was quiet this time of year but made good use of the winter, building up for the spring and summer. I looked around and outside at the blowing snow and cars slipping as they stopped at the intersection. I could not imagine anyone in town looking for an ice cream cone in the middle of this storm. *Perhaps I should take up sewing or crochet,* I thought.

"So, what do we do now?" I asked, more rhetorically, as in, *Is this it for the next four months?* Vivian looked at me and shrugged. Bruce and Buck thought I might invite them out for breakfast.

"Well, what do you think, Bucky? Is it too early?" Bruce asked in some sort of code. But Buck understood very well what Bruce meant. He walked behind the counter and opened a drawer.

"I brought the board in the other day, just in case," Buck said. He pulled out a small game board, rows of holes bored into the wood, and a few metal pegs. One peg was missing, and a plastic golf tee was used in its place.

"Cribbage?" I asked, recognizing the board from something I remembered in a buffet drawer as a kid but never saw in use.

"That's right," Bruce said. "This is what we do in the winter." He grabbed the old deck of cards bound with an extra-large rubber band. The deck came from the casino. The cards were worn and rough at the edges. The casino sold the old cards for one dollar but clipped the corners so they could not be brought back.

"This wooden bar is great for cribbage—especially for pairs, two on each side," Buck said and spread his hands across the expanse of the countertop.

"Do you want to play?" Bruce asked me.

"No, that's all right. Thanks," I said. "I don't know the game."

"It's easy! We'll show you, won't we, Buck? It's only a dollar a game." Bruce laughed.

"Don't listen to him," Buck said. "We just play for fun."

"Do you wanna play, Bimp?" Bruce yelled to Vivian, using an old nickname. I began to sense this was some sort of secret ritual—pervasive yet rarely discussed. How did I not know about this game? Was I the only person in town who didn't know how to play? Was a lamb or kitten going to be sacrificed when they were done?

"Maybe later," Vivian said as she rewashed some milk containers.

"How about if I watch to get the hang of it?" I said.

"Don't they play this in England? It's an English game," Buck said. He may have been right, and it had the look of a game some old-timers in the Cotswolds might play while downing a few pints. But I had not seen it in any of the pubs I saw in Britain—and I had been in many of them.

Bruce cut the deck. Buck picked a card. Bruce won the deal and handed out six cards like a pro to Buck and himself. Each discarded two cards face down in a pile, "the crib," Bruce explained, and moved them to his side. Buck threw down a card. "Nine," he said.

Bruce quickly dropped a six of hearts. "Fifteen for two," he said and advanced a peg two holes on the board. The primary objective was to lay a card that, when added to the others, equaled fifteen.

"I knew you'd have a six," Buck said.

Vivian came over to observe at the corner of the bar, glancing at both hands. "Oh, you've got a good hand, Bruce," she said, prompting a look from Buck. "Cecil and I used to play cribbage for hours in the winter when it was quiet at the carpet store," she reminisced.

I knew from that point that I was destined to become a cribbage player; it seemed a means of surviving the slow days of winter at the dairy. It beat knitting, and it looked like fun. I had never played many card games—it always seemed an activity reserved for people with much more time on their hands. I watched the hand and asked a few questions to understand some of the intricacies of the game, including the unusual combination of points.

Before long, as though he heard Bruce shuffling the cards, Little Bob walked in. The snow had not let up, and there were at least a couple of inches on the pavement. He shook the snow off his red wool cap with sheepskin earflaps by pointing his head to his chest so the snow fell on the wet floor. He did not intend to remove the hat.

"Just in time, Bob!" Bruce yelled. "Bucky and I are playing a practice hand."

"Oh, I thought you might get the board out today. It's a good day for cards." Bob spoke with as much enthusiasm as I had ever heard from him. In fact, everyone was in a jolly mood—and it was contagious. It was December, we were in the midst of a snowstorm, the last thing on people's minds was ice cream, but it was a good time for a game of cards.

"Oh, sure, but my eyes are pretty bad—cataracts acting up again," Bob warned.

"Would you like us to drive you later?" Bruce asked without explaining, but Bob must have understood him.

"Oh, that would be swell," Bob said.

I offered Little Bob my seat next to Bruce so he could play. He hunkered down with his eyes inches from his cards. He managed for the most part, but moving his peg proved difficult.

"Are you cheating there, Bob?" Buck joked as Bob missed a hole.

"Oh, no. Well, it's my eyes, you see. These damn cataracts. I think I'll go to the doctor next week."

"How about I do the peggin' for you, Bob?" Bruce offered.

I had watched enough. I found an old snow shovel in the back; bundled up with my scarf, hat, and parka; and removed the snow from the sidewalk to ensure people knew we were still open. I returned to the house, with a brief stop to warm myself in the post office.

"So, are the guys playing cards yet?" Al asked from behind the window.

"I guess the season began today."

"I thought it might—not good for much else." Al looked outside.

At McCormick House, Dean busied himself polishing silver in anticipation of our first guests, who were due to arrive in two weeks. He had bought six silver-plated coffee pots and wanted to get them ready.

"You're not going to believe it!" Dean shouted as I came through the door. "We booked our first wedding for next July. It's only a small wedding, and because it's our first, I agreed not to charge them for it, but they'll book all the rooms for Saturday night," Dean explained. He went on to say it was the friend of a friend of the woman who had taken our order for cable television. "The bride's from Rice Lake. And the best part is I took a deposit for the rooms—over a thousand dollars," he added.

"Now, that's great news!"

"We'll need to come up with a sound system. She asked that we play some Kenny Chesney song when she's walking down the aisle."

"Classy," I said. "Have the dogs been out?" I knew the answer by their dancing at the door.

"Well, it looks very cold, and I don't have a hat," Dean said.

I opened the back door. Spike and Freddie burst down the stairs. Spike dashed for the fresh snow, ran a series of crazy eights, and rolled on his back. Despite his age, at times he had bursts of puppy energy as he ran through the soft snow. Freddie hastily noted the zero-degree weather, pretended to do some business, looked at me, and raised her front paw in discomfort until I picked her up.

"Aww, c'mon, little girl. I got you."

Spike realized his age and stood, coughing as a result of too much activity. The episode lasted no more than a minute, and then they were inside, ready for lunch.

Back at the dairy, Pruny had joined the cribbage set. Pruny was married to Buck's younger sister. He was hefty, seventy or so, and spent a good seven months each year in his fishing boat. He wore a thick plaid wool coat and matching hat and smelled of mothballs and dead fish. No one ever gave me a straight answer as to why he was called Pruny.

They were playing in teams—Pruny and Buck against Bruce and Little Bob. Al from the post office looked on while he finished his chocolate malt. Pruny suspected Little Bob of cheating again even though Bruce had taken control of moving the pegs. Suddenly, Pruny erupted in anger over a perceived unauthorized move. For a moment there was tension until each player recapped his score.

"Sorry there, Pruny. It's just my eyes. I'm not cheating," Bob pleaded.

Pruny was not convinced. "Buck, don't you have a larger cribbage board so he can see the peg holes?" Pruny complained.

"It's getting very heated, the game," I whispered to Vivian.

"Well, Pruny is quite serious about his cribbage. He plays at the tournaments every Sunday at the Cruzin' Tavern, you know."

"I didn't know that. They have cribbage tournaments?" I asked.

"Oh, yeah. They're a big deal around here."

"Really," I said. I had been racking my brain to come up with ways of increasing sales at the dairy over the winter months. I suddenly saw dozens of cribbage players passing the day at a West's cribbage tournament. They'd drink endless milk shakes or one of our special caramel cream lattes. I imagined one of those sports/gambling cable shows coming to town. Players would wear sunglasses and hold an ice cream cone in one hand like a cigarette.

I looked at Buck, Bruce, Little Bob, and Pruny again. I came to my senses. They had not spent a dime and only drank the coffee I offered them free of charge, and the place smelled of mothballs and old men.

Later I returned to the shop just before closing. The snow had stopped for the time being but was predicted to start up again overnight. I thought I might be able to join in a game of cribbage. Buck, Bruce, and Bob had disappeared. Pruny was still at the bar, playing a hand with Vivian.

"I knew it," Vivian said. "I told Pruny, 'As soon as I sit down, the boss will come in.'" Vivian always had a smile, but now she had the cat-ate-the-canary grin of a good hand.

"She's beating me, Jeff. You should tell her to get back to work!" Pruny complained.

"You should know better. They call her the shark," I said. "Where are the others?"

"Well, you know, Bob is having trouble with his eyes," Vivian began.

"He can't see a damn thing! It was hell playing cards with him," Pruny said.

"Anyway," Vivian continued, "Bruce drove Bob in his truck to the edge of town so he wouldn't hit anyone, and Buck followed to bring Bruce back."

As Vivian finished, Bruce and Buck returned. I was struck by both the kindness they showed in taking a friend to the edge of town and concern that he may never make it home.

"Well, did he make it all right?" Vivian asked.

"We pointed him in the right direction." Buck laughed.

"The rest is up to him. At least it's a pretty straight road," Bruce said.

Pruny threw down his hand in defeat as Vivian pegged to finish the game. "Ah, shit! She skunked me!" Pruny shouted. "Buck, you need to find a bigger board so Little Bob can see what he's doing. He drove me crazy today."

Vivian returned to the counter to finish her closing tasks. I ran the tape from the cash register. The drawer opened to reveal a few dollars and two twenty-dollar bills. The tape told a story of eight customers all day. I might have made just enough to pay Vivian.

"A good day?" Buck asked, half joking.

"We've had better," I replied.

"Believe me," Bruce said. "There's not much you can do. Tomorrow, we'll get you started playing cards. Before you know it, it'll be spring."

I laughed. I hoped he was right.

We received four inches in the first significant snow of the season, just as Bruce predicted. It stacked neatly on everything it touched like a thick layer of marzipan on the tops of hedges, fences, and cars. Our neighbor brushed off his windshield and began to scrape the thin layer of ice on the surface formed after the snow melted on the warm vehicle and refroze.

On Main Street, shopkeepers resembled a shoveling brigade as they pushed the snow onto the road to clear a path to their front door. Inspired by the city's evergreen decorations and twinkling lights, the authorities at the chamber of commerce changed the music being played on the outdoor PA system to Christmas carols. With "Jingle Bells" in the air, shopkeepers began to put up their own decorations. At the electronics shop, which also sold a wide range of lampshades, the owner smiled, holding a string of lights while her husband stood near the top of a ladder attempting to secure them to the window frame. From what I could see, he was not smiling.

At the dairy, Buck watched the news and drank his coffee. He had placed a card I left for him upright on the counter. It was the old man's seventy-ninth birthday.

"Happy birthday, Buck!" I said as I came through the door.

"Oh, well, thanks. Thanks for the money, too."

"I thought you might try your luck at the casino."

"I've already been—to spin the wheel."

The casino gave players the chance to spin a wheel for prizes on their birthday. The idea was to provide a special treat for those gambling, but for locals, it was a required trip on their birthday to see what they had won.

"So, what did you win?" I asked

"A lousy roll of nickels!" Buck moaned and pulled out a roll of two dollars in nickels from his pocket.

"What's that?" I pointed to a cribbage board that had been bored into a plank of wood the length of a baseball bat.

"Oh, I had this at my house. I figured Bob should be able to see the holes on this one," Buck explained.

"Hey, should we play a game?" Buck asked. "See what you learned yesterday."

"Sure," I agreed. "Let me get a coffee." I'd thought I would never get to play.

Embrace It

In the weeks leading up to Christmas, the snow and cold brought to Hayward a small army of fuel-efficient vehicles with shallow coffins attached to the roof rack. The occupants were skiers. Despite its relatively flat terrain, the area was known as having some of the finest skiing in the country—cross-country skiing.

"It sounds like a lot of work," Dean said when I first suggested we take up skiing as a way to embrace winter and all that Hayward had to offer. "I like downhill skiing. Perhaps we could go to Colorado over Christmas," he suggested.

I tried to convince him of the health benefits of skiing and the beauty of the forest in the winter, but my attempts fell on deaf ears.

"I've decided I don't really like this extreme cold," Dean concluded by the middle of the month.

"They say you don't feel the cold once you get moving," I argued, but I wasn't quite convinced it was possible to stay warm, either.

Finally, I appealed to his vanity by pointing out that somehow over the course of the summer, between working at the ice cream shop and steak dinners at the Ranch, we had each put on a few pounds. It was inexplicable, and we were both baffled as to how this could have happened. Anyway, it did the trick.

I made arrangements for private lessons with a local ski instructor. We cobbled together from our spandex-free wardrobes something appropriate, picked up some rented skis, and headed for the trail. Our instructor was probably 102 years old but looked no more than fifty. He may have learned to ski before he knew how to walk. Even without skis, he seemed to float effortlessly above the ground.

We went through the basics before we put on the equipment—stance, movements, even falling down. He showed us where to find the "wax pocket" and expertly rubbed in a sticky substance to help us kick and glide, whatever that meant.

"Seems easy," Dean said.

The instructor told us to strap our boots into the skis and follow him to the trail fifty yards away. He disappeared in a flash, leaving a puff of smoke in his wake.

I managed to latch my ski boots into their bindings and briefly stood before one of the skis slid unexpectedly from under my body, apparently having made a decision to start without me. I fell back, ignoring the instructor's preferred technique of leaning forward, and the skis became entangled. I twisted like a pretzel.

"They're kinda slippery, aren't they?" Dean laughed.

"It's like someone put wax on the bottom of them," I said.

After some false starts, we got the hang of it. The trail was perfectly groomed and created a comfortable channel guiding our path. A three-inch track just wide enough for skis had been carved into the side of the trail for those of us who were skiing the classic technique instead of the free-skating style of the more advanced skiers. The sky was brilliant blue and the breeze invigorating as we began to work up a sweat.

We quickly moved along, and thanks to the helpful track and our relative youth, we proudly overtook a group of senior citizen women who were having a skiing coffee klatsch on the trail. Then we came to our first hill. Our instructor gave us some pointers for climbing it. None of the suggestions included the apparently easiest method of taking off the skis and walking. We awkwardly maneuvered our skis duck style up the hill—not exactly the "herringbone" pattern as the instructor wished.

At the top, Dean took off and descended the hill like a pro. Despite his objections, I knew he would pick it up easily. It could have been his downhill skiing experience. As I grew up in flat Minnesota in the

1970s, downhill skiing was still a sport for families with means. By the time I could afford to ski, I was too self-conscious to learn. In England, however, children from all backgrounds were bused off to France to learn how to ski in some sort of European rite of passage.

I hesitated, knowing my skill level was not exactly a match for the steep slope. With the instructor's encouragement, I bent my knees, lifted my poles behind me, and pushed off. I picked up speed, and as the wind blew over my head, I blanked on an important lesson—turning and slowing while keeping my knees bent. The trail veered to the left near the bottom of the hill. I knew I was expected to move one of the skis but could not remember which one. I had to stop, but I couldn't. I recalled something about pointing the skis, but was it inward or outward?

Dean was already at the bottom of the hill and gliding swiftly onward with the effortlessness he applied to many activities. Usually I was pleased with his casual skill, but at times like this it bugged me. I pointed my skis outward and stood up, locking my knees. Wrong move. As my legs began to spread, I headed for the edge of the trail and a large snowbank. To avoid greater injury to my widening groin, I leaned forward to take the snowbank headfirst.

I pulled my head from the snow and looked up at the instructor.

"I think you meant to point your skis the other way in a snowplow position," he said.

"Thanks. I'll remember that next time."

At the bottom of the hill, Dean waited. "Are you okay?" he asked.

"Yeah," I said with a blow to my ego

"Those ladies were laughing when they saw you fall," he said. I looked over at them as they loaded their skis into their old Subaru.

"Damn them."

Did the Big Fish
Eat Santa Claus?

We had no plans for Christmas. For the first time in ten years we would not be spending the holiday with Dean's family in the north of England. Dean would have liked to see his family in England, but our first guests at the B&B arrived just before Christmas. After a busy summer and autumn, we convinced ourselves it would be nice to enjoy some quiet time in our new home. We always spent pretty lavishly on gifts for each other, but that was then. We agreed the purchase of the ice cream shop and renovation of a Victorian mansion were worth about ten years of gifts. It would be a quiet Christmas. Little did we know our first Christmas in Hayward would feature a visit from an angel. But first there was lutefisk.

On the Monday before Christmas, Cheryl invited us to her annual Norwegian dinner. We spent many Mondays at Cheryl's enjoying her home cooking and sometimes a game of cards. She had been talking about her annual Norwegian feast for weeks and looked forward to witnessing Dean's face after his first encounter with the gelatinous Scandinavian seafood delicacy, lutefisk.

Like anyone from the Upper Midwest, I had had my share of youthful experiences with lutefisk. Along with the brutal cold, bird-sized mosquitoes, and distant yet polite neighbors, lutefisk was part of growing up. The states of the Upper Midwest—Minnesota, Wisconsin, Iowa, and the Dakotas—with their sizable Scandinavian populations consumed more lutefisk than anywhere else in the world. Apparently the good people of Norway and Sweden had lost their taste for the fish and now preferred tapas.

The Scandinavian presence was so dominant when I was growing up, I felt like a minority in a land of tall, blond Lutherans. Family friends, the Olsons, invited us to their home around Christmas for a traditional feast. Their children were young adults by then, and all were tall and stunningly beautiful. The girls had big blond hair and the attitude of someone who walked off the stage of the Miss World Pageant because the other contestants were too ugly. The boys were tall and good-looking, and I am convinced one of them may have dated Grace Jones later in the 1980s.

The Olson house was decorated in small, colorful Swedish ornaments, and tiny blue and yellow Swedish flags adorned the Christmas tree. The table was spread not only with turkey, potatoes, and cranberries but also a cold fruit soup and mounds of my favorite, lefse, the thin, crepelike potato bread. For much of the afternoon, I hovered around the food, devouring sheets of lefse spread with butter and dipped in cranberry sauce, lingonberry jam, or sugar.

At the other end of the table, Mr. Olson placed a large casserole dish with a well-sealed lid to ensure the foul odor of the lutefisk did not permeate the room.

"Olaf, keep that lid on the lutefisk," Mrs. Olson yelled at her husband, who helped himself to multiple portions of stinky fish. My older brother tried to hold my head to the open pan.

The Olson family piled mounds of the fish substance on their plates and ate with pride. My mother managed a small portion and complimented Mrs. Olson on the texture. I always tried a little, as I thought the lutefisk might be a key to greater height and beauty, but I always left it on my plate, covered by a small piece of lefse to look as though I had eaten it.

"Did you eat your lutefisk?" Mr. Olson asked. "Now you're an honorary Scandinavian."

At Cheryl's, the house was full. She came from a large family of Norwegians in the Hayward area. Her mother was at the head of the table. In the early stages of dementia, she sat with the distant and quiet look of Norwegian royalty. I recognized some Scandinavian sweaters from the *Syttende Mai* dinner at the Norske Nook back in May. These were worn by elderly cousins of Cheryl's who had actually been to Norway and complimented the cook on the authenticity of the food.

When we arrived, Cheryl was setting up the buffet on the island countertop in her small kitchen. The crowd milled around the kitchen and dining room, where Cheryl had placed some appetizers. She was a great cook, but she was no Martha Stewart, and the only evidence of the pending Christmas season was a tiny aluminum tree on an end table in the living room corner.

We mingled around the dining room table turned buffet of appetizers that, from the look of an empty sauce-smeared bowl, once included some tasty Swedish meatballs.

"Say, don't you own West's Dairy?" I heard a voice from behind me and turned to find a man with a paper plate holding a half dozen golf ball–sized meatballs.

"Well, you did well there," I said, pointing to his plate.

"Yeah, you should have been here earlier. You missed the venison sausage."

"I'll remember that next time."

"Anyway, great job on the dairy. I'm sure you had a good year," my new friend complimented me. Retired, he lived on Grindstone Lake and spent most of his time fishing. Even now he wore a fishing vest, perhaps in the off chance of stopping at his ice fishing shack on the way home from the party to check the lines he left in the water.

"Did you get much fishing done this summer?" he asked, assuming I too enjoyed his hobby. In his mind, it was the only reason to live in the area.

"No, I didn't. You know, I was just too busy at the ice cream shop."

Just as the conversation was screeching to a halt, he told me he volunteered at the Fresh Water Fishing Hall of Fame. Before I could get to the Louis Spray record controversy, I had to interject—

"So, I like the Christmas display at the hall of fame."

"You do?" he asked with great surprise. "Most people hate it."

The display consisted of a life-sized Santa Claus in his sleigh being pulled by several reindeer. The display itself was not unusual, but the fact that it sat in the mouth of the giant fiberglass musky gave the impression that this monster fish was about to eat Santa and ruin Christmas for the children of the world.

"Did that create a stir when it was put up?"

"Oh, for sure. We had kids crying. Parents phoned to complain they did not know what to tell their children. It was crazy. Of course, the fish is not going to eat Santa. It doesn't move for God's sake," he groaned.

"Anyway, we took it down for a few years, but you know those things are expensive, so we started to put it back up. People are now pretty used to it."

"Well, I think it's very clever."

"Thanks. That's good to hear," he said.

Cheryl began to dish up platters for the buffet. Soon the island counter in her kitchen was covered with food—bowls of boiled potatoes, white flour gravy, and a platter stacked with lefse.

"Now, I spent the entire day swearing at that lefse pan, so I hope you all enjoy it," Cheryl said.

Finally, she brought out a ceramic bowl of lutefisk. With no lid on the container, this was not a party for the fainthearted. The smell reminded me of the guys playing cribbage at the dairy—dead fish and mothballs.

The translucent, gelatinous mass resembled the cod from which it was derived as much as an old leather glove looked like a piece of grilled sirloin. Lutefisk was one of the few dishes in the world for which one stage in the preparation is deadly. First, the dried salt cod or other whitefish, also used by indigenous polar people to shingle their roofs, was soaked in water for a week. Then it was soaked in a solution of lye and water. It is at this stage when the fish becomes so corrosive, it could kill. Only after another soaking in water does the fish become—for the most part—edible. Still, cooks were advised to clean pans immediately after use and to avoid any silver utensils in serving the fish, as they could be ruined. I wondered if some of the guests were aware of these properties, given the generous servings of potatoes covered in lutefisk they prepared for themselves.

Cheryl insisted on dishing up Dean's plate, and she didn't skimp on the fish.

"Can I put some of this gravy on the lutefisk?" Dean asked, considering how he was going to master the task before him. I took a small, child-sized portion to be polite and an extra piece of lefse for potential camouflage.

A small card table had been set up in the living room. A woman in her late thirties sat by herself. We had not seen her before and knew she was not from around here. Her name was Elizabeth. She wore knee-high leather boots, a short skirt around a pencil-thin waist, and small denim jacket. Her lips and eye shadow were the shade of bruising. She could have been on her way to a trendy after-lutefisk club too cool for us to know about. She lived in Harlem and was visiting her parents, who had retired in Hayward. Her father had been a banker in the Twin Cities, and she had grown up in Edina, an exclusive suburb of Minneapolis, but preferred the slum-dwelling life she lived as an adult.

Not someone you would expect to meet at a lutefisk party in Hayward, Elizabeth worked in health care but also ran a business where she designed and created gowns and costumes for drag queens in Harlem. Dean lit up as though Elizabeth were an Amish family at an ice cream social and enquired as to the life and fashion needs of the typical Harlem drag queen.

Just as I clung to the odd English expression, Elizabeth had adopted a pattern of speech and slang more typical of the "'hood," as she called home. I described our new life in Hayward and was telling the story of my now-favorite pastime, playing cribbage, when she interrupted. "Now, this old man—Pruny—is he a cracker?" she asked.

"Cracker?"

"You know, white person?"

I confirmed that Pruny was in fact one of the whitest persons to walk the Earth.

And then, after trying her lutefisk, "This is some nasty shit! I wish I was packing some hot sauce in my bag." She added, however, very Minnesota nicely, "But Cheryl is such a sweetheart for doing this. My parents really enjoy this sort of thing. I think my dad might be Norwegian or some shit like that."

I agreed that hot sauce might have done the trick but knew it was not something on hand in the Norwegian household. Butter was considered spicy enough. Dean managed to find some pepper hiding in the back of Cheryl's cupboard.

"So, how do you like the lutefisk, Dean?" Cheryl shouted across the room, drawing attention to how he would respond.

"It's not bad," he replied semi-convincingly. "I think I'll have some more potatoes and gravy, though." He scooped a few more boiled potatoes on his plate and mixed them with gravy and the remainder of his lutefisk. He took his final bites, closed his eyes, and thought of England.

I tried my lutefisk. I wondered if my adult taste buds and openness to other cultures and traditions would affect my reaction to it. It did not. I tucked the slimy mass under a small piece of lefse and left it.

Once in the car, Dean looked at me. "I think I'm going to be sick," he said.

"Let's go to McDonald's."

We decorated McCormick House in balsam and cedar garlands adorned with tartan bows, pinecones, cinnamon sticks, and apples. A nine-foot fir tree filled the bay window of the living room. Dean hung a collection of new ornaments from atop a stepladder. "Do you like the colors?" he asked.

"It's unique" was all I could muster with respect to the brown glass and silk-covered ornaments. "I think the gold is a nice touch," I said.

"The tree looks fantastic with the new furniture," Dean said. Because we expected only a few guests over the holidays, it felt as though we were decorating for ghosts. Without presents for each other, we decided to wait until Christmas Day to open the gift box from Dean's parents. We knew it contained mince pies, Christmas cake, and other treats that would bring us some cheer.

Dean had randomly set the check-in time at McCormick House to between 4:00 and 6:00 PM. It was 6:30, and our first guests had not arrived. Dean paced the hall, checking that the lights were appropriately dimmed, the candles were lit, and the Christmas music—Ella Fitzgerald—playing over the sound system was not too loud. I sat in the library with a book and Freddie on my lap. Spike lay on the floor near the gas fireplace.

"Are you just going to sit there while I show them around?" Dean asked, irritated that the guests were late. I figured he was nervous about his innkeeping debut and hoped he would relax as we had more guests.

"I want to hear your tour. I won't say anything."

"This is typical, isn't it? She said they would be here at 5:00," Dean said, winding himself up even more.

"Oh, I think I see them." Dean changed his tone as he saw someone approach the house. "Uh-oh!" he exclaimed. "She slipped and almost fell. Did you check for ice on the walk?" Dean waited until they reached the front porch and then walked over to the door.

"Hello! Welcome to McCormick House!" I heard him say from the foyer without the slightest hint of irritation.

"Hello. Sorry we're late, but we got stuck at Angler's Bar on Main Street. It's a very nice place there, you know," the woman slurred. Her husband grunted in agreement. "Oh my God, John! This is beautiful," she said.

"Oh, thank you," Dean gushed. "Let me show you around, and then I'll show you upstairs."

"Oh, look, hon—there's wine!" Before Dean could begin his tour, the young woman with tousled blond hair piled on her head was already at the desk in the library, where Dean had placed a bottle of wine and two glasses. Her husband, frazzled and tipsy, followed with two bags and his wife's coat. He attempted to steer her away from the wine, but it was no use. She poured.

"Well, this is the library," Dean improvised after having the order of his rehearsed tour disrupted. He acknowledged me as some lump sitting on the sofa. Freddie was curious and tried to get off my lap to greet the guests, but I held her.

"Marybeth at the bar said you would have some wine for us." The guest giggled and topped her glass with the Pinot Noir.

"Did she?" Dean said, making a mental note to thank Marybeth for getting his first guest drunk on her way to McCormick House.

"The thing is"—she interrupted herself to take a sip—"this is the one night we get away from the kids over Christmas. You know, they say it's all about the kids, Christmas. But what about us?" Dean's eyes followed the glass as she raised her hands and nearly spilled wine on the new rug.

"So, you have children?" I asked.

"Two," she said abruptly. "Great kids, but hard work. Aren't they, honey?" She turned to her husband, who was joining her in a glass of wine.

"You're from Rice Lake?" I asked, moving the subject away from her poor children.

"Yep, not too far—but far enough."

"What do you do there?" I asked

"Oh, I teach at a Montessori school," she said.

"That's nice," I said, confused.

"Yeah, it's all right. More kids." She giggled.

Refueled, the guests took their glasses and followed Dean, who turned to me and held up his hands as if to say, *What can I do?*

I felt bad for Dean. He had been waiting for his first guests for six weeks like a young Conrad Hilton. The house was immaculate—not a speck of dust, not a cushion out of place. And in the end, he got a boozy preschool teacher from Rice Lake.

Dean went through the home's amenities—cable television, high-speed Internet, coffee service in the morning. I heard the teacher interrupt Dean's description of the breakfast menu. "Look, there's a hot tub!" she shouted from the end of the hall. "Wow, I'm going to be there later, for sure."

Dean quickly ushered them upstairs, gave them keys, and returned. "Let's lock the dogs away and get out quickly before they come down."

"What if they need something?"

"They have a bottle of wine. They'll be fine," Dean said, anxious to get going while the coast was clear.

We had planned on going out for dinner. We knew most restaurants would be closed for Christmas Eve and Christmas Day, and we wanted to thank Cheryl again for the lutefisk dinner now that the last of the lingering taste of old fish had left our palates.

The night was cold. I checked the northern sky to make sure the Big Dipper had returned, as it did every clear night.

A few regulars sat at the bar at the Ranch, all with the same intent to wish Cheryl and their other friends a merry Christmas. An office Christmas party was taking place in a small dining room off to the side of the restaurant that was used for such events as well as overflow seating on busy evenings. A large man with his shirt open and necktie askew approached the side of the bar with several empty glasses. "Cheryl!" he blared.

"Be right there, Chuck," Cheryl shouted as she finished a Cosmopolitan for a blond woman at the end of the bar.

"Hey, boys!" she greeted us as we pulled up stools. She took the bottle of cranberry juice and waved it over the martini glass filled with vodka for Dean's amusement. Dean teased her for the power she packed in her cocktails. She poured a splash of cranberry juice to finish the drink and carefully carried it to the customer at the end of the bar, who received it in both hands as she might a chalice.

Cheryl bounced back to the other end of the bar to service Chuck, who held tightly onto the corner to avoid falling into the doorway. "What do you need, Chuck?" Cheryl asked.

"Well, I'd like two brandy Old Fashioneds and"—he paused as he tried to remember what was in the other glasses—"one Manhattan and a vodka gimlet. Oh, and a Miller Lite for the lady," he said, referring to his wife. "And why don't you add one for yourself there, Cheryl?" Chuck added as a tip. "Dinner was fabulous."

"Don't mind if I do. Thank you very much," Cheryl said. From the way she poured the cocktails, it looked as though she had been tipped generously.

We ate our dinner at the bar and chatted with others. There was some reminiscing over the year that was about to pass. Many were local businessmen who thought it had been a good year for tourists, figured the following summer would be even better, and hoped it would get here fast.

"This is a long haul—May is nearly five months away," one shopkeeper, known for his pessimistic view of life and business, advised.

By 9:00, the restaurant was emptying. The office party stumbled out of the back dining room. Every fourth person had the erect stature and tired look of the designated drivers for the evening. They helped their drunken cargo out the door and gave Cheryl a serious thank-you.

We kissed Cheryl good-bye and wished her a merry Christmas before heading home.

Snow fell lightly into the beam of the headlights and lamps along Main Street. Partygoers left Angler's Bar and headed home to their families. We wondered if our Montessori teacher from Rice Lake and her husband were at the bar.

As we came through the back gate, we realized that was not the case. We heard laughter and giggling from the back terrace. The guests were in the hot tub. I went into the house to avoid them. Dean thought he should check on them.

As he approached the tub, our guest yelled, "Deano! Come on in!" and started to jump out of the hot tub. As her bare breasts bounced, her husband, in wet boxers, jumped to pull his naked wife back under-water. Dean made a hasty retreat to the kitchen, but our guest was loose. She managed to escape her husband's grasp, jumped out of the tub, and ran onto the snow-covered lawn.

"Let's make snow angels!" she yelled to her husband, in hot pursuit with a towel to cover her. Soon she was down on the ground, spread-eagled. Her arms flapped to form the perfect angel.

"Well, it's our very own Christmas angel," I said.

"I don't believe it!" Dean said, laughing at the absurd outcome of his innkeeping debut. "Will they all be like this?" We contemplated the pos-sibility that future McCormick House guests would be closeted streak-ers who gathered enough courage to run naked around the house.

"Perhaps we should open the box Mum sent. I think there may be some mince pies in it," Dean said.

"I think that'd be a great idea."

We returned to the kitchen, leaving our guests streaking across the yard. "She'll get cold sooner or later and want to come in the house," Dean said.

I opened our gift box from Britain. The mince pies were on top.

"Oh, they're from Marks and Spencer," Dean said.

I tore into the box to remove the pies from their foil tray. "I guess that makes it a very special Christmas," I said.

"It is indeed—happy Christmas." Dean raised his mince pie in a toast. I tore a bit of pastry off the edge to feed Spike and Freddie.

Not the Dog

By early January, a mild winter had taken hold of Hayward. Still, it was below freezing, and the days were short, gray, and damp. Those who ran primarily summer businesses hunkered down like hibernating bears, out of sight, conserving their resources for another four months. Contractors with only a few indoor projects were forced to lay off much of their teams for several months. The downturn took its toll on those businesses that remained open. Restaurants were often empty; some struggled to make it through the winter. It was a season that made apparent how Sawyer County was consistently named one of the two or three poorest counties in the state.

I had made no progress on improving the revenue streams at the dairy, but I was committed to keeping it open every day. I noticed many business people took on additional work. Would I ever need to find a job? If faced with a diet of cat food and turnips, would I consider taking the Wisconsin bar exam to qualify as a lawyer and hang a shingle? The fact that I had never written a will or a contract to buy a home or settled a marital dispute presented a steep learning curve. But then I thought how appealing the new cat foods looked—some were even organic.

Dean had already found a way to supplement our income, or at least his own spending money—eBay. He had been a casual user of the online auction house, more of a purchaser than seller. Over the course of a few weeks, however, he became a full-blown eBay merchant. He worked his way through boxes of clothes and items from the basement. He sold much of his corporate wardrobe and various items we had collected but not used in the house. He took detailed photographs and spent hours working on the descriptions to achieve maximum interest.

He staggered his sales so as not to be overwhelmed with auctions finishing at the same time. I helped with the shipping.

"You guys have been busy," Al at the post office noted. He had clearly seen this activity.

Once Dean cleared out his wardrobe, he started on mine. First it was the Hermès neckties—apparently still big in Japan. Cute pastel-colored ties with seals bouncing balloons or pandas frolicking had been some of my favorites. I had enjoyed wearing them because they gave my legal career a whimsical boost. I was sad to see them go, but Dean was right. "You're never going to wear these again. I can get almost as much as you paid for them and make money on the shipping," he said.

After the ties, there were dress shirts, Tiffany cufflinks, and my pen collection. Dean sold the briefcase that I had to have but rarely used because it was too heavy. The problem with listing your belongings on eBay is that you eventually run out of things to sell. One day, I caught Dean taking photographs of Spike. He denied vehemently that he was thinking of selling our pet of eleven years, but I kept an eye on the dog.

There was a group of people in Hayward who had found the answer to the winter slowdown and were willing to share it. As soon as we settled in the area and people assumed we had resources to burn, we received unusual phone calls. Some were from strangers and others from people we had barely met. They all wanted to get together to talk about a great opportunity, a way both to save and make money. They had found happiness in a "multilevel marketing plan," which was how they preferred to refer to this particular pyramid selling scheme.

In this get-rich-quick gambit—I mean *multilevel marketing plan*— one bought a membership for two thousand dollars. This membership permitted huge savings on a range of products from new cars to appliances, cleaning products, and printer ink cartridges. Some local restaurants offered a ten percent discount to members. While the price tag was steep, it seemed like a benign plan.

However, when we mentioned it to a few people, the reaction was almost universal—"Run!" It was as though an insidious cult had come to town and brainwashed a large portion of the population. Because many had already resisted the forces as best they could, cult members preyed primarily on new and unsuspecting arrivals, innocent or perhaps naïve, who used a lot of ink cartridges.

There seemed to be a few leaders in town who successfully sold the plan to a number of people. The new members began selling it to others and so forth. But Hayward was a small town, and a pyramid scheme required a large population filled with fools who were happy to part with their money, so the competition was fierce. In Hayward, there seemed to be ten people chasing us alone.

We were not interested. Neither of us was much of a coupon cutter, so discounts didn't matter. We had forked over thirty-five dollars to become members of Sam's Club in Duluth and already regretted it since we had used the membership only once in six months and had a five-pound bag of shredded cheese in the freezer to show for it. "Do you think that cheese is still good?" Dean asked from time to time.

As we did not know most of the callers, we initially quite politely and then rather rudely told them to get lost. In one case, we knew the caller, had been to his house for dinner, and thought his wife amusing. Every time we ran into him, he started in on this incredible opportunity. "Just let me come around to show you this video. It will blow your mind," he said. Neither of us had the courage to say we weren't interested, so he possibly got the impression we might be serious.

It was Sunday afternoon. We were in the middle of a gripping episode of *Law and Order*. It might have been from the *Special Victims Unit* series of the franchise. Dean was catching up on his eBay auctions. The phone rang.

"Hey, great. You guys are home. You're not doing anything, are you? No, I didn't think so. Look, why don't I pop 'round with that video? It will blow your mind," the caller said. Before I could say anything, he hung up.

"Dean," I said, "I think someone's coming 'round to see us." Before I could come up with even a plausible explanation of how I had allowed this guy to come by to show us his video on a pyramid selling scheme, there was a knock at the door. Dean answered. "Hi, Rick," Dean said, and then, "Chantal?" surprised to see our local pyrotechnic behind Rick.

"Hi, Dean. Jeff said it was okay to come over with the video I was telling you about," Rick said. "Chantal came with me to answer any questions you might have about the video. She's my mentor," he added.

"I didn't know you were involved in this," I said to Chantal as I came through to the door.

"Well, you know, the fireworks business is pretty seasonal, so this keeps me out of trouble the rest of the year," she bellowed with laughter. "And it's an awesome opportunity. I think it would be perfect for you guys. And this video—well, it's going to blow your mind." She put her hands above her head to imitate an explosion of fireworks or my head bursting from the excitement of it all. I wanted them to stop saying that. Unless the video had Matt Damon playing a character named Jason Bourne, it was unlikely to "blow my mind."

"Would anyone like a drink?" I asked. I opened the door to the refrigerator to see what we had.

"I would take a beer if you have one," Chantal said.

I handed her a Heineken and hesitated for a moment but took one for myself.

"Give me one, too," Dean said.

We led our visitors to the library. Rick held the explosive DVD and was anxious to get started. Dean, with his sales background, feigned interest in the scheme and asked for a description.

Chantal explained how, for a fee of two thousand dollars, members had unlimited access to great discounts all over the country—"cars, vacations, restaurants, ink cartridges, and so forth." I wanted to ask what the deal was with ink cartridges but figured it would be in the video and would blow my mind.

"But what do you get out of it?" Dean did not hesitate to get to the point.

"Well, as a member, if you recruit other members, you have the added opportunity to earn valuable prizes and cash," Chantal explained with a degree of delicacy.

"So, is it a pyramid scheme?" Dean asked without any hint of subtlety.

"No, it's a buying club that offers purchasing discounts to its members," Rick clarified. His explanation, of course, was inadequate. It was like saying, "Jeffrey Dahmer was not an evil, cannibalistic serial killer; he was a Lutheran."

With some help from Dean, Rick got the show started. The forgettable DVD was a series of testimonials of persons, more often than not from Arkansas, who had made a fortune selling memberships into the buying club. The testimonials moved from the fantastic merchandise savings to the extravagant lifestyle of those who committed to the product, sold memberships, and mentored others on the benefits of the club. There were endorsements by presumably famous NASCAR drivers appealing to a certain demographic and then back to the woman from Arkansas who had quit her job at Wal-Mart and moved out of her trailer to a new home in the Florida Panhandle. The people in the video spent their time going from one regional meeting to another, speaking to the converted.

As the video neared its climax, I heard light snoring. I looked around. Dean cringed and held back laughter while Rick bit his lip and held back his anger. Chantal was asleep in the corner chair with a half bottle of beer between her legs. Rick coughed and squirmed by the desk in an attempt to wake her. He pretended we didn't notice. Chantal's breathing became louder. Rick took the remote and turned up the volume on the DVD to drown out the sound of his mentor's snoring.

When the DVD was about to finish, rather than use the remote, Rick stood and walked past us to the television. As he passed Chantal, he gave her a sharp kick to her shin. She jumped, her breathing pattern broken.

"What?" she said, and without missing a beat, "Oh, what did you think, guys?"

"Great," Dean said.

Rick removed the DVD and put it in the case. He faced the bookshelf. His ears were red with a combination of hostility and embarrassment. He knew there was no point and looked for a way to get out of the room.

"Well, why don't you think about what you saw? We'll let you go back to what you were doing," he said as he walked past Chantal and gave her a signal they were leaving.

"Well, thanks for coming by," I said as they sheepishly walked down the hallway.

"Thanks for the beer." Chantal waved as Rick pushed her out the door.

We waited until they reached the bottom of the steps.

"That was pretty amazing." Dean laughed.

"Sure blew my mind."

West's Hayward Dairy Goes Global

The picture of our overall financial state was dismal, a deep hole in an unfamiliar forest with a gray background and only a hint of blue sky in the far corner. In preparing the year-end books for the accountants, I saw where the problems lay. For McCormick House, also known as the Victorian sinkhole into which most of our money fell, the financial prospects could only improve, but we recognized it could take one, two, or even three years before we reached the level of occupancy we hoped to achieve. It would take decades to recoup the investment made in the property.

The dairy was more of a mixed bag. While the wholesale milk business was relatively consistent, the margins were small. After accounting for the driver's salary, overhead costs of keeping the milk cool, and repairs to the old step van, I figured the entire business gave us spending money for the year.

The ice cream business, however, was surprisingly successful. The data confirmed what we knew—the bulk of the business occurred during the short and intense period between the middle of June and the middle of August. Approximately a third of the annual business was conducted in the month of July alone and another third during the months of June and August. We sold as much ice cream in December as we did on an average Tuesday and Wednesday in July. However, even with only Vivian managing the shop in December, fifty percent of the revenues went for labor compared to ten percent in July. If we measured gain in terms of my success at the cribbage board or the entertainment value of Buck's stories, December was a very good month, and January proved to be even better.

We racked our brains trying to figure out how we could improve the situation, to build on the successful ice cream business. We concluded that a drastic shift in the Earth's orbit to extend the summer months in northern Wisconsin would help. Another option was to move to Florida or another climate more conducive to ice cream consumption and vacationing. I looked out at the barren, snow-trimmed streets and recognized that perhaps Hayward was not the most logical spot to purchase an ice cream business.

Before heading back to Hayward after a day of shopping in Duluth, we stopped at a Starbucks for a latte and found our answer. We knew Starbucks as a nice coffee shop, a pretty successful chain with a few stores here and there. They had a good product and warm atmosphere, and people went out of their way to stop there, thinking or just assuming it was special. One could say Starbucks was the coffee equivalent of West's Hayward Dairy—give or take 12,000 locations and 150,000 employees and a fair amount of global recognition.

Over the course of the summer, I often heard people say they drove thirty, forty, or even a hundred miles not only for the ice cream but also for the unique experience at West's. The atmosphere was inviting and the staff personable. For many people, it was tradition. As we sat there dipping our dry-as-dirt biscotti that one would not consider eating anywhere else, we looked at each other, and Dean said, "We need to open another shop."

"It could be risky," I suggested.

"If we're going to be big, we have to start somewhere," Dean said.

The question became where to open our second location. Ideally, it would be in another tourist area but not too far from Hayward. We would need to factor in startup costs. Most likely, we would not want to—or would not be able to—purchase any premises. We would need to find a reliable manager; that would add to the expense.

Spooner, only twenty-seven miles from Hayward, was a possible market. We had a tip that a location was available on Spooner's Main Street, a potential launching pad for the global expansion of the West's brand. On a sunny late morning, we headed to town. The building sat at the end of Main Street across from the Spooner railroad station museum. It was a two-story brick structure from Spooner's heyday at the turn of the last century with a door on the corner. The building was originally a tavern and now housed a coffee and sandwich shop.

Inside, the ceilings were high and covered with their original tin. A long oak and walnut bar stretched into the large room. The wood had been scuffed and scraped by the boots of former patrons. Behind the bar hung a large mirror between shelves on which it appeared someone had hurriedly replaced the bottles of liquor with coffee mugs and flavored syrups. On the back bar, an espresso machine sat awkwardly.

In the window facing Main Street, a young woman wearing a black sweater and matching nail polish operated two grills, filling the window with steam and the room with the smell of cooked ham and cheese. A lone customer sat at a table reading the *Spooner Advocate,* drinking coffee from a large chipped mug, and waiting for his sandwich.

Dean and I stood, taking it all in. In the back was an old sofa with mismatched cushions next to a wooden granny-style rocking chair. They could have come from a loft in Haight-Ashbury thirty years ago. High-back wooden booths for secret conversations lined the outside wall. We knew without saying a word to each other that this was a perfect location. It needed a few gallons of paint. The bar required refinishing and extending to fit the ice cream dipping cabinet. New menu boards could go behind the bar, replacing the chalkboard easel in the middle of the floor. I didn't want to imagine the condition of the restrooms.

Our sandwich maker turned, revealing a pierced lip and a tattoo on her neck. Her dyed black hair was tied behind her head in a steamy ponytail.

"We're looking for Catherine," I said. "Or perhaps it's Cathy?"

"Which one?" our Goth sandwich maker asked. "Cathy is next door at the gallery. I think Catherine stepped downstairs and should be up shortly." She returned to her grill.

"Oh," I replied. "I guess either would be fine."

From the back of the shop came a tall woman around sixty years old with a long gray witch's mane. She wore a floor-length caftan-style dress in a rich red and black pattern above sneakers. She carried a cauldron-shaped pot of soup or possibly a secret potion.

"Hello, hello," she greeted us, knowing already who we were. "I'm Catherine. You must be Jeff and Dean. It's such a pleasure to meet you. You know, we've heard so much about the fabulous things you've been doing in Hayward." She spoke softly, elongating every syllable as though she had spent a life on the stage.

Catherine explained that her partner, Cathy, ran the small art gallery and framing studio next door, and we could buy that building, too, if we were interested. She laughed. She gave us the story of how they fell in love with the building, how they wanted to live in Spooner but would only do so if they could get a decent cup of coffee. She laughed again. And that was why they opened the coffee shop. She extolled the virtues of Spooner and the coffee shop's business but was reluctant to reveal any figures until she had some sort of commitment from us.

We explained that we proposed to add ice cream to the current business of sandwiches, soups, and coffee. We thought of calling it West's Ice Cream Café. We had only been thinking about the concept, but it clearly struck something in Catherine. I thought she was going to cry, she seemed so moved by the suggestion. Looking back, perhaps she was more moved by the possibility of ridding themselves of a big building.

"Oh my gosh, that would be so fabulous! You will do amazingly well here in Spooner. You know, there is no ice cream in town," she said, as though the city's founders somehow had banned it.

Catherine was less enthusiastic when we explained that we would not be in a position to purchase the building, including the three-bedroom tenement apartment upstairs, but would lease the premises with an option to purchase. She looked serious and quiet. I thought she might cry again. She rose to stir the soup, or potion, behind the counter.

"Well, I'll need to discuss this with Cathy, but perhaps we could work something out." She spread her palms across the counter as though she were spreading her tarot cards. She got up and walked through a doorway to Cathy's gallery next door. We didn't know whether she would return or not.

As we got up from the bar, I saw Matt approach the door. As he was instrumental in our purchase of West's, we thought it would be good for him to see the building and give us his opinion. He checked his hair in the reflection off the glass door.

"Great ceiling," Matt said, pointing to the deeply patterned tin some fifteen feet above our heads. "Could use painting. Keeping it?"

"Of course," I said.

"What about the Goth chick in the window?"

"Not so sure."

The bright sun over Spooner was a shock to the eyes after sitting in the dimly lit coffee shop.

"Let's go for a drink to talk about it," Dean suggested and pointed to a tavern across the street.

"Big Dick's Buckhorn Bar." I read the sign above the door. "That's where you want to go?"

"Sure—great name for a bar."

"And a great place for a murder," I added.

Big Dick's was an old-style small-town bar. The building was of the same era as Catherine and Cathy's building. It sat between a pet store and a vacant building. It was impossible to see what was inside from the street. The only windows were mere slits of glass and revealed a few neon beer logos and neglected hanging plants. A schedule for the previous summer's softball league covered the glass door to the street.

Inside, the limited natural light struggled to find its way through a cloud of stale smoke. After walking through Big Dick's shrine to the fallen deer and other wildlife of Washburn County, we reached the bar—rich walnut with ornate carving that was difficult to see because the cheap lights were directed on the bottles of gin, vodka, and whiskey. The bar was more elaborate and in better condition than the one across the street at the coffee shop.

A Native American girl with long hair in pigtails worked behind the bar. The patrons consisted of a few men in either denim farming over-alls or thick insulated pants worn by workmen who spent hours out in the winter cold. They leaned over the bar in various stages of late-morning inebriation. In the dim light, it was hard to tell whether they were awake or even alive as they sat silent and lifeless, propped up with elbows on the bar.

"This place is scary," Matt mumbled under his breath.

Our barmaid approached and placed three cocktail napkins in front of us. "Our special today is one-dollar tap beers—Leinies," she added, referring to Leinenkugel's, the local beer of choice.

"Sounds great," Dean said. "Make it three. I'm buying."

She smiled and began to pull three beers into small six-ounce glasses. She wore a tight pink tank top. She caught us staring at her breasts. Over the right breast was a logo for Big Dick's with the more than suggestive slogan, "Good to the last swallow."

"Do you like my shirt?" she asked. "We sell them in all sorts of styles." She pointed above the bar. Her T-shirt was the tamest of the bunch. Others were simply vulgar and offensive, including one featuring a nun. "We have some more in the back if you're interested, but they're, you know, X-rated."

"Perhaps before we leave," Dean said. I couldn't tell whether he was being polite or curious.

We moved from the bar to a small high-top table so as not to arouse the others, who were beginning to stir. We quickly debriefed Matt on the global expansion of West's Dairy, beginning in a tired coffee shop across from Big Dick's Buckhorn Bar in Spooner, Wisconsin. Dean had already decided on colors for the walls and the tin ceiling. I had an idea for how to extend the bar to the door for the ice cream dipping cabinet. We were not sure about keeping the food but hoped to find a manager with experience at running a sandwich shop in order to maintain it.

"Well, it sounds like you have it figured out," Matt said. Perhaps he thought we were rushing ahead of ourselves. "How much do you think it will cost?" he asked. Although conservative with his own money, Matt was usually very happy to see us spend ours.

"Well, the building requires only a bit of cosmetic work, and we're not buying it. I think we can keep it down to ten to fifteen thousand."

"That's if Catherine can convince Cathy to lease the building," Dean reminded us.

"Oh, they'll lease," Matt said. "I did some research. The place has been for sale for two years. They're desperate."

One of the regulars at the bar began to rumble. With his upper body lowered over the bar so as to shorten the distance his head would drop in case he passed out, he attempted to make an introduction across the room. We at first ignored him, pretending he was talking to someone else. He only spoke louder. "Hey, I was talking to you fellas," he slurred.

Dean decided to take a look at the barmaid's T-shirt collection and went over to the bar to avoid what was about to come our way. At the bar, he asked not only about price and available colors but also manufacturer and whether there were any in Sea Island cotton. However, this display of shopping seemed to captivate the attention of the man at the bar, who watched Dean with great interest. Matt and I thought we were safe given the man's focus on Dean, but when the man stumbled to his feet, he began a circuitous journey from the bar to our table, bumping into barstools and securing his stance with the help of a few tables. He finally landed against the wall nearest our table.

"Hey, fellas, how you doin'?" His words slopped as he leaned in our direction.

"Okay," I replied timidly.

Matt was a bit spooked, but having lived in the area, I felt I could handle this. We spoke briefly about Spooner and all it had to offer. I told the drunk what we did in Hayward, knowing he would not remember any of it. The trick was to overwhelm his anesthetized sensibilities so he would retreat back to his drunken stupor. But in the case of our friend in Spooner, he seemed more curious with everything I said.

He moved in closer as he dragged a stool from another table. He began to sway, and I thought he was going to collapse on top of me as he hoisted himself onto the seat. Suddenly, he interrupted my description of the proposed West's Ice Cream Café.

"Say, is he gay?" he asked, pointing to Dean, who was examining T-shirts in the natural light provided by the open front door.

With that, Matt rose and rushed to Dean's side, leaving me with this curious drunk who began a line of worrisome questioning about what three good-looking guys were doing at Big Dick's Buckhorn Bar in Spooner on Saturday. "You don't look like you're from around here." He shook his head from side to side.

I did my best to convince him we were just some guys drinking little beers. Dean and Matt purchased their T-shirts and hovered by the door waiting for me, anxious to make a run for it. It became clear, however, that my curious friend was less likely to take me out to the woods, tie me to a tree, and slit my throat than he was to take me out to the woods, tie me to a tree, and, well, you know . . .

I made an excuse that we had to get back to Hayward, finished my little beer, and said good-bye. I was pretty certain he would not recall anything I had said about West's Ice Cream Café in downtown Spooner.

Where's Spike?

The dairy ticked along at a pace just above a standstill. I gave up on the idea of high-stakes cribbage tournaments. I made enough to pay Vivian and buy coffee for my cribbage partners. There may have been ways of increasing business over the quiet winter, but life at the dairy was comfortable. I became quite a good cribbage player and could attest to the game's addictive qualities. I often joined a game late in the morning after *The Price Is Right*. There was usually a break for lunch while Bob went to the co-op for a cup of soup and Buck went to the senior center. I returned just before closing to pick up a game with Buck, Bruce, or even Vivian; by then they were tired and just a bit off their game.

McCormick House began to receive sporadic guests. After the visit by our Christmas angel, I was wary of spending time with any guests. I moved around as a ghostlike figure, closing doors and rushing away down empty hallways to avoid them. I helped Dean with breakfast in the kitchen, but that was about it.

At the end of January, Dean came to the dairy with some big news. "So, this is what you call 'paperwork'?" he asked. I may not have told him the extent to which I spent hours there playing cribbage.

"Hey, stranger," Buck joked. With the onset of winter and the opening of the B&B, Dean's visits to West's were limited to the coffee run.

"Oh, ignore them, you blue-eyed devil. Would you like a coffee?" Vivian asked with a gentle rub on his back.

"Thank you, Vivian. That would be lovely," Dean replied.

"Oh, I just love your accent," she purred.

"Yes, Vivian, another cup of coffee here would be *lurvly*." Bruce mocked an English accent and laughed.

"You can get your own," Vivian retorted.

Dean had big news about a booking he had taken and could not wait to share it. A woman had called to make a reservation for the upcoming weekend. She did not give any information other than her name, but thanks to caller ID and the Internet, Dean discovered she was a travel writer for a major Twin Cities newspaper.

"This could be really big for business!" Dean said. "So long as she likes it," he added.

"She will love it," I assured him.

"We have only one other couple this weekend."

"Well, let's hope they're nice. They aren't from Rice Lake, are they?" I asked.

With only four days to prepare the most perfect environment for his special guest, Dean spent most of the day and evening cleaning and going over his plan for the reporter's visit.

Dean upgraded the reporter to one of the suites, arranged flowers in the room, and placed a nice box of chocolates on the bedside table.

"Do you think the box is too big?" he asked. "I don't want her to think I'm trying to bribe her or anything for a good review." I thought he might be right but said she would appreciate the chocolates.

As far as we knew, our travel writer assumed we had no idea who she was, but in addition to Dean's investigation, we had reconnaissance reports throughout the afternoon once she got to Hayward. First, Ann from the bookstore telephoned to give Dean the scoop on the reporter in town. "She said she was staying at McCormick House. I told her she picked a great place."

When I closed the dairy, Buck told me a woman had come in for an ice cream and coffee. "Some lady was here asking about you," he said.

"Really?" I said, fearing what Buck might have told her.

"Well, she had a thousand questions about the dairy and about you guys and the mansion," Buck said. "I hope you guys aren't in trouble with the FBI." He laughed. It sounded pretty harmless—I hoped.

At McCormick House, Dean had welcomed the other guests for the weekend, a couple from St. Paul. Before they arrived, they told Dean they had stayed here many times when the B&B was known as Lumberman's Mansion.

"I hope they aren't offended by the changes," Dean had said. "Some people like that old Victorian style."

But there was no need to worry. The couple was duly impressed by the complete transformation of the property. "Feel these new floors, Kent," Cindy said. "We won't have to worry about slivers coming through our knit booties," she said, noting the basket of hand-knit slippers was gone.

"Yeah, guys, this is amazing," Kent said. I heard Spike scratching at the kitchen door, so I let him out. He and Freddie darted down the hall to greet the guests. *Hope they like dogs,* I thought.

"Look at this—a welcoming party. How sweet," Cindy said as she kneeled on the floor to greet our canine ambassadors.

The couple had spent the day on the ski trails and were looking forward to a relaxing evening. They were on the youthful side of middle age, with about six ounces of fat between them and a showroom's worth of skiing equipment, maps, and guides. They took quickly to the bottle of French wine Dean had placed in the library.

"Oh, Kent, they have the *Pioneer Press.*" Cindy picked up her hometown newspaper. We informed them that the travel writer from the newspaper was expected any minute.

Our featured guest and her boyfriend arrived promptly at 6:00 PM. I thought it appropriate to join Dean at the door.

"Hello, I'm Beth." She extended her hand. "I'm from the *St. Paul Pioneer Press,*" she announced immediately. "And I'm going to write a story about you and the incredible things you've done in Hayward," she said before she took a tour of the house or had a chance to dip into the box of chocolates in her suite.

"Well, hello!" Dean said. "We had no idea you were from the newspaper," he lied boldly yet convincingly. The reporter's German boyfriend followed, carrying their bags.

"This is incredible." She looked around and up the stairs. "You've done a great job."

"Oh, thank you," Dean said.

Dean showed our special guests to their suite. I hoped he had not strewn rose petals on the bed. Before they returned to the library, Dean popped into the kitchen for some cheese and crackers. "A standard feature at McCormick House," he improvised.

"So, we would like to go skiing tomorrow," the reporter told me. "Do you have any idea what the conditions are like on the Birkie Trail?"

I should have known. Most guests this time of year were skiers, but all I could think about was my face imbedded in a snowbank. I thought "cold" was not the report she was looking for.

"We were out on the trails all day, and they were great," Cindy said, looking up from her paper. "Hi, I'm Cindy, and this is my husband, Kent." Our guests introduced themselves. They began a conversation on ski conditions throughout the Upper Midwest.

"You know, we love your column," Kent said. "We often follow your suggestions."

Knowing our special guests were being glad-handed, I said I would check on Dean in the kitchen. Cindy turned to me, winked, and gave me a thumbs-up to suggest that they would take care of the reporter.

"Isn't it amazing what they have done to this house?" she said. "We can tell you what it was like before Jeff and Dean got here." *She's good,* I thought.

Kent and the reporter's boyfriend were already engrossed in a detailed discussion of waxing skis and sharing funny stories about some of their experiences skiing the Mora Vasaloppet.

On Saturday morning, breakfast went smoothly. There had been hiccups in the kitchen with some of the earlier guests. Dean's offerings were based on a combination of the breakfast menu from the Mandarin Oriental in London and the Four Seasons in New York. The menu looked nice and was designed to impress, with "freshly squeezed juices" and "organic, farm-fresh eggs." The problem was that neither the chef nor sous-chef from either the Mandarin or Four Seasons was free to take a position at McCormick House in Hayward, Wisconsin.

Dean was a fine cook but had no restaurant experience. He was not accustomed to preparing several different items at the same time or timing his preparations to meet someone's request to eat at a particular time. In addition, while Dean was certainly a master of the "Full English Breakfast," which was central to the menu, he was not familiar with American classics such as pancakes, streaky bacon, or breakfast links. For him, eggs came either fried or scrambled. Requests for "over easy," "over medium," "over hard," "basted," or "sunny side up" required translation and a bit of experimentation. Needless to say, yolks were broken, spatulas flew, and the eating habits of Americans were generally trashed.

In Britain, omelets were considered French, or at least foreign enough to be eaten only on rare occasions and typically not at breakfast. For Americans, of course, omelets were a breakfast standard. While the concept of an omelet was basic, making one required the correct technique. The key was to get the pan very hot with just enough butter or oil to prevent sticking but not enough to affect the taste. While one could attempt to flip the omelet in the pan, the easier and more effective method was to hold the pan under the broiler for a minute before folding in order to cook it and the toppings thoroughly.

Unfortunately, Dean was not aware of these techniques when he started. For his first omelet, he made four attempts and used a dozen eggs, but he had since mastered the craft. He folded our reporter's spinach and feta omelet—a classic combination. "Perfect," he said and tossed the sprig of parsley I handed him in the trash, replacing it with a bouquet of parsley with the stems tucked under the edge of the omelet. "There. Now it's ready." I took the plate. "Without garnish," I said, remembering Larry's quip at Thanksgiving.

In the dining room, the reporter, her boyfriend, and our other guests continued a nonstop discussion of skiing and other outdoor pursuits. I could not add much to the conversation, but it didn't matter. They were enjoying themselves.

"The English breakfast is fantastic," the reporter's boyfriend commented. "It's so rare to find English bacon in America."

I described how we had located an English butcher in North Carolina and had the bacon shipped to the house by Federal Express. My description sounded like a review from a newspaper and a bit pretentious, but the reporter nodded and made a note on her pad. "How was everything in your room?" I asked.

"Oh, it was wonderful. The beds are so comfortable, and the champagne truffles on the pillows were a decadent touch," she added. I imagined the description in the article.

"That's nice," I said, unaware that Dean had used the chocolates his grandmother sent me for Christmas.

Back in the kitchen, Dean was waiting for an update on how it was going.

"Well, she liked the champagne truffles," I said accusingly.

"Oh, sorry about that," Dean admitted. "But it was for a good cause. A good review could make a big difference for us." I let him off the hook.

Our guests spent the day skiing and visiting some of the other businesses in town. Later in the evening, I saw the reporter in the library making some notes on a pad. I thought about interrupting. Instead, I opened a bottle of wine and placed some glasses on the desk. She seemed exhausted but was quite relaxed. She thanked me for the wine and the very enjoyable stay, and she meant it. It was nice to hear—not simply because she was a reporter and might say a kind thing or two in an article or because it felt good that the efforts we made were so appreciated. I was happy she was comfortable. I could get used to innkeeping.

I woke in the middle of the night. While in the kitchen looking at an open refrigerator, I remembered we had not retrieved the completed breakfast menus from outside the guests' doors. I tiptoed upstairs, hoping not to wake anyone, especially as I was in only my underwear. With the menus in hand, I darted back to the kitchen. I looked them over. I would do any necessary grocery shopping in the morning. On the reporter's menu, she had checked "Fresh Bakery Basket." I had not seen the item on the menu before, and so far no one had requested it. I remembered Dean saying we could simply go to the bakery and pick up a few things in the morning. However, it was Sunday morning, and the bakery was not open. It was 3:00 AM, and there was not much I could do. I reset the alarm for 6:00 AM and went back to sleep.

Later, while Dean slept, I snuck off to the supermarket to fill my bakery basket. I bought flour, blueberries, and other general baking ingredients in hope of finding a recipe and time to prepare homemade muffins before breakfast. I had plenty of time to mix ingredients and bake muffins but not enough time to acquire any significant experience at baking to ensure success. I located online what appeared to be a basic, foolproof recipe for blueberry corn muffins. I got my ingredients together, measured them carefully, and was beginning to mix when I heard barking from our room.

"Spike! Be quiet!" Dean hushed.

I interrupted my muffin baking to feed the dogs. I placed the muffins in the oven before taking Spike and Freddie for their walk. A fresh layer of snow gleamed in a bright, cold sunshine. It was too cold for Freddie, who pulled to get back inside. Spike was curious and preferred to wander. The soft snow seemed to comfort his arthritic legs as he bounced back and forth and shoved his muzzle in the fresh snow. I had read that moles, gophers, and other small vermin locked out of the frozen earth made "subnivean" homes between the ground and the layers of snow. If this was the case, I doubted they appreciated Spike's snout at the door of their igloo.

"Come on, boy. My muffins are almost done." I explained to the dog my need to get back inside.

Dean had made his entrance into the kitchen and had begun to set up. There would be French toast, two omelets, and an English breakfast. He prepared the custard for the French toast, yawning and knocking things over. He wasn't a morning person.

"What's that smell?" he said as though one of the dogs had passed gas.

"My muffins," I said. I explained the glitch in the plan to buy baked goods on Sunday morning.

"Ah, right," he said. "That's a problem."

The muffins should have been ready. The kitchen smelled of sweet, warm blueberries. I opened the oven expecting to find giant golden muffins with thick, toasty tops. Instead, the mixture had risen only slightly, not even to the level of the muffin pan. I was gutted. I took them out of the oven and lifted one to see if they were done.

"They're not burnt—at least," Dean said.

"They look like hockey pucks." I cut one open. The taste was not bad, but it was very dense. I would need to make sure plenty of water or coffee was on the table to wash them down.

"We can sprinkle some powdered sugar over them before we serve them. They'll be fine," Dean assured me, but I knew he was concerned. The reporter's stay had been going very well. I was sure a missing bakery basket would not be the end of the world. I feared the story would read, *Nice décor, but don't even bother with the bakery basket!*

"We would still be sugarcoating hockey pucks," I said.

I set the dining room table. The table was mahogany, circa 1840. It was not meant for daily use any longer. A vice grip held one of the joints together under the table. I placed a thick insulated mat on the surface to protect the wood, followed by a white linen tablecloth, starched napkins, and new cutlery. The setting was almost enough to mask the muffins I was about to serve.

With forty minutes before the guests were scheduled to have breakfast, I showered and changed. When I returned to the kitchen, the exhaust fan was roaring like a jet engine, the outside door was propped open, and the dogs were on high alert in their basket as the smell of burnt bacon hovered above them in a fog.

"I forgot the bacon was in the oven," Dean said. "At least I had another pack."

I looked at a plate of charred and shrunken meat. "Crispy," I said.

My role was part waiter, part kitchen supporter. I mixed pancake batter if necessary; prepared juices, coffee, and toast; and served the meal. If it went well, Dean came out at the end to take a bow and chat with the guests.

Everyone was bright and cheery.

"Smells wonderful," Cindy said in response to the lingering smell of bacon. I served the drinks and began with orders of toast and crumpets.

Dean finalized work on the bakery basket as he might have been arranging flowers. The muffins were strategically placed in the center under a small baguette and toasted English muffins. He pulled the linen napkin that lined the basket over the bread to keep it warm and prepared an assortment of jams and a plate of unsalted butter. "Presentation is key." He handed me the basket.

The guests were delighted, especially with the Sunday *New York Times* and *St. Paul Pioneer Press* to read over breakfast.

"It's so civilized," the reporter said. "Who would expect to see the *New York Times* in Hayward, Wisconsin?"

I poured the coffee and put the basket of bakery items in an awkward position at the corner of the table just out of the reporter's reach.

"Yumm. They smell wonderful. I can't wait to dig in," she said.

"Would anyone like any juice, extra water?" I pushed.

In the kitchen, Dean was finalizing the French toast under the broiler. I looked around. Freddie was asleep in her basket. "Where's Spike?" I asked.

"He was here just a minute ago," Dean said.

I looked around the corners of the kitchen and then over to the door. The outside door was still propped open with a stool. There was a small gap, but it looked too small for a dog to get through. I looked outside but didn't see anything. "I'll check the garden," I said.

The yard was fenced in on three sides but open at the side of the house. The fresh snow should have made it easy to find any new tracks, but there were none at the side of the house, nor could I see anything in the yard.

"Spike!" I called. "Come here, boy!" This was pretty much useless as Spike was never one to respond to such requests, even when he was young. As he grew older, we suspected he was either losing his hearing or had become especially obstinate.

I returned to the house, thinking he might have managed to slip through the door into the dining room while I was serving the guests. I walked through as though I were checking on the guests.

"Breakfast will be ready in just a minute," I said as I looked around the corner of the room. I didn't say anything. I didn't want to disturb the guests' breakfast, alarm them about a missing dog, or give the impression that they were otherwise taking part in an episode of *Fawlty Towers.* I went to the living room and then into the library.

"Spike," I called in a hushed tone and looked around the sofa and under the desk. There was no response. My heart started to race.

I went upstairs. If the guests had left their rooms open, Spike could be in their trash or their suitcase or in anything else they might have left on the floor. The doors were closed, and he was nowhere to be found. I called again. My palms began to sweat. I reminded myself not to panic.

Downstairs, there was one place I had not looked, but it would be difficult to do so without raising the guests' suspicions. Without any excuse, however, I simply approached the table, stooped as though I might be tying my shoe or picking something off the floor, and lifted the tablecloth to see if Spike was lying at someone's feet waiting for a treat. All I could see were four sets of legs and feet, some with shoes, some in slippers, and the reporter's German boyfriend in plastic flip-flops as though he were going to the pool. No Spike.

I rose from the floor, forced a smile, and returned to the kitchen. Dean was anxious for me to serve the breakfasts he was plating. "These are going to get cold," he warned.

"We need to find Spike!" I said, panic beginning to set in.

I took another look outside. I scanned the yard. The oak fence had been installed late in the autumn and was still unpainted. At the back of the yard against the wood tone of the fence, I saw what looked like a mound of snow moving along the fence.

I ran out through the snow. As I approached Spike, he seemed unaware that he was doing anything out of the ordinary. When he saw me running toward him, he figured I wanted to play and went down on all fours, scrambled from left to right, and ran in a circle in the snow. He stopped briefly for me to grab him and grumbled as I picked him up, but then he licked my cheek.

"You're a bad boy," I said in a tone that did not convince anyone.

With the dogs all accounted for, I served the breakfasts. The reporter was nibbling at a blueberry corn muffin, but I didn't care.

"Here you go," I said as I put the plates on the table. "May I get you anything else? Juice?"

"No, thanks," the reporter said. As I turned toward the kitchen, she added, "Did you find your dog?"

"Yes." I smiled. "He's fine."

Are You Here for the Birkie?

They said it was the mildest January Wisconsin had seen in 160 years. I questioned the accuracy of some French fur trapper with a thermometer, but needless to say, it had been warm, and snow cover had been spotty. Since the beginning of February, however, winter had returned with an Arctic fury. Temperatures plummeted to twenty and even thirty degrees below zero for an entire week. It was how I remembered winter as a child in Minnesota—within minutes of exposure to the cold, my nose became stiff and numb, crystals formed on my eyelashes, and the bitter breeze burned the back of my throat and lungs. It always seemed worse on Sunday mornings, when I had to deliver the *Minneapolis Tribune* to the old people on my street before the crack of dawn. Mom helped by assembling the papers while I delivered to those houses in the immediate neighborhood. She then drove me around to those further down the street.

I knew it was coming . . .

"How do people live here?" Dean shouted as he ran from the car to the front door. "This is bloody insane!" he complained and grabbed my parka.

Freddie began a boycott of any outdoor activity by taking care of her business inside the kitchen door. Even hardy Spike came down with an unusual bout of constipation.

As the local conversation turned to one topic, the cold and snow was nevertheless welcomed in Hayward like a warm spring day. A year ago in February, we had been in town for the closing of the cabin. No one recognized us, so they all asked, "Are you here for the Birkie?" This year, we knew everyone considered us locals, as their question became, "Do you think we'll have snow for the Birkie?" As we had never seen a Birkie, we didn't know what to expect or how much snow was required. A shrug with some raised hands was an acceptable response, suggesting we had seen it all before.

The American Birkebeiner, the largest cross-country ski marathon in the country, was by a long shot the biggest event of the year in Hayward—even bigger than the demo at the Sawyer County Fair. Every year the event attracted up to nine thousand skiers, including many professionals from Europe and around the world, and twice as many spectators to Hayward and nearby Cable for the last weekend in February. It made sense: Hayward has the perfect climate for such a race, and the terrain, free from large mountains and big oceans, was suitable. Cross-country skiing had grown in respectability in recent decades, and with plenty of Scandinavians in town you could say the event was an extension of their heritage.

Back in 1973, however, when the race started, cross-country skiing was as alien to Americans as soccer and espresso, and elite skiers from Norway and Sweden would scoff at an event in Wisconsin as Brits might a cricket tournament in Nebraska. For me, the most curious thing about the Birkie was how one person first convinced the townspeople of the merits of an idea crazier than a giant fiberglass fish and then enticed the world to come to it.

The Birkie was the brainchild of one person who more than any other since the logging era left his mark on the community—even more than Louis Spray or the clever folks who built the giant fish. Tony Wise was born in Hayward and served in World War II, including a temporary stint as mayor of a Bavarian village in the American-controlled sector of postwar Germany. As mayor, he enjoyed spending free time at a ski lodge and thought, *This is what we need in northern Wisconsin.*

When Wise returned to the United States, he bought a 120-acre plot of land east of Cable on which he found a hill, or at least a mound of earth rising just over three hundred feet into the air. With a gift for marketing, he called this mound of earth "Mount Telemark" after the region of Norway known for skiing. Notwithstanding the geological challenge, Tony proceeded to create the first downhill ski resort in the Upper Midwest at a time when downhill skiing was reserved for the wealthy or those who happened to live on or near the mountains. Before long, Tony's Telemark Lodge became a destination for people from all over the region. He even brought big-name musicians such as Count Basie and Duke Ellington to the lodge for part of the après-ski atmosphere. I remembered the television ads for Telemark from the 1970s and what a glamorous hotspot it must have been.

Tony did not limit his enterprise to Telemark. His mind never stopped scheming of new business opportunities and ways to promote tourism in the area. It was said he spoke in rapid-fire sentences and often missed syllables of words as though his vocal apparatus was too slow for his brain. In 1960, he organized the first Lumberjack World

Championships in a small lagoon on Lake Hayward. The thought was not only to pay tribute to Hayward's logging past but also to promote a new sporting event that involved pole climbing, logrolling, and wood chopping. He managed to secure national television broadcasts, and the Lumberjack World Championships remained another annual spectacle in Hayward.

Nearby on Lake Hayward, Tony owned a successful tourist restaurant known as the Cook's Shanty, housed in a restored lumber camp bunkhouse. Young men and boys wearing lumberjack costumes served pancakes and burgers on simple metal trays to the tourists who lined up to get a seat.

"I worked at the Cook's Shanty for years," Vivian once told me. It seemed Vivian had worked most everywhere in Hayward, and if she hadn't, Buck had. "He was such a wonderful man, Tony," she remembered fondly. "Whenever my kids came to see me at the restaurant, he told them that if they helped me clean the kitchen, he would give them a hamburger and a ride on the *Namekagon Queen*."

The *Namekagon Queen* was a Mississippi riverboat with a large paddlewheel at the back. Tony offered tourists rides around Lake Hayward. One day, the *Namekagon Queen* left the Cook's Shanty for a trip around the perimeter of Lake Hayward. Twenty feet offshore, however, the boat began to take on water. Crowds standing on the deck of the flat-bottom boat saw water rise around their feet. The boat was sinking in four feet of water, so there was little panic on board. Rowboats came to the rescue while some folks simply stepped into the water and walked ashore as the mighty riverboat sank in the sandy bottom of Lake Hayward. The *Namekagon Queen* sat partially submerged for several weeks. With the costs of repair prohibitive, Tony turned his riverboat over to the Hayward Fire Department to hone their skills at fighting fires aboard riverboats on Lake Hayward.

Such a loss was insignificant given the success of Telemark Lodge, but Tony saw the writing on the wall—other resorts had opened in

Wisconsin and northern Minnesota. In addition, as visitors to Telemark got a taste of the sport, they began to seek out real mountains out West.

After a skiing vacation in Norway, Tony saw a future in Wisconsin for Nordic-style, or cross-country, skiing. Norwegians told Tony about the Birkebeiner ski race in Norway, a marathon open to citizens of all skill levels. The race re-created a famous event in the Norwegian Civil War of 1206 when two soldiers, known as *birkebeiners* because of the birch leggings they wore, rescued the young Prince Haakon and skied with the baby through the woods to safety.

When he got back to Wisconsin, Tony hired a Norwegian skier to set up a trail through the woods between Telemark and Hayward using primarily old logging routes and snowmobile trails. In 1973, he held the first American Birkebeiner. There were fifty-three participants, but that was just the beginning.

Dean and I had no idea what to expect. It was hard to imagine a large number of Europeans descending on Hayward. I was certain the Italians would seek out the dairy for true Italian cappuccino and perhaps an *affogato*. With the finish line for the Birkie only a city block from McCormick House, Dean envisaged hosting VIPs or Olympic skiers. With all the competitors and thousands of skiers and spectators, finding accommodations in the area was next to impossible. Lodging was so scarce, people opened their homes to skiers in what became literally a cottage industry, and the school allowed people to camp on the gymnasium floor.

On Wednesday evening before Saturday's race, the City of Hayward closed Main Street, and a convoy of dump trucks carried loads of snow to cover the street. For hours, all one could hear was the warning beeps of trucks packed high with snow as they backed into position. When they reached the desired spot, the drivers raised the back end of their truck and opened the hatch to release a ton of snow. Large tractors and plows followed to groom the ground for skiing. The plows looked like something out of *Aliens,* with hooks and rakes and blades at the front and the back. The machines were outfitted with large flood lamps to light the thick blanket of white in front of them. Groomers followed to flatten and grade the snow. The skiers referred to the groomed snow as *corduroy.* To me it looked more like a beautifully iced cake or, better, with the flags of participating countries lining the street, a white carpet for visitors from around the world, than an old pair of pants.

On Thursday, the Sons of Norway, the Norwegian American cultural organization, sponsored a children's race, the Barnebirke, beginning on Lake Hayward and ending on snow-packed Main Street. Sponsors collected hot water from the dairy to make hot chocolate to give away at the finish line. At West's, pairs of small, brightly colored skis and poles rested against the building as children were treated to ice cream. Buck came around the counter to help Vivian and me meet the rush of young customers.

"Did you finish the whole race?" he asked a young girl who approached the counter. She nodded. "Well, what color would you like, dear?" he asked. The girl looked confused by his question but settled on vanilla.

Later, as the kids were leaving the dairy, Buck took his position at the bar. "Look at the little bastards!" he said with a chuckle. "They're so happy they got a damn medal."

"So, you like the Birkie, Buck?" I asked.

"Oh, it's probably the biggest thing in town."

"Did you know Tony Wise?" I asked, not knowing what kind of circles Tony or Buck moved in.

"Oh, for sure." Buck raised his hand and brushed the air. "Everyone knew Tony. You know," he added, lowering his voice, "he kinda lost it in the end. He had long, scraggly hair." Buck tried to raise his hand to show how long Tony's hair might have been. "You know, he had a lot of debt at the end. In fact, he owed money to just about everyone in town—that was the problem." I wondered what had happened—how someone so successful could let himself go. I looked at my reflection in the window. Maybe it was time for a haircut.

With the success of Telemark and the American Birkebeiner, Tony built a new lodge at the base of his mountain and a conference center modeled after the Colosseum in Rome. People joked it was the only ski resort where the lodge was larger than the mountain. When it was complete, the lodge employed over four hundred people, about half the population of Cable, Wisconsin.

In the end, the expansion was too much, and Telemark was forced into bankruptcy. With eight million dollars of debt and six thousand creditors, Tony Wise lost his cherished Telemark while the colosseum was demolished and sold for scrap.

"Everyone thought he would bounce back," Buck said.

"Were people angry?" I asked.

"Oh, sure, but you couldn't blame Tony. He was such a character." Buck grinned at the thought. "Tony was a real character, wasn't he, Bruce?" Bruce had just come in the back of the dairy.

"He was," Bruce acknowledged. "Say, you working the Birkie this year, Buck?"

"Of course. I'm handing out bananas at Fish Hatchery Park to the crazy bastards who make it that far," Buck said. He and Bruce were some of the two thousand volunteers who helped organize and run the event, including six hundred volunteers handing out water, bananas, and oranges at stations along the race as well as hot soup and donuts at the finish line.

"That's the other thing about Tony. He always got as many people as he could to work for free," Bruce joked.

By Friday, the town was abuzz with excitement. With limited skiing experience, I had a hard time imagining the race, but I could read it on the racers' nervous smiles. For those who had skied the Birkie—and many had done so ten, fifteen, even twenty times—it was their favorite time of year. It was like their Christmas and birthday wrapped into one, but it would also test their endurance and skill like nothing else. If it was their first Birkie, they looked anxious and somewhat terrified that they might miscalculate the wax given the temperature on race day or might consume insufficient carbohydrates the night before the big event. They had heard about the hills and the effect of the cold temperatures on snow conditions. Their fear and trepidation added to the harried atmosphere of the race.

I could spot the Europeans—tall, lean, and focused. Only a few wandered around town taking in the sights. I never caught an Italian at the dairy, only a few old Germans who must have been from a remote corner of the former East Germany as they spoke no English. When I didn't understand them, they only spoke louder. They must have picked that up from some Americans in their village. I gave them a cappuccino.

There were no VIPs or beautiful Olympic skiers at McCormick House. Before we knew it, our place was bursting with a family of four sharing a small room and crowds of people arriving with air mattresses and spare pillows. The front of the house soon looked like a used Subaru dealer's lot, while inside resembled an overcrowded halfway house as guests traded packets of protein-filled gelatin known as GU and small blocks of wax for their skis in a seemingly illicit manner, or a military camp as they compared strategies for attacking "Bitch Hill" on Saturday.

Dean was tearing the remainder of his hair out as his guests were negotiating breakfast arrangements for the morning of the race. The Birkie race guide provided helpful tips and rather graphic descriptions of the stages of digestion, including the amount of time the food spent in your stomach, small intestine, and colon—twelve to fifteen hours. Depending on the time they started their race, which depended on skill level, the skiers needed to eat three to four hours before their start.

"You've got to be kidding me," Dean pleaded. Many of the guests customized their breakfast order to load up on fruit, oatmeal, and pancakes, while one requested a baked potato, melon, and kiwis. A couple from Colorado, intense in their belief that they would do well, indicated their secret fuel to a successful race was a large plate of *huevos rancheros.* I assumed by "fuel" they meant methane.

"Huevos what?" Dean exclaimed. Although he came from a country maligned for its culinary traditions, his tone managed to convey to the guests that they might as well have ordered dirt for breakfast.

On Saturday morning, after our guests had eaten and by the time their food had begun to make its way into the small intestine of their digestive tract, they left for Telemark. It would be a cold race. The temperature at dawn was minus ten Fahrenheit. Our guests from Colorado had never skied in such conditions and wondered if they had consumed enough refried beans for breakfast.

As the race started, spectators began to gather downtown. The dairy filled up with people watching the clock so they knew when their spouse or friend should be approaching the finish line. The local radio station broadcast the race live. A helicopter buzzed overhead to track the lead racers. The elite skiers would fly along the trail and complete the fifty-six-kilometer course in approximately two hours.

People began to line the barriers on Main Street. These makeshift walls were plastered with advertising from Birkie sponsors, including local businesses but also national ski manufacturers, Subaru, and GU. The snow had been re-groomed to perfection, with only a few holes and footprints where people had gone around the barriers to cross the street.

Many spectators held actual or small plastic replica cowbells to ring as skiers passed. I walked up Main Street toward the post office, where a blue ribbon had been stretched across the finishing line. Two small raised wooden structures had been placed at the intersection of Third Street and Main for race officials to oversee the finish. A large television monitor stood near the finish line so people further down the street could see the skiers cross it. It was an impressive display of professional sports for our little town.

Tony Wise died unexpectedly in 1995. He was seventy-five years old, but many had assumed he would live much longer. Even though he had been heralded as one of the greatest promoters of this health-conscious sport in the United States, it appeared he did not ski much himself and may not have been in the best of health. Despite his losses and debts, he devoted his life to promoting his town, and the people of Hayward lined the streets as his funeral procession passed. Many rang cowbells. In the years since his death, the city had considered an appropriate memorial—perhaps a park or statue. But it would seem this annual gathering on Main Street was about the best tribute the town could give Tony Wise. Everyone who participated, volunteered, or simply stood by and watched knew that if not for Mr. Tony Wise, there would be no Birkie.

As temperatures failed to reach twenty degrees, ice cream was a hard sell at the Birkie, but the dairy was packed with people drinking coffee and tea and staying warm. I turned on the local radio station so customers could hear the race announcers.

Excitement grew as the announcer indicated there would be a close finish. The lead skiers had just reached the shore of Lake Hayward and wound their way around the back of the supermarket to Main Street. I told Jen and Liz I was going over to Main Street, where I was meeting Dean for the finish.

The sidewalks were packed—three or four persons deep. I found Dean near the front of the bakery.

"Can you believe this?" he shouted over the screams and cowbells. "This is huge," he said. I stood on tiptoes and could see three figures turn toward Main. Two skiers were literally neck and neck. By their uniforms, you could see they were both from the Italian team. They sprinted as though they had just entered the race, their strides long and smooth. The finish was so close the announcer struggled to identify the winner, and then struggled with the Italian names of both the first- and second-place finishers.

Soon there was a nonstop rush of race finishers. After the professional and elite skiers, the super-fit citizen racers came through over the course of the next two to three hours. They all had the look of exhilaration and smug accomplishment. Next came a large category of men and women eager to prove something—perhaps to their spouse, their children, their doctor, or themselves. They looked beaten, with ice forming on their hats and beards from hours of sweating in the cold weather.

As the afternoon progressed, the crowds thinned. People packed their equipment and left to shower and get something to eat, though not necessarily in that order. I closed the ice cream shop and headed home. The light was fading, and the race officials began to dismantle their equipment at the finish line. The American Birkebeiner would officially close at 6:00 PM. The city's snowplows waited at the side streets in order to remove the snow and reopen Main. A few people walked up the course rather than go around the barriers between the track and the street pavement.

A woman was talking to an official at the finish line. "Oh, I see him!" she shouted and pointed to the end of Main Street, where a dark figure was seen prodding the snow and moving ever so slowly on his skis up the street.

How it took him so many hours to complete the race was hard to imagine. Perhaps he had stopped and ordered a pizza or taken a break at Turk's for a Blue Hawaiian cocktail. He was not exactly the picture of cross-country skiing, with a graying beard and expanded spandex. On the verge of collapse, he stepped his skis across the finish line and fell into his wife's arms. He had made it. I thought I saw tears on his face, which was otherwise the picture of exhaustion, pride, joy, and accomplishment. He looked up to some being, perhaps Tony.

A race official handed him a medal strung on a red, white, and blue ribbon. "Congratulations."

"Thanks," was all the exhausted figure could manage.

The Potluck and
Paws of Appreciation

Within hours of the Birkie's finish, crews cleared Main Street of the packed snow. By Sunday, skiers and visitors were trickling out of town. The guests thanked Dean, many crediting his breakfast for their success. We ran out of soy milk at the dairy, suggesting a connection between skiing and lactose intolerance. In the days following the Birkie, Hayward seemed aglow in a collective good mood. Certainly some were happy to be rid of the sixteen thousand people who descended on town; others looked to spring, which seemed just around the corner. For the rest of us, there was a satisfying sense of being part of a small community capable of pretty big things.

After eleven months in the north woods of Wisconsin, we received our first potluck invitation. The Northwoods Humane Society was holding its annual Paws of Appreciation. We were tipped that Dean might be receiving a Paw of his own.

The event took place at the First Lutheran Church, just up the road from McCormick House. First Lutheran was one of a dozen or so churches in Hayward, or at least those churches that could afford to put their name on the billboard as you entered town. The number of churches seemed high by any standard but especially for a community as small as Hayward. Apparently, one of the original lumber barons was a staunch prohibitionist and was concerned about the spread of taverns and consumption of alcohol in the area. Rather than limit the number of beer halls, the city attempted to create a balance by adopting an ordinance limiting the number of tavern licenses to the number of churches in town.

The community center next to the First Lutheran Church was packed. Two large round tables were set up at the back for the potluck. On one table, heated baking dishes and large casserole pans featured a history of savory dishes or salads with plenty of cranberries and wild rice. The other table was reserved for desserts, pies, and trays of bars— lemon bars, Rice Krispies bars, and brownies. We brought ice cream, of course. I carried a three-gallon tub, including plastic cups and spoons, and looked for a place to put them.

Deanna ushered people in and advised them to get a plate of food and sit down so she could begin her presentation.

"Hi, guys!" she greeted us cheerfully. "I'm so glad you could make it. Oh, is that Almost Sinful you brought?" she asked. "That's everyone's favorite, you know. Let's make room for the ice cream." She instructed a volunteer to help. I felt bad—clearly people had spent hours baking pies and bars, now pushed to the edge of the table, while I had merely scooped up some ice cream from the freezer.

We grabbed some plates, and Dean investigated the offerings. Like most northerners, he was wary of unusual food combinations. On the other hand, I could not believe my eyes. I had not seen many of these delicacies in years—the Frito salad, the classic tuna casserole topped with potato chips, and a three-bean salad that I still found an unnecessary use of kidney beans. I had a sudden craving for tuna casserole. I hadn't had any since mom made it on a Friday during Lent in 1980.

At the edge of the savory table, since it was still considered a salad, was another one of my favorites. In a large ceramic bowl, untouched, was a lovely Watergate salad. I begged my mom to make this as a child, but she told me it was too sweet. The Watergate salad was introduced in the 1970s when Kraft began producing pistachio pudding mix. For the most part, Americans were unfamiliar with pistachio, and the manufacturer published recipes to increase consumption of their exotic product. Kraft denied naming the salad after the political scandal that brought down a president, but the name stuck. Canned pineapple and a box of pistachio pudding were mixed with miniature marshmallows to create a green fluff—the perfect complement to my tuna casserole.

"That looks absolutely disgusting," Dean whispered.

Before we took our seats, I peeked at the desserts. In case I didn't get back to the sweet display, I grabbed a lemon bar. They weren't one of my favorites. I always suspected Mom made them for herself. Then I saw—hidden behind a large tub of ice cream—my favorite childhood dessert. I asked Mom to make it instead of birthday cake. It went by many names—seven-layer bars, seven-layer magic bars, or coconut magic bars. Unlike the twelve days of Christmas, I could still remember each layer—graham cracker, sweetened condensed milk, coconut, walnuts, butterscotch, and chocolate chips. I was pretty sure the last, or first, layer was butter. It was a small square tray of perfectly baked gems, the cream caramelized along the edge. The last time I saw the bars had been at Dean & DeLuca in New York during the early 1990s. They had a brownie base and cost as much as a new shirt. I took two of the bars. I considered giving Dean one of them.

Long cafeteria tables had been set up for the dinner. They were those sort of tables where the benches are attached so the table could be folded and stored into spaces in the wall of the building. We sat next to the editor of the *Sawyer County Record*. He had a large camera with a telephoto lens to record the event.

Deanna moved to the front of the room to begin the presentation even though most people were either still eating or milling around the dessert table.

"We have a lot to get through tonight, so please take a seat," she requested and asked someone to dim the lights for the slide show.

Behind a lectern, she stood with notes and clicker and began the show. The slides included photographs of every cat, dog, kitten, puppy, and bunny that had gone through the shelter over the course of the year, including a description of the animal, a cute story if any, and details of the adopters, who were invariably "a very nice family."

With every slide, there was either a general "aww," or in the case of an especially cute puppy an "ohhh," and for particularly special animals, Deanna gave them the designation "cutie patootie." The humane society, fortunately for the sake of the slide show, did not euthanize any animals but cared for them at the shelter until a suitable home was found or Deanna took them home.

After about twenty minutes of animal photographs, the crowd grew weary and their enthusiasm waned. It reminded me of the Musky Festival parade. "Just a few more," the host encouraged because honoring the animals was an important part of the event.

I enjoyed the Watergate salad. I thought how I might be able to replicate the flavor in ice cream. I moved to my collection of bars. I asked Dean if he would like one.

"That looks good." He took the lemon bar, leaving me the two magic bars.

"Ohhh—these *are* good," he whispered.

"What's that smell?" Dean asked. "Do you smell that?" he continued. "It smells funny," he added and wrinkled his nose.

"Shhh," the editor whispered. "It's Teddy." He discreetly pointed to the end of the table where an elderly man sat enjoying his third helping of food.

I knew Teddy from the dairy. He had some mobility issues, which may have affected his bathing or showering schedule, but he was usually seen driving around town. He and a few other old guys who were oddly attending the humane society dinner were present wherever there was free food on the go.

One day at the dairy, Teddy drove up to the front door and honked his horn. I went out to see what the problem was.

"Could I get a vanilla cone, please?" Teddy requested from inside his car.

Not sure how to respond, although *This is not a drive-through* came to mind, I returned inside, scooped his cone, and delivered it. He gave me a dollar and some change (but not enough) and drove off. Since then, every couple of weeks, Teddy drove up to the dairy for his cone. The staff knew what to do and didn't bother counting his money since they knew it would not be enough, yet it seemed inappropriate to ask for more.

Teddy looked over at us and waved. "Thanks for bringing the Sinful," he said through his cupped hand.

The program was moving on, and Deanna began to thank all of the volunteers at the shelter and describe the events that had helped raise funds over the course of the year. The recent Turkey Bowl on the Chippewa Flowage had been the best ever, she indicated, as it had raised over four hundred dollars. I found this popular event, where frozen turkeys were used as bowling balls to knock down pins on a stretch of frozen lake, a curious undertaking.

The highlight of the evening was the awards, or Paws, to key volunteers, including a twelve-year-old girl who worked after school to clean kennels and play with the kittens. The girl stood nervously as the president praised her, and smiled from ear to ear when she was presented with a wooden plaque.

"Now I would like to bring a new friend to the podium. Dean Cooper, could you please come up?"

Dean mumbled something under his breath, walked the center aisle to the stage, and stood next to the young girl. Dean was used to accepting awards. At annual sales conferences, he regularly received commendations for performance. We had a drawer full of plaques, trophies, and crystal bowls. We figured the humane society award was in regards to the donation Dean made to the society from the proceeds of the auction last spring, but Deanna's words went beyond the donation.

"Now, some of you may not know Dean or Jeff, who have only been in Hayward a short while. Has it been a year?" she asked. "But you certainly know what they have done." She went on to describe in the kindest and most glowing terms how we had restored the local institution, West's Dairy, for generations to come and how we had taken an unsightly mansion on the hill and did what few could imagine. "They brought to this town a vision and purpose that we have not seen in a long while, and it is just amazing what they have accomplished in such a short time," she said. I saw others in the room nod in agreement. Some looked around to see if they could find me.

"Anyway, one day last spring," she said, to change the subject. "This tall Englishman came into the shop. He said he was Dean," and in a mock English accent that sounded more like Helen Mirren than Dean, she continued, "'I am the new owner of McCormick House. We are going to have an auction and I would like to donate some of the proceeds to the humane society.' I thought," returning to her own accent, "Who is this angel and where did he come from?" She moved closer to put her arm on Dean's back as though she were presenting him to the crowd and laughed.

She concluded her tribute by thanking Dean for the donation and added, "On behalf of all of us, I would like to welcome you to Hayward and thank you for what you have accomplished and added to the community." He smiled broadly as he received his Paw of Appreciation and a hug.

I could tell he was touched by the tribute, as was I. The young volunteer and fellow Paw holder next to him shook his hand. There was applause. "That's nice," I heard someone say.

At home, Dean hung his Paw of Appreciation in the office next to his desk.

Spike and Freddie acted all suspicious. "We were only looking at pictures of other dogs," I assured them. Perhaps they could smell the Frito salad.

The Anniversary

It was March already. In most parts of the northern hemisphere, spring was around the corner. On Saturday, we woke to eighteen inches of fresh, wet, heavy snow. It was the largest snowfall of the season. I started to clear the path around McCormick House but gave up after twenty minutes. *Surely,* I thought, *it will warm up and melt in a day or two.*

Buck managed to get to the dairy through the snow.

"You should have been a mailman, Buck. No sleet, snow, or rain will keep you from *The Price Is Right,*" I joked.

"Well, I figured you would be snowed in at the mansion."

Vivian was going out of town, so I had agreed to cover for her. I would have closed for the day but knew Buck would be there. I made coffee and uncovered the ice cream. We had cut back to only twelve flavors to ensure freshness. It was still a hard sell. I checked the cash register for change and made myself a cappuccino. Buck had bought some donuts at the co-op and offered me one.

I sat in my favorite leather chair next to the old guy. He was chastising people for driving too fast on the slick street. "There's going to be an accident. Mark my words." He raised his finger.

"Say," Buck said. "We're coming up to your anniversary at the dairy, aren't we?" He had suddenly remembered.

"End of the month," I said.

"Time flies when you're having fun, heh?" Buck laughed.

"Yes, something like that," I said. He was right. In many ways, it seemed like only yesterday that I had walked through the door, taken one look at the dairy, and felt like leaving. In other ways, it seemed like light years since we had left London. Already, I was forgetting names of people I had worked with for years or the restaurants we ate at every couple of weeks.

"You and Dean have done real good," Buck said. "Bruce and I had our doubts. We didn't say anything, of course, but you did come across as a couple of real city slickers." Buck laughed. I had always suspected those initial misgivings. I was glad we had overcome them.

"Thanks, Buck. That means a lot to me." And it did. "I'm glad you decided to stick around."

"Well, I like it at the dairy. It has always been part of this town—you know what I mean?" Buck said.

"Just like you," I said. He laughed.

"And you're already expanding?" Buck said. "I don't know, Jeff. Spooner is a tough town to crack. It always has been," he cautioned.

At the end of February, we had signed the lease on the premises in Spooner across from Big Dick's Buckhorn Bar. We took over in April with a goal to open by the middle of May. I tracked down painters and other workmen to complete the project. I found a manager, a young woman from Hayward who once ran a coffee shop in town. She could cook and make coffee and was willing to drive to Spooner every day.

"Well, time will tell," I said. I imagined Buck traveling the country and globe teaching young recruits at new West's Hayward Dairy outlets how to make malts and play cribbage.

Notwithstanding the blanket of snow, the people of Hayward began to gear up for the summer season. The chamber of commerce revealed the slogan for the upcoming Musky Festival—"Reel in a Good Time"— and kicked off the contest to design the logo that would be used in advertising and Musky Festival merchandise. The prize was a hundred dollars. A representative from the chamber board approached us about sponsoring a tent at the Musky Festival next summer. He also mentioned there was talk of nominating Dean or me to the chamber's board of directors in the upcoming elections.

The *Sawyer County Record* reported that the Fresh Water Fishing Hall of Fame and Museum board, after commissioning its own report on the veracity of Louis Spray's 1949 musky, announced it had rejected the claims of the World Record Musky Alliance and that Spray's fish would remain on the books as the world's largest musky. Hayward would remain the *home of world record muskies.* "So nothing really changes," Buck said, and that summed up the reaction in town to the hall of fame's decision.

Following a feature story on how *Hayward Broadens Its Appeal* in the *St. Paul Pioneer Press* by the reporter who had visited McCormick House, bookings at the B&B began to take off. While the reporter described other new businesses in town, she focused on West's Hayward Dairy and McCormick House and the story of how Dean and I had come to Hayward. She described the changes at West's, including "leather chairs in which customers can sit while reading the *New York Times* or work on laptops." The greatest praise was reserved for Dean's pampering of guests, including offering "evening truffles and hot chocolate imported from London's Bond Street." Some of the guests who called indicated they looked forward to the fancy chocolates. Dean reminded his grandmother my birthday was approaching and how I had enjoyed those truffles she had given me for Christmas.

"So, you leave tomorrow? Going all the way to London?" Buck asked, still watching the traffic on the snow-covered street.

"That's right."

"Do you think you'll come back, or have we worn you out this year?" He laughed. He still liked to think I couldn't keep up with him or Bruce.

"Of course," I replied. "Who would run this place if I wasn't here?"

Vivian came in the front door, and I said, "I thought you were going to see your daughter?"

"I changed my mind after I heard the forecast. Glad I didn't go in this mess," she said. "I just wanted to come down to say 'good-bye' before you leave on your big trip." Vivian walked over to give me a big hug.

"Now, you boys have a good time in London. Don't worry about us," Vivian said, looking over at Buck.

"Yeah, me and Bimp can take care of things," Buck added.

I was not worried about leaving for a week. I left contact details, but even if they managed to dial the international number correctly, it was unlikely there would be anything that could not wait until my return. After all, it was only ice cream.

Given the snowstorm, customers were few and far between. While Buck was at lunch, I paid some bills that could not wait until we returned from the U.K.

A woman with a snow-covered beret and denim jacket came into the dairy. "Do you have coffee?" she asked from the door so as not to track snow on the floor in case we couldn't honor her request.

"We do," I replied.

"Well, I'll have a large one with lots of cream. Actually"—she stopped herself—"do you do espresso?"

"Yes, we do," I replied again.

"Well, then, I'll have a white chocolate raspberry mocha—with whole milk, please," she requested and began to unwrap her jacket and series of scarves. "I get enough exercise with my dogs. They're sled dogs," she explained. I thought a moment. Perhaps she saw that I was puzzled, but she did not elaborate. "I'm having my car fixed next door. You don't mind if I wait here, do you?"

"Of course not." She was very tall—well over six feet—and when she removed her hat, she revealed thick, long, gray hair. I had not seen her before, but she must have been local if she was having her car fixed in town, and she dressed as though she shopped at Mennonite garage sales.

She took out a small blue wallet from her large bag. It overflowed with receipts and papers and revealed only a few dollars. She gave me three dollars for her coffee. Her hand was large enough to grip a basketball. I then noticed the light springtime floral scarf wrapped tightly around her neck. The scarf was useless in practical terms given the day's weather.

"I'm Sam," she said, introducing herself.

I introduced myself and stumbled. I was not sure what to say. I thought that in the course of the year, I had seen it all. Tourists of all shapes, sizes, and ages. There were farmers, lawyers, accountants, bikers in leather chaps, snowmobilers in Michelin Man outfits, the Amish family from the Fall Festival, and even a few attractive, young Mormon missionaries who handed out postcards of the Mormon Temple in Salt Lake City to my customers. But Sam was my first transsexual.

"Are you from Hayward?" I asked.

"I'm originally from Spooner. I came back to the area about ten years ago. I live on Moose Lake," she told me. Moose Lake was a remote lake over thirty miles from Hayward and known primarily for its aging population. "I was in Vietnam for a long time—far too long," she said.

She began a description of her time in Vietnam that was far more detailed and gruesome than I had ever heard. "The horrors I saw there would blow your mind," she emphasized. I suddenly thought of Chantal and the DVD for the pyramid selling scheme.

I noticed she had more or less chugged her espresso. "Would you like more coffee?" I asked. "There's some regular coffee on the counter. Refills are no charge."

"Thanks, man," she said. She pumped the lid of the air pot as though it were a weapon. She filled her cup to the brim. I could not help but wonder. I had to ask.

"So, if I may ask, why did you choose to come back?" I quickly tried to adjust my question. "I mean Hayward's so small and all."

She looked me up and down. She smiled. Perhaps I had been too forward. I regretted my question.

"I could ask you the same thing," Sam replied. I smiled. Perhaps it was the thick navy turtleneck sweater that gave me away, or how I finished my coffee drinks with whipped cream and a bit of pizzazz. *Touché,* I thought.

"Actually, it's pretty big when you get out there." She arched her long arm as though it followed the horizon, suggesting there was room for all of us. "I can hook my dogs to a sled. There's nothing like it. Do you have dogs?"

I nodded.

"Sled dogs?"

I laughed at the thought of putting a harness on Freddie and Spike to pull Dean and me around the yard on a sled. "They're not exactly big dogs."

"But I bet they love it here," she said. She was right. Spike and Freddie had adapted very well to the north woods.

As Sam took a seat to read the paper, Suzi came in and smiled at her. School had been cancelled for the day due to the snowstorm. She wore a white powder puff ski jacket and pink mittens but no hat.

"Hi, Jeff."

"How are you, Suzi?"

"Great. I just got my driver's license. But I can only drive my dad's truck because it has four-wheel drive."

"Be careful today. The roads must be slippery."

"I will." She had heard it already. "I wanted to check with you about working this summer. You're going to have me back, aren't you?" she asked as though I might have reconsidered.

I hesitated for effect but confirmed I would have her back.

"Oh, thanks. I really like working here," she said. "It's fun, isn't it?"

I laughed at her question, thinking no one at the bank ever suggested it was fun to work there. "Of course, it's fun—best place in town to work," I said.

"And I'm thinking of signing up for the Musky Queen Pageant," she said.

"That's great," I said. "What would you do for your talent? Make waffle cones?"

"No, I'd play the trumpet—not sure what, though. But I've been working on my wave. Look." Suzi stepped back, put her head in the air, and moved her arm as a robot might clean a window.

"You're a natural," I said.

Suzi looked over at Sam in the chair and leaned over the counter toward me. "That lady over there," she whispered. "She's really tall, isn't she? It's funny how some women can be really tall, isn't it?"

I smiled. "Yes, it is."

The Return

We arrived in London on Saturday, March 18, 364 days after we had left the city. We spent some time in the north with Dean's family, enjoyed some fish and chips, Lancashire hot pot, a *Coronation Street* omnibus, and rain. We planned a long weekend in London before returning to Hayward.

The sky was gray outside St. Pancras and the temperature unusually cool for spring, but the forecast was good for the next few days. The station was crowded with commuters who looked pleased the day was over but did not welcome the journey home. We felt a bit like bumpkins as we weaved through the crowds, unaccustomed to the direct, head-down, damn-the-torpedoes method of walking through a crowded station.

"Reminds me of Musky Festival," I said.

"Or the Birkie, even." Dean laughed.

"For sure," I said in my best Wisconsin voice.

With plenty of taxis dropping travelers at the station, we didn't wait long in the queue. As I stepped in, the driver pulled down his window.

"Claridges, please," I said.

"Oh, now that came very naturally," Dean said. In fact, it didn't seem natural. We always thought London would be a place we could slip back to as though we had never left it. Suddenly, I was self-conscious that we didn't belong here, and certainly not in a luxury hotel.

We had splurged and redeemed the bulk of our remaining corporate air miles on a few nights in posh surroundings. Dean viewed it as important research for McCormick House. I was always intrigued by Claridges, a London hotel that hadn't been completely modernized and clung to its traditions.

The cabbie weaved and turned through Mayfair, avoiding the congested avenues, and took a shortcut through an alley lined with small cottages—mews houses, converted from what would have been stables. He crawled across an intersection on Oxford Street to avoid running down any tourists before soaring down Bond Street, took a quick right, and made a U-turn in the middle of the street to drop us at the entrance of the hotel.

"You picked a nice place," he commented after I gave him an American-style tip.

Inside, the lobby was typical of any five-star London hotel. French and Italian tourists visiting London for the weekend sat among assorted international businesspeople attending a conference. An elderly English couple, he in a tattered jacket and she in clunky jewelry from India, waited to be served afternoon tea in the dining room off the lobby below a black-and-white photograph of Winston Churchill at a formal event at the hotel. They sat near a table of footballers' wives from Liverpool or Manchester. The women sipped champagne and discussed where they should eat dinner. And then there were the air mile millionaires, innkeepers, and ice cream makers from Wisconsin.

We spent the weekend doing those things we had taken for granted over the years—walking in Hyde Park, looking at shops along Bond Street or bookstores on Charing Cross Road between brunch, lunch, and dinner with friends we had not seen in a year. Dean insisted on a Sunday roast dinner at a favorite pub near Lot's Road. The crowd seemed younger, louder, more confident, and more hung over than I remembered. We strolled through the auction houses, but nothing tempted us.

After a morning shower, the sun came out. Magnolia trees bloomed behind wrought-iron fences in front of what might have been workmen's cottages at one time. We walked down the King's Road and past our old home on Limerston Street. Locals pulled chairs outside the Sporting Page Pub for a long afternoon session. Our old home sat on the west side of the street. It was part of a row of unique stucco cottages built to house Italian workers who had come to build the Great Exposition of 1862. Curtains were drawn across the large window on the raised ground floor where Spike used to sit on the back of the sofa for hours waiting for us to return in the evening. The wooden blinds to the window on the lower ground floor were also shut, concealing the new kitchen we had installed. We had sold the house to a couple from Malaysia with Swiss connections. They were likely traveling. We regretted the new owners had removed the daffodils that would have been blooming in the window boxes and had replaced them with a plastic box hedge.

We thought of dropping in on our old neighbors whose young children had enjoyed yelling at the dogs across the fence in the garden. Their house looked conveniently quiet, so we walked on to South Kensington Station. On the Fulham Road, we walked by what were some of Dean's favorite shops for home accessories and furnishings.

"Would you like to go inside?" I asked.

"No, I don't think we need anything," he said. It wasn't clear to me if that was the case or if he had lost interest in such things since moving to Wisconsin.

Dean perked up when we passed La Brasserie, where lunchtime crowds cut into their *steak frites,* prompting him to ask, "I wonder who will be at the Ranch tonight?"

We had gone to the Ranch the night before we left Hayward. Like Buck, Cheryl wanted to make sure we were coming back. "You are leaving the dogs here, right?" she asked. I discussed the history of Watergate salad with Chef Jeff. He reminded me of the salad's cousin— Watergate cake—and promised to make it sometime.

On Monday, I planned to meet a former colleague for lunch near the office in Canary Wharf. I walked to the Underground station at Green Park to catch the Jubilee Line. It was late in the morning, after the rush hour crowds were already behind their desks. A few men and women in suits were headed to the office quite late, perhaps after a dentist appointment or interview. In casual attire, I could have been joining the other Americans on the train heading for the Tower of London, and many assumed I had forgotten to get off the train as it left tourist London behind for the commercial district of Canary Wharf.

I was originally meeting my friend for lunch, but she had left a message for me with the hotel to say she could meet only for coffee because she was involved in a high-level compliance investigation. Without going above ground, I went to a coffee shop in one of the large subterranean shopping malls below the office towers. After fifteen minutes or so, my friend arrived, out of breath in a tailored black suit, blond hair tied back in a businesslike manner, wearing tortoise-shell glasses.

"Jeff!" she called and air-kissed my cheeks. I had bought her a cappuccino, which she usually had had when we took our breaks from work, along with a piece of cake to share. "It is so good to see you. I cannot believe it's been a year already," she said before going into her workload at the moment.

We quickly turned, as usual, to the important matters of office gossip that I had missed over the year. There were the leaves of absence for stress, and someone would be getting a large settlement after a claim of sexual harassment. Another colleague was distraught after her stay-at-home husband had run off with the nanny but didn't even bother to take the kids, leaving her to find another nanny.

She updated me with news of her children and shared photographs from her phone. She had her own problems with a nanny who insisted on speaking Polish to the children. "I'm afraid they won't understand me come Saturday after what she's been teaching them all week," she said. "But what about you? How's life in Wis-con-sin?" she asked in an American drawl. "The photos of the lake are beautiful. There's nothing like that here."

I told her about the dairy, the changes we made and how busy the summer was. For whatever reason, I felt the need to impress her with how much ice cream we made and the number of customers we served. Perhaps I thought she would tell people I knew. I described McCormick House.

"I saw the website. It's beautiful—like a larger version of your house in London."

I told her about the people at West's and some of our new friends in town, how we frequented the Ranch for dinner and visited friends to play cards, and how I played cribbage with Buck, Little Bob, and Pruny.

"So, you're telling me you spend time playing cards with old men? Oh, darling! I can't imagine you doing that," she said in disbelief.

"It's not so bad, really," I tried to convince her.

"But do you feel as though you belong there—part of it?" she asked. "I'll always think of you as the American in London."

Before I could conjure up a response, she looked at her watch. "Oh, but I've got to run," she said. "I have a meeting in five minutes." She jumped up. "Next time we must do dinner," she proposed. "We'll have sushi."

We kissed again and said good-bye.

I grabbed a sandwich and finished my coffee. I went above ground and looked at the new developments. I tilted my head back and looked up at one of the towers. I tried to make out the seventeenth floor where my office sat. I walked around to the lobby. I thought I would go up to the floor to say hi to a few people. However, my friend said she had heard reviews were under way in the legal department, and they were in the midst of an FTE (full-time employee) reduction.

I decided against a visit as it might be considered inappropriate. I also knew that there was little point. I had not heard from most of my former colleagues in a year, nor had I been in touch with them. In any case, if I did go up, I would have to arrange for someone to come down to greet me at reception, complete some forms, proceed through screening, and offer up a child or puppy before I could get into the lift.

I stood outside the door of the building and watched people returning from or going to lunch. They were dressed in similar styles and walked with the confidence and determination of members of the USS *Enterprise* as though they were all headed for the bridge.

As I turned to leave, I heard, "Jeff, is that you?" I looked and saw a short woman with dark hair whom I recognized as my first secretary at the bank from ten years ago.

"Tracy!" I was surprised I remembered her name. "Hi! What are you doing here?" I asked. Shortly after I started at the bank, Tracy had married and returned to her native Australia. I had heard she had returned to the U.K. but was living in East Anglia.

"Yes, I'm back. I'm even working for Lorraine," Tracy said, referring to the other manager she supported. She spoke in a resigned tone as though returning to the bank had not been part of her life's plan. "How are you? I heard about your exciting move. Are you happy?" The question was oddly direct. She was Australian, of course, but I sensed she was asking out of her own experience of moving home after many years, only to return to Britain again.

"It's going well," I said. *Could I do what she did—return to London, the bank?*

"Were you coming up?" she asked.

"No. No, I've got to get back. I just met someone for lunch."

"Well, take care," she said.

"You, too."

On the way back to the West End, I got off the Tube at Westminster. The sun peeked through an abundance of clouds. I decided to walk through St. James's Park. People fed the birds in the pond, and, between Polish language lessons, nannies watched children run after the ducks and geese on the ground. I turned to walk through Green Park and along a field of daffodils that spread every year closer to Buckingham Palace.

At Piccadilly, I stopped at my favorite coffee shop, which was now a chain on nearly every corner of the city. I ordered a latte. I imagined Vivian behind the counter, wiping the surfaces. When she handed me the drink, she would warn me, "I make them hot. Be careful." Instead, a surly Spanish boy with unfulfilled beard and dreams handed me luke-warm coffee and grunted in European.

I sat in a familiar-looking leather chair in the window. I imagined Buck next to me, watching the traffic on Piccadilly. "Look how fast they're going! There's going to be an accident. Mark my words." He would point his crooked finger down the street. The phone would ring. "It's Fortnum's. They need a poly," he would say and wheel a bag of milk down Piccadilly toward Fortnum and Mason. Bruce might come in and ask if we needed to make more green tea ice cream for Nobu, the Japanese restaurant around the corner. And there was Cheryl, working behind the American Bar at the Savoy. I am certain her Manhattan could rival any bartender's in town.

I finished my coffee and walked down Bond Street toward the hotel. A wind picked up, a light mist fell from the darkened sky, and moisture trickled down in my face. I was smiling as though I had skied the Birkie for the first time. I thought of my friend's question—*Do you feel as though you belong there—part of it?*

I wasn't sure I would ever feel part of Hayward. I appreciated that West's and McCormick House were considered essential elements of the community, but I thought I would always stand apart and look upon my new home with a certain detachment. I would enjoy particular moments—such as watching the demo at the county fair or a streaking Montessori teacher at the B&B. Dean and I would laugh and ask ourselves—*How did we end up here?*

Our friends Matt and Dave joked that we were losing our big city ways whenever we complained about city traffic or that restaurants in Minneapolis didn't offer a salad and choice of potato with dinner. They were under strict instructions to intervene, with firearms if necessary, if Dean and I ever considered buying a pickup in order to haul stuff or suggested a road trip to see the Packers in Green Bay.

But even if I didn't feel part of Hayward, Hayward was certainly part of me. Buck, Bruce, Vivian, Cheryl, Ann at the bookstore, the tellers at the bank, and even the guy at the bait shop who sold me ice were part of my life now. Hayward's traditions—celebrating fish and fried food— were part of my routine. I may never understand why I chose to come home to Hayward, but as I walked back to the hotel, I was glad I had.

At the hotel, Dean was watching television and studying the room-service menu for breakfast ideas.

"Do you think guests would like an egg-white frittata?" he asked.

"That could work," I said. "We don't have a healthy option other than oatmeal."

"So, how was it?" he asked, referring to my visit to the office.

"Strange, I guess," I said.

"I know what you mean," he said. He had spent the day with former colleagues as well.

"Do you think it's time to go home? To see those little dogs," he added.

"Yes, I think so." I smiled.

"I think there's a *Law and Order* on TV." Dean grabbed the remote control.

And Then . . .

We returned to Wisconsin feeling refreshed and ready for another season, another year. And when it was done, we did it again. While every year brought changes to the businesses, we grew accustomed to the rhythm of the seasons, and we marked time in Hayward by its annual traditions—Memorial Day weekend, Musky Festival, and so on through the Birkie.

There would be many more stories and more characters. We stuck our toes in local affairs. I was a member of the chamber of commerce, and Dean was appointed to the visitors and convention bureau. Someone heard about my interest in Hayward's history and invited me to join the board of the Sawyer County Historical Society, which I dubbed the "hysterical" society after they suggested that I, as the youngest board member, could look at those new-fangled technology issues. Dean's work as an international judge was in demand, peaking with the Musky Queen Pageant, where there wasn't much judging: once a contestant shot an arrow through the small hole of a Life Saver candy, the contest was over. She had a weapon.

There were ups and downs for our business. Buck was right—Spooner was a tough nut to crack. After this setback, we scaled down our global ambitions. We figured any expansion would require a significant investment in new equipment. If it failed, we could lose everything. Ben and Jerry could relax—poolside—as there was little risk to their market share from northern Wisconsin—for now.

We focused our efforts on the shop in Hayward. Every year, we promoted new flavors until we offered forty flavors—or "colors" as Buck called them—of fresh homemade ice cream. For two years, Coconut Magic Bar and Church Basement Lemon Bar had been among our strongest sellers, and my personal favorites.

McCormick House proved to be all Dean and I could have imagined and exceeded the expectations of most guests. It was named "Best New Business" by the Hayward Chamber of Commerce and was featured on the cover of a regional magazine. Over the years, there have been a few unusual and mysterious visitors and at least one other case of public nakedness. I learned to appreciate the company of strangers in our home. Many guests returned a few times each year and became good friends. I liked to think our visitors enjoyed themselves. Many were curious about our story, and if they asked about a particular painting or object, I shared how we managed to lug the thing to Hayward.

We didn't go back to London very often, and when we did people commented on Dean's increasingly American accent. Over time, people forgot we weren't from these parts as we became part of the fabric—albeit the shiny, sequined part—of the community. There was one serious conversation with Matt and Dave after we spent an afternoon watching a Packers play-off game at the local veteran's center. We argued that we went only for the free buffet and that we didn't focus much on the game. They agreed there was no need for further intervention—this time. We never revealed that we might have been disappointed the Packers lost.

During our third summer in Hayward, Buck fell while stepping out of the walk-in freezer. He had a small gash in his forehead. I rushed him to the emergency room in Hayward. His head was fine, but his vitals—sugar levels, blood pressure—were all out of whack. I took him to a hospital sixty miles away where they admitted him for observation. After a week, he was released. He came back to work but was never quite the same. Shortly after that, a police officer, knowing Buck did deliveries for me, told me he saw Buck run a red light. I had to tell Buck

I would take care of deliveries going forward. I explained I was afraid he might fall. I didn't mention what the policeman had said.

Perhaps he felt he wasn't needed. Buck began spending more and more time away from the dairy, much of it at the senior center, where he enjoyed playing cards. This past summer, our fifth at West's, I saw Buck only a few times. He seemed weak and frail. I heard his daughter was moving back to Hayward to help take care of him.

It was another hot summer—ice cream sales were up considerably as customers sought a bit of sweetness and light from the economic recession that took hold across the globe. Banks had been hit particularly hard. My friend in London e-mailed to tell me that my successor at the bank lost her job. Shares of bank stock—which had formed the bulk of my savings and which I had sold at a good price to purchase West's—lost ninety-eight percent of their value. No one, including me, had thought selling those shares to buy a small ice cream shop in the north woods would be a wise financial decision. At times, fate can be a curious thing, but it made me wonder. While I'm not one to look to the skies for answers, perhaps someone up there was looking out for me.

At McCormick House, there were two large weddings over the summer. The second went smoothly until a mini-tornado blew through while the guests were finishing dinner. Everyone, including a forty-piece orchestra, ran for cover under a small tent set up for the bar. The last I saw was the caterer, in tears, catching the wedding cake while the table supporting it collapsed. It was a memorable wedding. It was a summer where many things seemed to be collapsing.

After failed attempts to embrace the outdoors—banana boats and snowbanks—I may have found the perfect pursuit. On my way back to town after delivering ice cream to the casino, I saw someone biking along a small road near Spring Lake. I turned our new dairy van around and drove to the nearest bike shop. They were having a sale, and I even got a kickstand and water bottle thrown into the deal. For a pint of Red

Velvet Cake ice cream, they agreed not to mock me when I brought the bike in to check the tires for air.

I spent many afternoons pedaling around the area, taking a break from all that was going on. I found circular routes out of town that took me by Smith Lake, Nelson Lake, and even Buck's Chippanazie Lake. I might get off to dip my toes in the water or even take a short walk or ride into the woods—no longer as terrifying to me as they once were.

It was a warm Sunday in early October. I sat by the pond in the McCormick House garden. In the spring following our first year, we created a contemporary-style English garden with lots of symmetry and open spaces. Rows of arborvitae trees were clipped into short hedges to form borders. A tangled vine of Concord grapes grew against the southern fence, producing juicy fruit for birds and for our house-keeper, Charlene, who made her own "grape juice." Parallel paths stretched from the back of the house and terrace to the garden wall and were each lined with six littleleaf linden trees. In the October sun, the trees resembled giant over-ripened pears on sticks—their gold and yellow flesh flaking away in the breeze.

The garden was an unexpected sight in Hayward. It was one of the last reminders of a former life. People said we should plant large trees to block out the county buildings behind the fence, but then we wouldn't be able to see the water tower with its message—*Hayward: Home of World Record Muskies.*

Bright goldfish and a few koi perused the pond. A large fountain in the pond's center sounded like a summer shower and blocked the noise of any traffic on Kansas Avenue. Freddie and the puppy, Georgie, raced around the pond with screeching cries of exasperation as they attempted to herd the fish. Georgie, another Norfolk terrier and a true cutie patootie, was three but still had the energy of a litter of Labradors.

Spike sat on my lap. He squinted as the sun warmed his arthritic bones. He had just turned fifteen, and this would be his last autumn.

Pretty much deaf, he ignored the fish-herding chaos around him. I had been sitting a long time, staring into the fountain on one of the saddest days.

It started in the spring. We hadn't taken a big trip in a few years and decided to go back to Hong Kong and then Shanghai. It seemed like a great time, but when we returned everything changed. A gulf grew between Dean and me as wide as the Chequamegon National Forest. I spent most of my time at the dairy, while he ran the B&B. He seemed so unhappy. Finally, he got a call from his old boss. There was a job for him if he wanted it. It was a great opportunity—in New York City.

I didn't see it coming, either. He said he didn't know what he wanted, but I knew he didn't want to stay in Hayward. We agreed he should take the job. I would stay to run both businesses. He had been to New York to find an apartment, sent some boxes, and was leaving. This was it.

I heard him come into the garden. As he approached, Freddie, distracted, lost her balance and fell into the pond. Dean ran to fish her out. When he set her down, she shook and sprayed his jeans.

"Freddie!" Dean shouted. "Now I'm all wet."

I smirked. "They'll dry."

"I guess I should get going—I need extra time to return the rental car," Dean said. I continued to stare ahead. He sat in the chair next to mine and reached over to stroke Spike between the ears.

"You okay?" he asked.

"I'll be fine," I said. What else could I say?

"I'll be back in a few weeks," he said. "Then I should get back every month or whenever you need help—like the Birkie." I didn't say anything. He continued, "You know, I think you are going to be great at the B&B. And you have a lot of support here—Matt, Dave, Vivian, Bruce. Kent and Cindy will be here next weekend."

As these things go, our separation was nothing special. There were no tirades, ultimatums, or outrage. We weren't giving up completely, we'd see what effect being apart would have, but I knew the end was near. He wouldn't be coming back. While on my bike rides, I tried to compare the breakup to losing a limb, to cancer or the death of a loved one. But it wasn't like that. All limbs were intact, no one was sick, and no one had died. It was sad, but it would get better.

"What about breakfast?" I asked. Dean had been teaching me how to prepare our time-tested offerings. I didn't enjoy it and was struggling. "You'll get the hang of it. It took me a while. With the omelets, you just need to make sure the pan is hot." He stopped. He knew it wasn't the time for a cooking lesson.

"The key thing is the guests like you. You seem to enjoy them, and they appreciate your funny stories about life in Hayward—especially when we first arrived from London." Dean chuckled. "You should write them down."

The dogs began to tire. Freddie came over and sat by Dean's feet. Georgie lay on the edge of the pond, her head near the water, on the lookout for an errant goldfish.

Dean chuckled again. "Do you remember our first McCormick House wedding?"

I laughed. "You mean the endless Kenny Chesney wedding march?" I said. "Well, it was a four-minute song, and the bride only had to walk twenty feet."

Now Dean was laughing. "It wasn't all bad," Dean said. He looked at his watch. "I better get going." He stood. "Hey, maybe you could come to New York for Thanksgiving." He gave Freddie and Georgie a squeeze, rubbed Spike's muzzle, and gave me a peck on the forehead. After sixteen years, we didn't say it was over—not then.

"Bye," I said.

"I'll give you a call when I get to the airport."

The dogs and I stayed in the garden. It seemed a long time. It may have been shock. It reminded me of a car accident we had before moving to Hayward. We were visiting in the winter. We had a rental car, and Dean hit some black ice on Highway 70. The car swerved into the other lane, spun, and hit the ditch. It rolled twice and landed on the passenger side. We had our seatbelts on and were fine. The windshield had shattered in place with only a few shards of glass falling into the car. There was that period of time when you weren't sure it had really happened. All I could do was try to pick the few shards of glass from my exposed hand.

I heard the kitchen door open. "Jeff," Charlene shouted. Charlene came every Sunday to clean the house. She was another mother figure. She brought us baked goods and talked to the dogs. "Are you okay?" she asked. "Dean told me to check on you."

We had told Charlene and others in town that Dean was taking this job because it was too good to pass up. Until we knew exactly what we were doing, it made sense, but it didn't explain my sad-dog behavior.

"I'm coming in, Charlene," I said and set Spike on the ground. I took a deep breath, wiped my eyes, and got up.

Charlene was finishing for the day and wrote her time on a card we kept in a box by the kitchen door. "I left you some cookies. They're chocolate chip. I made them this morning before I came."

"Thanks," I said. "I'll have one later."

"He's coming back in a few weeks," Charlene said to cheer me up as she grabbed her cleaning supplies to leave.

"I know," I said.

I followed the dogs into the living room. I lifted Spike so he could lie on the back of the sofa. Freddie jumped up as well to look out the window over the front lawn. I looked at the blue and white porcelain Chinese figure on the table next to the sofa—it was from a street market in Chengdu on the way to the panda sanctuary. The memory was like a shard of glass under the skin.

I looked outside. "What do you see, Spike?" There wasn't anything outside—not even a squirrel. I heard Georgie in the kitchen. I was afraid

Charlene had left something on the floor, so I followed the sounds. Georgie sat by the kitchen door, looking up with chocolate-drop eyes.

"What's this? You were just outside." I picked her up. She gave me a lick on the cheek. I closed my eyes, sighed.

"Okay," I said and looked at Georgie. "We'll go out again." I grabbed one of Charlene's cookies and opened the door.